No Trifling Matter:
Contributions of an Uncompromising Critic to the Democratic Process in Cameroon

Godfrey B. Tangwa
(alias **Rotcod Gobata**)

Langaa Research & Publishing CIG
Mankon, Bamenda

Publisher:
Langaa RPCIG
Langaa Research & Publishing Common Initiative Group
P.O. Box 902 Mankon
Bamenda
North West Region
Cameroon
Langaagrp@gmail.com
www.langaa-rpcig.net

Distributed in and outside N. America by African Books Collective
orders@africanbookscollective.com
www.africanbookcollective.com

ISBN: 9956-717-47-9

Dedication

To

Albert Mukong
Ni John Fru Ndi
Pius Njawe
Charlie Ndi Chia
Bate Besong
Rene Philombe
Celestin Monga

and all other Cameroonians who are willing and ready to stand by their convictions in spite of inconveniences.

Preface To The New Edition: Background To Gobata Columns And Essays

I started writing under the pen-name Rotcod Gobata in the early 1990's, as an attempted contribution to the democratization struggle in Cameroon, following the so-called "wind of change from the East", in the wake of the collapse of the dictatorships of Eastern Europe, most notably that of the communist Soviet Union, and the awakening effect it seemed to be having on political systems around the world, particularly in Africa. The release of Nelson Mandela from prison around the same period, followed a few years later by the truly miraculous democratic breakthrough in South Africa, added great impetus to this wind of change. In Cameroon, the sudden voluntary resignation of Alhaji Ahmadou Ahidjo, and his handing over of the reigns of dictatorial power to Paul Biya in 1982, had ushered in great euphoria and optimism. Paul Biya rode on the crest of mass popularity as he made some moves, under the slogan "rigor and moralization", to democratize and liberalize the hitherto heavily autocratic and centralized state structures.

I was a University student in neighbouring Nigeria between 1974 and1984. I used to come home to Cameroon on holidays as frequently as I could, but home-coming was not an easy affair, because getting out of Cameroon legally was a Herculean task. An exit visa was needed by Cameroonians legally to cross any of Cameroon's borders. In West Cameroon (the English-speaking part of the country), one applied for such an exit visa in Buea or Bamenda, but such application was referred to Yaounde, the governmental seat of the French-speaking dictatorship, for approval or rejection. Very often Yaounde took months to respond, if it responded at all, keeping applicants in a state of worrisome stress and anxiety. As a consequence, to come home on holidays was always to take the risk of not getting back in time for resumption of term. Many other Cameroonian students in Nigeria at the time used to opt for trekking "exit-visa-less" across the border through the thick bushes separating Cameroon and Nigeria, or bribing their way through the border posts, but I could not bring myself seriously to even consider such options.

Once, I came from Nigeria and went right to Yaounde to apply for a multiple entry and exit visa to enable me carry out field work in Cameroon for my Master's thesis. I instead got a good rude introduction to the Francophone system of public administration, general orientation, mind-set and way of doing things. I was given a long list of documents to compile, for my visa application, including a fiscal stamp of 8000 francs (quite a fortune for a self-sponsored student like me at the time). After submitting the *"dossier"* and following it up daily for about two weeks, the visa was finally refused on the grounds that I was not a Government-sponsored student!

In 1986, after having earned my PhD degree two years earlier from the University of Ibadan, I quit a lectureship at the University of Ife and returned definitively to Cameroon, under the impression that I had been recruited at the University of Yaounde. I was in for a shock. On arrival in Yaounde, bag and baggage in tow, it turned out that the supposed recruitment had got stuck at the very last stage of the process. I landed into plain joblessness, which lasted for over a year before my recruitment *"dossier"* (not without the kind intervention of friends and secondary schoolmates well-placed within the system) was finally positively sorted out. You would therefore understand that I felt personally very concerned about the prospect of democratization and liberalization in Cameroon. Some fans of Gobata are wont to refer to me as "the hammer of the New Deal regime" but any careful reader of my narratives would realize that, far from being the hammer, I have been the nail.

By the dying years of the 1980's, Cameroon's economy had started nose-diving, and corruption, as never before witnessed, had set in at the highest ranks of Government, and Cameroonians were becoming increasingly uncertain as to whether the peaceful revolution of 1982 was a blessing or a curse. In 1990, some Cameroonians, mainly Anglophones, boldly decided to challenge the one party dictatorship in Cameroon by launching a political party (the Social Democratic Front – SDF) in Bamenda.

The first Gobata essays were published, at my own initiative, in a column headed "NO TRIFLING MATTER", in the *CAMEROON POST* Newspaper, published by Pa Augustine Ngalim and edited by Paddy Mbawa, and which used to appear weekly, if and when its dummy had been censured by the administrators and it had been authorized to appear. The column proved so popular with readers that many claimed they were buying the paper for the column and, whenever my piece was not ready, the paper was reluctant to go to press.

In 1993, I was persuaded by many readers to make a book of the essays, in the interest of readers who had not been able consistently to keep cuttings of the column. The result was *THE PAST TENSE OF SHIT (Book One): Contribution of an Uncompromising Critic to the Democratic Process in Cameroon.* Comprising 75 essays, the book was published by Nooremac Press in Limbe. A public launching, to have been presided over by Dr. Simon Munzu, who at the time was the spokesperson of the Anglophone problem and struggle in Cameroon, was planned for 18 June, 1993, in Yaounde. But the "administration" frustrated the launching by sealing the proposed venue and by seizing the entire stock of the books on their way from the Press in Limbe to Yaounde.

NO TRIFLING MATTER, however, continued appearing in the *CAMEROON POST* until 1994 when I felt I had exhausted my originality and would only be repeating myself if I continued writing. I stopped writing, but not before publishing a book of the 50 essays that had been written since the seizure of THE PAST TENSE… The book was given the title: *I SPIT ON THEIR GRAVES (Book Two of the Past Tense…): Testimony Relevant to the Democratization Struggle in Cameroon.* Chairman Ni John Fru Ndi, the charismatic "book seller" of Bamenda and hero of the defiant launching of the SDF on 06 May, 1990, accepted to write the *Preface* to the book and Simon Munzu wrote the *Epilogue*. This time around we were cleverer than the agents of repression and kept both the time and place of publication a closely guarded secret.

I was, however, not allowed to take my well-deserved rest from scripting. Tremendous pressure from all directions – publishers, editors, readers, friends, colleagues, etc. - was brought to bear on me to continue writing. I reluctantly gave in and resumed writing a weekly column in the *CAMEROON POST* under the new rubric *COCKTAIL…From the Son of Gobata.* The column was short-lived (flourishing only between March and July 1994) and this owing to the instability of the newspaper itself and the fact that towards the end of 1994 I left Cameroon for Germany on a fellowship of the Alexander von Humboldt Foundation. The fifteen essays of the Cocktail are published as the Appendix to my book *Democracy and Meritocracy: Philosophical Essays and Talks from an African Perspective*, Berlin, Galda & Wilch Verlag, 1996.

On my return from Germany in 1996, I resumed writing in the same newspaper whose publisher-ship had now been acquired by N. N. Susungi. I wrote under the new rubric: *IN THE SPIRIT OF GOBATA*, until around June 1997 when the *CAMEROON POST* collapsed under its own weight from internal problems, and virtually ceased appearing. *THE POST*, with Francis Wache as Editor-in-Chief and Charlie Ndi Chia as Editor, got erected on the ashes of the *CAMEROON POST* and I eventually resumed writing infrequent but well-highlighted Gobata essays in *THE POST*, until around 2001 when other time-consuming commitments and frequent traveling made it impossible for me to continue writing in a regular manner. In 1998 I published the last 33 Gobata essays of the *CAMEROON POST* as Part Two of my book *ROAD COMPANION TO DEMOCRACY AND MERITOCRACY (Further Essays from an African Perspective)*, Bellingham, USA, Kola Tree Press. The occasional Gobata essays of *THE POST* are the only ones which have never otherwise been published as a collection.

I am particularly happy at the republication of these first 75 Gobata essays, seized on first publication by Governmental authorities. There is some anecdotal evidence that the authorities in question read carefully through all the essays in question. Well, I have neither been rewarded nor directly further punished for writing them, but some their concerns and recommendations seem to have been addressed. It is only right that the public to whom they were primarily addressed and on whose insistence they were collected for publication in book form, should at last have them at their disposal. The change in the title of the collection will, no doubt, please many among the readers.

For the rest, the central concerns and themes running through these essays – democracy, meritocracy, public fair-play, development, accountability, unity, assimilation, etc. – are as urgently critical today as they were when the essays were first written. The New Deal regime of Paul Biya has been completely successful in its immunizing and immortalizing tactics, thanks in part to unprecedented emigration of young people out of the country, since the early 1990s, impoverishment of the rural and urban masses, and the survival strategies of the parasitic elite classes. Given its enormous resources, Cameroon is nothing if not one of Africa's paradigmatic cases of spectacular failure. In many parts of the country, for instance, 50 years after so-called independence, the roads are worse than in colonial days and inhabitants have never seen a water pipe, let alone an electric pole; and yet there is scarcely any other African country with as many publicly enormously enriched individuals as in Cameroon. No Cameroonian today can pretend to predict the further evolution of the country.

Godfrey B. Tangwa, alias Rotcod Gobata
Yaounde, 18/06/2010

Table of Contents

Foreword

My pen name is ROTCOD GOBATA. Today, an enlarging circle of readers of CAMEROON POST have come to know my real names. For those who don't know, I will prefer to leave them undisturbed and I encourage them to remain peacefully in their blissful ignorance. You can never predict the results of any 'revelation'. After all what's in a name? The cat was let out of the bag through the *Campost* editorial house itself by people who could not have helped knowing my true identity.

The only Cameroonian known to me who on his own divined my true identity is Dr Joseph B. Jumbam of CLINICA SANTA MONICA, P.O Box 30, Jakiri. I was not very surprised because Jumbam and I have been very intimate friends from our secondary school days. There is a childhood 'secret document' which we 'kept safe' periodically exchanging it between us for twenty years before finally deciding to destroy it in a mock solemn ceremony. On 17 September, 1991, Dr Jumbam wrote to me *inter alia:* "Whenever I buy a copy of the Cameroon Post I first read "NO TRIFLING MATTER" by ROTCOD GOBATA. When I consulted the gods, they guessed that GOBATA could be (and here he deciphered the code accurately) but they couldn't guess who ROTCOD could be. Have you anything to say to clear their doubts?" I wrote back to congratulate him and gave him a single clue to help decipher ROTCOD and thus his solution of the puzzle.

Left to me, even the gods themselves would only have had to guess. One day my wife excitedly rushed into my study, a recent copy of Cameroon Post in her hands: "G.B! G.B! have you read Cameroon Post of today? You really need to read this columnist called GOBATA!" I calmly asked her what it was all about. She read out excerpts of it for me and I said: "Sounds quite interesting, when you finish reading, let me also read it." On several occasions I found myself in situations where people were discussing NO TRIFLING MATTER and whenever my opinion was sought, I would always say something fairly non-committal. This gave me wonderful opportunities for honest feedback.

Why did I choose to write under a code-name? Simply to escape the nuisance of professional congratulators. Before becoming a columnist for Cameroon Post, I used occasionally to write articles for Cameroon Tribune. On one occasion in 1987, some university lecturer, a supposed intellectual, saw me and warmly congratulated me for my article in the newspaper. When I tried to get his critical opinion on my views, I discovered that he had not read the article in question and could not even recall what it was all about. He had simply chanced to see my name in print and came to congratulate me! I was sickened.

NO TRIFLING MATTER has been my own contribution towards positive change in Cameroon. It was conceived as far back as 1986 but it was not until 1990 that it found an Archimedean foothold in the Cameroon Post. At first I tried doing it through Cameroon Tribune but discovered that if they didn't like what you wrote, the entire manuscript simply "got missing" within their spacious editorial rooms. That way I lost irretrievably two of what I would consider the best essays I have ever written. Shey Peter Mabu could confirm this. I sincerely thank Paddy Mbawa, Editor-in–Chief of Cameroon Post for his act of faith in unhesitatingly granting a complete stranger a column at a time he could not have known whether it would help or mar circulation and readership.

The scaffolding of the philosophy underlying NO TRIFLING MATTER was sketched in the piece: 'GOBATA ON GOBATA by Rotcod Gobata (see Campost, July 16-23, 1991). The modest objective of the column was to rouse Cameroonians from thirty years of lethargic slumber. That objective has been largely achieved. I believe that the momentum towards a just, democratic and prosperous Cameroon is now unstoppable.

But as I start humming my *nunc dimitis*, it must not be forgotten that the struggle will continue even after this highly kleptocratic Biya regime has been routed. The price of liberty is eternal vigilance! The struggle must continue against those who committed or commissioned horrendous atrocities - maiming, killings, abductions, beatings, raping, detentions, incarcerations etc., to maintain the *status quo* and so safeguard their stolen wealth. *A lutta continua*! equally against those within the anticipated new regime who may turn out to be wolves in sheep's clothing. The struggle must continue until ... we spit on their graves!

Rotcod Gobata

Preface

My first encounter with Rotcod Gobata's writing was neither direct, immediate, nor intended. It came two issues after the debut of the column "No Trifling Matter". He was recommended to me by HRH Fon Angwafor III of Mankon. I had brought back from town a couple of newspapers for the Fon. Skimming through one of them, Cameroon Post, his attention was caught by a headline which he read aloud: "No Trifling Matter: Those Billions in Foreign Banks. By Rotcod Gobata." Then he exclaimed: "Rotcod Gobata! I like his writing. I enjoy his arguments. He doesn't quibble!" Thereafter, I set out to bring the column home to myself. And when I noticed I had fallen in love with Rotcod Gobata's weekly menu of enriching insight and alternative interpretations of topical issues, I sought to know the face behind the pen. For a long time I suspected Dr Tata Mentan, until the day I met with a TV producer, Kwasen Gwangwa'a, at his office. "Rotcod Gobata is a good friend of mine. He doesn't know that I know his real identity," said Mr Gwangwa'a in response to my question on the identity of Rotcod Gobata. A few days later, Shey Anthony Kimbi, a student journalist on internship with Cameroon Post, volunteered insider information. And so my curiosity got satisfaction.

Perhaps some who have read Rotcod Gobata with attentive interest and scrutiny, might think that I took a rather roundabout way to narrow down my short list of possible "Rotcod Gobatas." His writing is full of clues that point to his "Banso origin" they could claim, and proceed to substantiate by citing *inter alia*, his intimacy with the Nso and his more than cursory knowledge of what goes on in the Bui Division in particular. With such examples as eating "Kimbur" with Cardinal Christian Tumi in Garoua, the anecdotes by little Kiven and others, his Banso friends and his being generally very informed about the atrocities committed by the "foxes of loo and udder" in the Nso area, they could consider their case proven.

And if one where to read into these clues that Rotcod Gobata is a tribalist, one would be going counter to the columnist's ardent stance against tribalism. His views on the issue are without equivocation. He believes that any man of reason would have nothing to do with tribalism, which is principally a man-made problem created to promote "false consciousness", and "sustained by politicians who are destitute of the sterling qualities of leadership or who want to cover up a hideous path of personal corruption." He considers himself "completely detribalized", not in the sense that he does not cherish his father's name and place of birth, but that tribalism as the practice of granting or obtaining favours simply because you share the same ethnic origins, "cuts no ice" with him.

Rotcod Gobata comes across as a man of courage and resolve; one ready to swim upstream in a manner of a desperate midwife eager to prevent a still birth (in this case, of democracy). His column is as daring an embarrassment to Biya's "démocratie avancée" as the radio programme "Cameroon Report" (later "Cameroon Calling"), was to Presidents Ahidjo and Biya in the hey days of the "parti unique". Rotcod Gobata believes the time has come for Cameroon to graduate from a country over milked by mediocrity and callous indifference, to the paradise that it was meant to be for the poor and downtrodden. In this regard, he belongs with that rare breed of intellectuals who are genuine in their pursuit of collective betterment, and who in consequence, have opted to distance themselves from the stomach and all its trappings. This position is to be commended and encouraged, especially in a system where explanation is often mistaken for subversion, a system where the stomach is about the only political path-finder - the sole compass in use, a country where the champions of falsehood want all at their beck and call, and where a handful of thirsting palates daily jostle to share with Count Dracula the blood of the common and forgotten.

Rotcod Gobata wants the new Cameroon to be rid of the ills and failures of the past three decades that have made it impossible for Cameroonians in their millions to live productive and creative lives. The new Cameroon should therefore be free of political demagogy, double standards, stoogery and sycophancy. It should be a Cameroon where people are moved by principle and love of country, not propelled or remote-controlled by the whims and caprices of self-serving dictators and schizophrenics, or worse still, by their foreign paymasters and overlords. It should be a Cameroon void of censorship, even the symbolic; a Cameroon where there are no political inquisitions, and where no one is forced underground or into exile because of his or her opinions and beliefs. The new Cameroon should be BMM free, not on paper but in fact.

In contemporary Cameroon few personalities or institutions connected with the status quo have been spared Rotcod Gobata's virulent pen. The Fons, in the main, have lost the glamour and esteem that went with their traditional office, and are reduced to "professional congratulators and handclappers" by a regime that has neither respect nor compunction for the persons or institutions. J. N. Foncha is criticized for not resigning from the CPDM much earlier than 1990, and accused of myopia, naivety and simple-mindedness in the dangerous, rough and slippery terrain of post-Foumban politics. S. T. Muna is "a self-serving political prostitute" who sold "his own people and patrimony for a mess of pottage". Jean Zoa, "His lostship" the Archbishop of Yaounde, is not only a secular priest renowned for his masses in service of Rosicrucians and the beleaguered CPDM, he also is a chronic sufferer from the regime's "verbal equivocations...conceptual mirages and gerrymandering." The police, gendarmes and armed forces are far from being "forces of law and order". If anything, they are "foxes of loo and udder" or members of the "harm forces"; for is it not true that they have rendered the term "security" meaningless by the repeated violations of privacy and the arbitrary arrest, detention and torture to death of often innocent citizens? The students of the University of Yaounde have, for thirty years, "watched with complacency and complicity the rape and spoliation, the sapping and draining" of Cameroon. Having thus proved themselves impotent before the country's political problems, they should spare the public their "occasional collective idiocies" or so-called "strikes", and grant passers-by the "right of innocent passage". As for the University, it is an "embarrassment", "an antiquarian and authoritarian institution" whose senate is little other than a political playground where pseudo-intellectuals are locked in combat for political sinecures.

The whole of Biya's New Deal is given the place it deserves in history's basket of waste and irrelevance. Rotcod Gobata gives it a thorough flogging. In a decade, Biya and his "associés" have, like locusts, devastated the economic and political vegetation and reduced

Cameroon to a laughing stock in international circles. They have transformed a potential paradise into a hellish Sahara. They have frauded and embezzled with impunity, mismanaged with stubborn arrogance and reckless ignorance, and bled the commonwealth dry, with systematic disregard for he expressed wishes of the drowning, disillusioned bulk of Cameroonians. And at the height of it all, at the very heart of their much heralded democratization process, when the entire world expected them to pass from rhetoric into action, they made a volte-face, and, far more than Ahidjo could ever contemplate, have excelled in repression, coercion, intimidation, and blackmail. They have opted for disinformation, monologues and propaganda, to the detriment of information, debate and truth. They have, as Vaclav Havel would say, chosen to live a lie. And in all this, the public media have served as real apologists, often bending over backward to defend the undefendable.

In sum, Rotcod Gobata argues, "the verbal sterility of the New Deal regime is glaringly evident. No other regime has been so full of rhetoric about rigor and moralization, responsibility and accountability, efficiency and democracy, liberalization and national integration, etc. And yet no other regime has been so wide off the mark in these matters". Biya clearly, much in contradiction to his declarations, shows himself against any meaningful change in Cameroon. His failure to heed, inter alia, Rotcod Gobata's advice on numerous occasions, his rejection of the national conference as "sans object", his controversial hotly contested victory at the October 11, 1992 presidential elections, his declaration of a state of emergency in Bamenda under the flimsy excuse of guaranteeing "national security", and in general, his foolhardy disregard for national and international concern over the New Deal's dictatorial excesses, are all the indications of Biya's profound reluctance to go beyond the cosmetic in the process of the democratic rebirth of Cameroon.

Rotcod Gobata has a political cure in which he believes without reserve: Ni John Fru Ndi and the SDF. He has no doubt whatsoever, that these two would fetch Cameroon out of its present mess. In his writing, Ni John Fru Ndi and the SDF are singled out for unqualified praise. These two, thanks to what Rotcod Gobata has termed the "Ntarikon formula" ("democracy cannot be given on a platter of gold. It has to be taken and there is a price to be paid for the taking"), have woken Cameroonians from their deep slumber and political apathy. And any Cameroonian who really sweats for his/her daily bread cannot but feel identified with the SDF and its daringly bold challenge of the status quo. If Ni John Fru Ndi is a "simple bookseller" and if for thirty years and more the PhDs (Pull Him Down Syndrome) have, instead of bringing about "the good life" compounded the misery of the majority, then "it is about time we tried a bookseller. Let us try a bookseller". And indeed, but for the corrupting influence of the absolute power of the incumbent, the simple bookseller would be president in Cameroon today, trying in a simple way to give his country a new look.

Rotcod Gobata's writing is bound to be controversial. As the Fon of Mankon so shrewdly pointed out in those early days of the column, he does not quibble. But no one has summed the columnist up better than he himself. In "Gobata on Gobata", he compares himself to a meal set before many people. "Some would taste the soup and impatiently shout for salt, declaring that the cook forgot to put any salt. Others would taste the soup and wriggle the nose and declare it over salted. And yet others will relish the meal without any complaint." Which may suggest that "the taste may be more in the palate than in the meal". Read him and situate yourself; that is the challenge.

At the level of discourse, Rotcod Gobata is unimpeachable, academic. His ideas are enlightening, his arguments rigorous and persuasive, and his positions clear and consistent. It is difficult, for those with no vested interest in the status quo, to find fault with his words. One would have to see him in action, to be able to say whether between declaration and deed, there are any contradictions. For, as he so aptly remarks, "between word and action, between concept and reality, between desire and gratification, stand a wide, deep chasm and a thousand and one obstacles."

Dr Francis B. Nyamnjoh
Bamenda, December, 1992

1

An Open Letter to Pa Foncha
(Published October 11-18, 1990)

Dear Pa,

I hope that this letter will meet you in good health and enjoying your voluntary retirement from the rough and tumble of active political life. For some time now, I had thought of writing to you privately. But on further reflection, I am convinced that a letter to one of the founding fathers of the nation, precisely in his capacity as a founding founder of the nation, cannot be a private affair. That is why several thousand Cameroonians will be reading this letter with you.

The year 1990 will probably go down in our political annals as a landmark year, comparable to 1961 and 1972. 1990 has witnessed a quickened tempo, temperature and pressure in our political affairs that would have appeared impossible even to an optimistic dreamer a few years ago. All this is in a positive direction. At long last, Cameroonians have awoken from a deep slumber and political apathy and are poised to take their own destiny in their hands instead of leaving it as heretofore in the hands of self-appointed messiahs and autocrats.

By far the most important event in this process of reawakening was the launching on May 26th of the SDF party in Bamenda against fierce opposition and intimidation. Another was the unprecedented memorandum of the Mezam section of the CPDM to the Head of State on the events of May 26th. The third was your own resignation on June 9th from the CPDM party as a sequel to the events of 26th May and their aftermath.

I last wept in 1970 on the occasion of the tragic death of a young sister. Since then I had resolved never again in my life to weep for any cause. But when I read your letter of resignation from the CPDM of which you were the First National Vice President and your memorandum entitled "A Brief Account of the Events Which Took Place in the Bamenda Township on Saturday 26th May, 1990,

Culminating in the Shooting and Killing of Five Innocent Young Men and One Girl," tears involuntarily flowed from my eyes.

We all knew you had been marginalized and rendered irrelevant since the time Mr Ahidjo, in his political wisdom, carefully manoeuvred you out of power and replaced you with a self-serving political prostitute who helped him in completing the sell-out of his own people and patrimony for a mess of pottage. But who could really have imagined, Pa, until you yourself put it down in writing, that as first National Vice President of our single party, requests by you "for audience with the Chairman of the party to discuss issues were systematically turned down" or that "several memos and presentations you made in writing on several national issues were ignored"? Eh Pa, who could really have believed before you yourself confessed it, that in this our Republic you used to be summoned to meetings in Yaounde by radio or that members of the Cameroon armed forces could actually stop your car, knowing fully well who you were, and subject it to a meticulous search before "scornfully asking you to go"?

Your resignation was thoroughly justified though not timely and history will never forget your courage at this particular point in time nor your place as one of the founding fathers of the nation. You were the architect of Reunification although after that momentous event you seemed to have been rendered completely impotent and your pet projects – a deep sea port for Limbe, CamBank, marketing board, WADA, Cooperative Movement, Ring Road, Mamfe Road etc. – all abandoned. How indeed, Pa, is it that, thirty years after independence and Reunification, all the roads in your primary constituency, Northwest Province are in a much worse condition than they ever were when you used them while campaigning for Reunification?

Politics is a game of numbers and a politician within a democratic set-up, true to his calling, is the representative of his people. This means that if the collective interests of those people are threatened or violated, he cannot afford to practice the virtue of quietism, much less engage in stoogy handclapping. A certain Fon of the North West Province once removed a medal with which President Ahidjo had decorated him and sent back to the President through the SDO in his Fondom because, in his view, the president had taken an action he considered inimical to the interest of his people. Ahidjo was reportedly shocked at the effrontery but thereafter always greatly admired and respected this particular Fon. Of course there no longer seem to be any Fons of that calibre around to today as most of the Fons, for unfathomable reasons, now turn themselves into professional congratulators and hand clappers.

However, the fault, dear Pa, is not in our stars but in ourselves that we are underlings. That is why it must be said that although you did the right and honourable thing, you did it far too late. You should have protested in this dramatic and efficacious fashion long long ago. To be candid with you Pa, I think that your fundamental fault has been too much patience, too much trust, too much wishful thinking, too much eagerness to show that often praised Christian side of you which tends to leave everything to God. It is this fundamental weakness, I believe, which led you into political myopia, naivety and simplistic approach in dangerously rough and slippery terrain.

Let me illustrate what I am saying by asking you to take your mind back to 1961 during the pre-constitutional talks in Barmenda, prior to the Fumban conference. That conference brought together representatives of all the political parties in the then Southern Cameroons, the ten Native Councils and the Government under your leadership. The main purpose of this conference was, ostensibly, to prepare a bargaining position for the Foumban conference. Now, living participant witnesses at this conference can testify that you were so naively enamoured of reunification that you were very displeased with those who tried to argue that safety valves should be built into the proposed union. At least one of the native councils, as well as one of the parties represented, presented strong memoranda to this effect. But you personally made sure that these suggestions were defeated and the radical elements proposing them excluded from the Foumban conference. Your main concern then was that there should not be any stumbling block on the way of unification and that, as a Christian, you should not be seen as lacking in the virtue of human trust by your Moslem counterpart. You forgot that an emergency exit is never provided with the hope that it will be used. Rather, the hope is that it should never be used. But it is a necessity all the same, just in case... Is all this true or false, Pa?

3

It is said that he who fights and runs away from the fight lives to fight another day. And here you are today, Pa, fighting again whereas, if you had fought to a finish in 1961, you wouldn't have needed to be fighting again today. This column believes that many of the problems plaguing our political landscape today were sown much earlier during the pre- Foumban constitutional conference in Bamenda. There were serious errors of omission committed which the Fonlon-inspired KNDP memorandum of 1964 attempted unsuccessfully to salvage. It was already too late. A careful study of the proceedings of that initial constitutional conference would certainly throw plenty of light on our present political travails. But, in a system in which records are not kept, it is doubtful whether all or even part of the documentation of that historically important event is anywhere still extant.

Pa, do you perhaps have anything in your personal files on that event? If you do, please, do posterity the favour of letting us have a look at it.

Highest regards and very best wishes.

Yours Truly,

ROTCOD

2

Begging the Question
(Published October 18-25, 1990)

There is a fallacy which lawyers and logicians term *'petitio principii'* or "begging the question." Technically, the fallacy consists in assuming as a premise the very conclusion which you want to prove. If, for instance, in trying to prove that someone is a thief, you use as part of your evidence the fact that he is accused of being a thief, you commit a *'petitio principii'*. Similarly, if I argue that God must exist because the Bible which is the word of God Himself says so, I commit the same fallacy. But the fallacy can be extended to include any claim, action, procedure etc., which immediately raises many pertinent questions.

In these first few months of our *"democratie encore plus avancée"* too many question-begging issues have been very apparent even to the casual observer.

Let us begin with the press conference granted by the Minister of Territorial Administration to members of the private press on August 7, 1990. For several days before this conference, the national radio, whose advertisements are fast becoming an index of veiled apologia for discredited courses and persona, had enthusiastically advertised it, with insinuations that it was going to be a lambasting of the private press.

One of the questions that the honoured (if not quite honourable) minister's conference begged in its advertisemental stage was the following which sprang to mind immediately: a press conference for the private press alone? Usually, a press conference is meant to divulge information that is of interest to the public at large for dissemination. So why would a purported press conference exclude the official and international press? As a matter of fact, the press conference itself turned out to be a series of admonitions to the private press to eschew false reports, unfounded rumours, intoxication (whatever that means), etc.; in short, a plea for responsible journalism in the face of increasing liberalism. Now, why would anybody exclude the official press from such admonitions

5

when it has been the worst offender in those regards? The minister of Information and Culture (recall the open letter of Zacharie Ngniman and Antoine Marie Ngono) was even present at this conference, not in his capacity as one of the journalists needing admonition but as co-admonisher! Haba! Of course, members of the official press did (stubbornly?) attend this conference. But that is beside the point.

After the aforementioned conference, the national radio again started advertising a certain forthcoming issue of one of the private newspapers, *Le Democrate*. The questions that immediately sprang to mind were: why should the national radio be advertising a private newspaper in such a blatant and avid manner? Or is <u>*Le Democrate*</u> (which has now become *Le Patriote)* a privileged newspaper? The particular issue being chanted about on radio was that of August 9th, 1990. I fell for the propaganda and rushed for a copy when the issue came out of the press, spending my last 200 francs in the process. And what did I read in the headlines? The following cynical question and statements: "**Who has looted the Public Treasury**? In a state of law, it is necessary to provide proofs. No ethnic group has the monopoly of uprightness."

"Wonders," I exclaimed, "so all those alleged public thieves belong to one ethnic group?!" How could one really have known or imagined? A thief is a thief and no one ethnic group has a monopoly of thieves. Which is not to say that special circumstances may not make an identifiable group to excel in thievery or that the big time thieves of a particular epoch may not in fact belong to one ethnic group if such had monopoly of access to what was to be stolen? But the way, *Le Democrate* went about expressing these truisms leaves the impression that it might be gunning for the unenviable title of "defender of public thieves."

By the bye, another elaborate radio programme about the same period spent much time and energy trying to prove how impossible it would be to carry milliards (Billions) of francs out of the country. Here it was maintained that anyone who has ever been anywhere near a bank should know that such a "feat" would require several suitcases. The question again that sprang to mind: Is there any law against carrying several suitcases out of the country? And even if

6

there were, who would enforce it against the of type special breed of Cameroonians likely to be carrying out milliards of francs?

The last story that we'll mention here that raises a catalogue of questions was on television news of Thursday August 9, 1990. According to this story, supported by camera shots in some of which custom officers posed for pictures with samples of contraband with the air of national heroes, a lorry-load of "Elephant" brand of detergent, smuggled from Nigeria, was apprehended somewhere in the Central province. Now, note that this heavily loaded lorry was not caught anywhere near our borders. Questions: How did a heavily loaded lorry carrying contraband manage to travel all the way to the heart of the country before being caught? Could it possibly have been dropped from an aircraft? Given that even a private motorist cannot travel from Bafoussam to Yaoundé without being stopped and searched at least half a dozen times by the "law enforcement agents," is it rather not more plausible to believe that this 'Elephant' detergent lorry got caught only at the point where the owner of the contraband ran out, not of luck but of the ability to "*parler bien*"? In any case, the economically sensible thing to do is to force the illegal importer to pay duty on the stuff perhaps, with an appropriate fine. Failing which, the goods can then be sold (auctioned) to the public. They should not be given to "the poor" for free. The government is not a Father Christmas, and even if it were, it may be hard to determine who the poor are, and even if they could easily be determined, it is not likely that what they need is detergent. In our situation, "the poor" will likely turn out to be the big men and officials charged with the enviable duty of dispensing this extraordinary piece of government charity. The goods will surely end up in their well-stocked shops down town.

Which brings to mind this SONARA TV advert against "Federale." How does this contraband get here in the first place? And why, in spite of the much vaunted virtues and advantages of SONARA refined fuel do most motorists compulsively go for "Federale" wherever and whenever it is available? The answers may be blowing in the wind. But how, in fact, do we explain the fact that in two neighbouring countries, both oil producers and refiners, it takes less than 1000 francs. to fill your tank in one against 20000

7

francs in the other? A putative smuggler is thus enticed by 2000% gain and his customers save comparatively by patronizing him. Such temptations should not be placed even before saints.

3

Mondial 90 and the Success of Success
(Published October 25-November 1, 1990)

Before "Italia 90" takes its allotted space in the store room of memory and history, we can draw salutary lessons. One of these lessons is that nothing indeed succeeds like success.

A hundred advertisers would probably have needed two decades to achieve for Cameroon the world-wide publicity the Indomitable Lions achieved in a fortnight.

The instinct to identify with the winner must be second only to the instinct for survival. Or how would you explain the outburst of an English fan during the most thrilling quarter final duel between England and Cameroon on Sunday July 1st? The English fan is reported to have declared that he wants to become a Cameroonian and some young Nigerian girl is simply dying to be Mrs Roger Milla. I can bet my last 10000 francs that by now some street somewhere other than Cameroon is already named after Roger Milla.

One thing for which I had always admired the English people is their spirit of adventurous pragmatism. It is this spirit which led them to nearly conquer the world through colonialism under the concept of "British Empire." This failed on the brink of success on the strictly political level. But, at the cultural level, no one can doubt that the English have actually conquered the world especially through their language.

As I was reading through some very flattering write-ups on Cameroon's World Cup performance in some British newspapers and magazines, one story particularly caught my attention. This story is in the *Times Saturday Review* of July 7th, 1990. The World Cup spotlight on Cameroon had sent a certain Briton by name Alan

Franks searching for an atlas. Once he ascertained where Cameroon is, he immediately packed his travelling bag and set off for Cameroon! Can you beat that? Well, his enchanted adventure brought him right here and as far as via Mudemba to the Korup National Park which has been described in Britain as a "priceless national asset."

The opening of Alan Franks' account of his adventure to Cameroon entitled "A Short Walk In an Enchanted Rainforest" is very telling. Writes he: "Cameroon has suffered from a sub-section of the Falklands factor: it is one of those places that sounds as though it might be found up among the ragged bits in the top left hand corner of the British map, only to be hiding in one of the most outrageous, if original, spots on the globe, well beyond the scope of our insular sightlines. Then something big occurs in the place, or concerning the place, and there is a general buying of time while we all go in search of an atlas and re-order our topology. Of such alarms are adult Geography lessons made.

"Just as the Falklands conflict did wonders for our knowledge of where the Falklands are, so the World Cup has put Cameroon unto our blinkered map, as the small Central African nation with a population of 10 million which not only made it to the later stages of the competition but also had the temerity to beat the reigning champions Argentina."

The Britons generally have shown more than a passing interest in the Korup forest. In fact, it can be said that when British royalty in the persons of the Prince and Princess of Wales, Charles and His charming wife, Lady Diana, came to Cameroon for the first time ever, a few months ago, it was mainly to see Korup for themselves. If I know the Britons, there must be something in Korup beyond monkeys, giant apes, ants and vicious wasps. Does any Cameroonian know what it is?

But to get back to "Mondiale 90," the success of success and compulsive identification with victors, let us note that everyone has actually forgotten the dismal performance of the Lions during the African Cup of Nations in Algeria only a few months before the World Cup. Of course there are always plausible retrospective explanations. But as long as performance and achievement are the only criteria for credibility, one cannot but side with those who blame the Cup of Nations' fiasco on the absence of Roger Milla, the African super star of Mondiale 90.

Some Nigerians have long had the theory that, without Milla, the Indomitable Lions are quite domitable. This is a plausible theory which the Lions can only labour to falsify in the future. In the meantime, the Milla fever continues as even scientific theories are postulated to explain how a man of nearly forty can exhibit the physical qualities associated with teenagers. Personally, I don't believe that Milla's performance has anything to do with the structure of his bones or the shape of his legs. One palpable truth is that those who had ruled out Milla on grounds of age failed to take into account the difference between chronological age and what we should call physical age. A man of forty could be physically as young as a normal twenty-year-old. Some men below thirty have bodies which physically are close to sixty, having been wrecked by excessive drinking, eating, smoking, womanizing and sheer inactivity. Another palpable truth is that talent, skill, and especially genius are not a function of age, whether physical or chronological.

The Milla fever has not spared anyone. Recently, our own very Head of State himself, during his "famous" Radio Monte Carlo press conference in France, disclosed that the inclusion of Milla in the world cup team was his own "l'idee originale." (The cousin in Television House is certainly losing monopoly over this domain!).

In his policy speech during the (first?) Congress of the CPDM party, the Head of State used the Lions as a model which can be applied on the wider socio-politico-economic level. The model is very compelling. But why has Cameroon football flourished so much over the years? My guess is that the success of football is directly related to the **freedom** that has been allowed in that domain over the years, in contrast to the no-dare situation in other domains. In all domains where Cameroonians have had the liberty to operate freely - sports, music, drinking, womanizing - the results are uniformly remarkable. Contrast these permissible domains with those which are anathema. It is a near impossible task in this country to form a scientific or professional association or even a serious discussion group and, up to the present, (hopefully) it has been a suicidal task to express well-thought opinions of any sort if such were contrary to official doctrines or positions or even the mere opinion of someone within the ruling power structure.

All Cameroonians owe the Head of State three hearty cheers for having had both the idea that Mila should join the World Cup squad and the means and will to have that idea translated into action. How fortunate indeed would we be if such positive and efficacious interventions were more common. Suppose, for instance, he had positively intervened at Bamenda on 26th May to prevent the murder of seven innocent citizens by people armed and paid, in fact, to protect these very citizens. Suppose he had intervened to tell one of his lieutenants who cried out that that there were enemies in the mansion, that the mansion neither belonged to him personally nor were there any enemies in it. Or suppose, he had reminded the other one, who with reckless arrogance asked those not happy with the status quo to go elsewhere, that a modern state is not a feudal chiefdom.

Just suppose that he had stepped in when the official mass media started singing about 10,000 Nigerians infiltrating into Bamenda, Uniyao students chanting the Nigerian anthem, six people being trampled to death etc. Just suppose he had stepped in then and asked the unimaginative authors of those incredible falsehoods to stop over-stretching credulity, what a great country might we be living in!

Performance and achievement, in short, success, is equally the only criterion of credibility in the socio-politico-economic arena. Here, like elsewhere, no amount of high-sounding declarations or promises or even mere good intentions is enough. When mere declarations, promises and wishful intentions are translated into reality, no one needs persuasion to applaud or to compulsively identify with the architect of such achievement.

For the Milla miracle at Mondiale 90, my vote goes to the Head of State, if indeed Milla's last minute inclusion in the team was his making. But as for who shall be remembered for bringing democracy and prosperity to Cameroon, I say I am no futurologist. My guess may be as good as yours. This is mine: For prosperity, I offer the medal to all Cameroonian peasant farmers whose toil has flooded our country with food. As for forcing the beginnings of credible democracy and liberalism, my vote is reserved for the SDF and the seven martyrs of its launching in Ntarikon Motor Park, Bamenda, on May 26th, 1990.

4

Those Billions in Foreign Banks
(Published November 1-8 1990)

Are there Cameroonians with billions in foreign banks? This is a multi-billion hard currency question. But the initial answer to this question is not far to fetch and requires no pondering. The simple answer is "Yes." How do I know? By simple deduction. The banks and parastatals have been looted and the economic crisis proves that the loot is nowhere near our borders.

In their June 3, 1990 Pentecost Sunday Pastoral Letter, the Catholic Episcopal hierarchy highlighted three questions which are on all desperate lips: Why are the banks empty? Who have emptied them? Where are those who emptied them?

In trying to answer these questions, some newspapers have named names. The very nervous reactions from high quarters to this name-calling shows that it is the tip of a veritable iceberg that has been touched. For now, it seems prudent to avoid the hyper-sensitive tail of puff adder. More dancing around the real issue seems not only necessary but inevitable for the time being. But those billions abroad will remain a skeleton in our national cupboard until we decide to bring in the exorcist and give it a decent burial.

How do I mean? The magnitude of our present economic travails cannot be explained away in terms of falling prices in the world market. We are not the only country which sells and buys in the world market. Some of our neighbours who have nothing better than, say, groundnuts, which they can hawk at the world market, are still managing to get on in spite of the world economic crisis.

In Cameroon, we can boast of timber (even if we lack men of calibre), cocoa, coffee, tea, cotton, banana, palm produce, rubber, etc,

12

and several minerals including the "black gold," petroleum. To crown it all, our population is only around ten million and we are self-sufficient in food production. So why really should our economy be so badly off? It seems more palpable than a coloured butterfly, then, that our economy has been wrecked by large-scale fraud, embezzlement, mismanagement and reckless looting of the national treasury.

This is not very surprising, really. For over two decades, we have been running a single party system within which it is absolutely anathema to ask questions or otherwise probe into any issues. This always leaves people in positions of power and responsibility to act with reckless abandon in erecting what Cameroon bishops, following Pope John Paul II, have termed "structures of sin." Furthermore, kleptocracy has been identified as an African problem even where plural democracy operates. The question we shall never be able to run away from nor sweep under our carpets is: Who have emptied our national treasury and what is to be done about it?

We already have some indications about the first part of this question. I would like to offer some suggestions about the second part. The first thing to note carefully is that we cannot, like the President of the National Assembly in his November 1989 opening speech simply call "on Cameroonians who have large sums of money saved in foreign banks to repatriate some back to the country so as to revamp our economy by creating enterprises." It is those who never listened carefully to this speech and who never read it in print that got the mistaken impression that the Honourable President might be harbouring some repressed or suppressed elements of radicalism in him. We have no business asking Cameroonians who have saved money abroad to bring some to revive our ailing economy. No self-respecting country can depend on this sort of individual philanthropy for its economic well-being or survival. What we are or should be talking about is our stolen money banked in foreign countries.

You don't beg a thief to bring back part of what he stole from you and invest it in a business so that you might indirectly benefit from the good effects of his successful business. Stolen money cannot be legitimized by being kept for a while in a foreign bank and then brought back and invested in enterprises. Nor should we make

13

the mistake of focusing our attention only on those who have banked the stolen money abroad. Those who have invested or banked theirs right at home are no less guilty. In fact, such "structures of sin" at home should naturally be our first targets in the just process of recovery. There is absolutely no need calling on these thieves to bring back the stolen money. If they heed such a call, it would be generally against human nature and particularly against the psychology of a thief. When someone steals something from your house, you don't send a radio message to him that he should "please" bring it back. Instead you take your club or whatever and pursue and, if you catch up with him, just too bad for him.

Some Cameroonians have already indicated that they know the banks and account numbers where our stolen monies are being kept. If the government were serious, it should commission these people and give them all necessary means and protection to carry out a thorough investigation in full public view. At the start of such an investigation, opportunity should be given to those who may have undergone a veritable *metanoia* to confidentially confess their holdings and voluntarily to bring them back. Any such could be rewarded with, say, 10% of their loot and a medal for moral bravery. Repentance always involves three stages: confession, restitution and penance, including a firm purpose of amendment.

Next, all means at our disposal should be used to get back the holdings of those who had not undergone the radical moral transformation. At this stage, culprits who fully cooperate in the exercise should also be rewarded with, say, 2.5% of their recovered loot but without any decoration for bravery.

But for those who refuse to cooperate, all coercive means should be used, including *Umaru-Dikkoing* them and their loot from wherever they may be hiding at home or abroad. And if any of such turn out to be people who had sought the exculpating services of a Charles Ndongo and publicly declared (say, on radio, television or the print media etc.) that they had never stolen a franc of public money, they should further be imprisoned for criminal incorrigibility and for adding insult to injury.

5

I Doff My Hat to Mr. President

(Published November 19-26, 1990)

I doff my hat to Mr President of the Republic as he celebrates his eighth anniversary of accession to the pinnacle of political power. If one were to be looking for a nail in conceptual space on which to hang the last eight years, that nail would without dispute bear the tag "Democracy and Liberalization." Indeed, if we limit ourselves to the level of pronouncements and declarations, the Biya regime will have no rival anywhere on the African continent regarding its obsession with Democracy and Liberalism. But alas! Between word and action, between concepts and reality, between desire and gratification stand a wide, deep chasm and a thousand and one obstacles.

Mr President has himself openly declared that he would most like to be remembered as the person who brought (back?) democracy to Cameroon. On my part, I would be content to be remembered as the person who remembered to tell Mr President how easily he could achieve this deep-seated wish of being remembered as the person who brought democracy to Cameroon. This humble column would, therefore, humbly like to suggest how the President's wish can most assuredly be translated into reality.

The ball for multiparty politics has already been set rolling. The road to immortality for Mr Biya lies in neutrality. As the architect of this whole process, he must afford himself a circumambient vantage position from where to view the unfolding impartially. He needs a "God's eye view," as it were. Running with the hare and hunting with the hounds would be equivalent to an attempt to square the circle. In no true game can the umpire be at the same time one of the contestants. The sure path to the objectives which Mr Biya has never stopped proclaiming since his accession to the presidency, objectives which he now seems poised to realize, that sure path lies in **not** seeking another term in office. In the next two years or so he could concern himself with organizing free and fair elections within a democratic set-up. That would bring his longevity at the summit of

15

power to an ideal ten years. Indeed, if Mr Biya could refrain from seeking another term in office as President of the Republic, he would surely become a political hero and immortalize himself in the annals of our history. This would clearly prove beyond a shred of doubt that his commitment to democratization/liberalization is not just immunizing tactics for staying in power against the inevitable forward march of objective events. If he bows out now when the ovation is still loud and clear, he would prove that he is not only a politician but the statesman that we have always suspected him to be. Cameroonians will completely forgive, if not forget, any errors he may have advertently or inadvertently made during his incumbency. He would be idealized and idolized. He would remain in peaceful retirement like a refuge to which the people may run as a last resort, if those now rehearsing in the wings to take our collective destiny in their hands should disappoint our hopes.

But one fears that the political chameleons and professional praise-singers who populate our political landscape may not allow Mr Biya to take or even contemplate this very honourable option. They will drown him with cries of his indispensability. Well, let him remember, how, about eight years ago, the same people openly wept for and declared that Cameroon could have no future without his predecessor in power when the latter wisely decided to hand over power.

Today, his body lies amouldering in a shallow grave in a foreign country, but his spirit, unlike that of John Brown, does not go on marching anywhere, and none of these his former flatterers gives him even a thought.

Let's be done with political demagogy, chameleonism, stoogery and sycophancy. Let's be done once and for all, with these fellows who preface everything they utter in public with "As His Excellency the President has said..." (Haba! You mean you never have a personal opinion even in the area where you are an expert?). Let's be done with people who, their voluminous agbadas billowing in the wind, sing today, avidly condemning a proposition they suspect His Excellency does not like, only to re-sing in support of the very same proposition tomorrow when his Excellency finally declares his position. Let's be done with these fellows who blank fairly innocuous stories in newspapers because of some imaginary threat to national security whereas all they want to do is advertise themselves as busy bodies for the regime. Let's be done with people like the hatchet man of Mballa II who in his dimitial dance sees subversives everywhere, distributing hundreds of queries, transferring to punish and generally turning an important national corporation into a haven of professional mediocres and court jesters.

Paul Biya should not listen to these people when they chant their choruses of praises; he should not look at their crocodile tear-covered faces. No, Paul Biya must not take the path of the Boignys, Bongos, Does, Mombutus, the Eyademas of Africa. Cameroon has always been something special on the African continent. Let Paul Biya opt for statesmanship and political immortality. Let him join Mwalimu Julius Nyerere in his solitary camp.

> Fly, Paulus, fly
> Up up to the skies
> Of political stardom.
> Tarry not to listen
> To the cacophonies
> Of stooges and sycophants
> Seeking to lead you down
> The path of political perdition.
> Stay firm on your chosen path
> Which leads to immortality.
> Seek not another term of office.
> The ovation is kissing the summit.
> Bow out, Paulus, bow out!

6

The Day I Ate Fried Corn With the Cardinal
(Published March 6-13, 1991)

Long time no see and happy new year in arrears!! This column has not appeared for quite some time, which might have set you wondering whether, in spite of its respectful approach, those who think that respect can be enforced by law had, nevertheless, detected some disrespectful statements in the column and accordingly moved against the column or columnist. Well, both column and columnist are hale and hearty although the recent "suspended conviction" of Pius Njawe and Celestine Monga of the *Le Messager* newspaper does give one cause for concern as to whether the obviously erroneous view that a journalist is a professional praise-singer would ever be successfully combated in this country.

NO TRIFFLING MATTER only ran into some "bad weather" which created enormous procedural problems. It is remarkable to what extent this business of sitting down with a pen to put down ideas on paper is dependent on a serene mind in a healthy body. The Greeks who discovered the joys of writing and reading long long ago, centuries before Christ was even born, realized this and captured it in the maxim: *mens sana in corpore sano* – a healthy mind in a healthy body.

When you run into mental or bodily bad weather, this is always equivalent, from the point of view of creativity, to the portion termites have eaten off your life. The casualties are here in front of me in the form of two half written essays, one trying to assess the year 1990 which ended the penultimate decade of our millennium, and the other on the celebration mania of Cameroonians. We will probably come back to the latter issue in future. As for an assessment of the year 1990, I can only now relate what I considered personally as the most significant event of that year: the day I ate fried corn and groundnuts with Cardinal Christian Tumi! This was in April, nearly a year ago now, but it is still very fresh in my memory. It was my first visit ever to Garoua. My host in Garoua thought that I should not go back without "sampling" at least one Bororo girl. But I thought instead that I shouldn't leave without shaking hands with the Cardinal.

The strides that this country has made with regard to the progress and development of the Church, especially the Catholic Church, are simply mind-boggling. If anything comparable had been achieved in any other facet of our national life, ours should be a very remarkable country indeed. But alas! nearly all other aspects of our lives have all but stagnated.

As recently as the time Cardinal Tumi was born, no one in this country could have believed that a Blackman could become a priest - a Catholic priest? Man, stop dreaming. But today, we have countless priests, numerous bishops, several archbishops and a Cardinal - Prince of the Universal Church, member of the College of Cardinals who elect a Pope from among themselves whenever the seat of Peter becomes vacant.

When the appointment of Christian Tumi as the first ever Cameroonian Cardinal was first announced, I told a group of friends: "By the year 2000, we will have the first African Pope," which made them roar with laughter. Until the present Pope, who hails from what they call the Eastern bloc of countries was elected, it appeared as though a Pope not only had to be an orthodox, white Western European, but even specifically an Italian. Today the possibility of an African as Pope in Rome may still appear to some people as remote as the possibility of having a real change in the political and administrative landscape of Cameroon. But prospective and retrospective insight and foresight should warn us that both are imminent possibilities.

However, to get back to my story, I showed up at the Cardinal's residence with a lot of apprehension. I was expecting "Spanish Guards" at the gate and had carefully rehearsed what I would tell them to be allowed in. First shock: No Spanish Guards, no *megida* gateman, no *chien mechant*. As if I dreaming, I just walked up to the little bungalow - no Episcopal palace - no one stopping me, shook my dusty feet on the veranda and went through the open door without even knocking. He raised his head from behind the table where he was sitting reading, beamed a radiant smile, came up to me, hand warmly out-stretched.

We sat down on armchairs and, immediately, he brought out a tin of fried corn mixed with groundnuts, called *kimburr* in his native *Lamnso',* which his mother had sent to him all the way from Kikaikelahki and we ate it and washed it down with Fanta.

This was indeed the most moving experience I've had in a long long time. I've continued reflecting on it and asking myself why a little success, if success indeed it can be called, turns the rest of us into demi-gods who completely forget their humble roots and origin. Sometimes, here in Yaoundé, I have waited for more than two hours at the mercy of some capricious little girl called a Secretary to see a secondary school contemporary (since I cannot dare go his house for fear of his *chien mechant*) only to finally go in and be dismissed perfunctorily within 60 seconds.

For the Cameroon of my dreams, I offer you Christian Cardinal Wiyghan Tumi.

7

What Do University Students Really Want?
(Published March 14-21, 1991)

A few days after "Youth Day" on 11th February this year, the students of the University of Yaoundé went on rampage, blocking roads and burning cars, sequel to one of their members being crushed and killed by a taxi driver right inside the campus. This very unexpected action of the students really begs a lot of questions. This action was completely unexpected because it came only a few days after the Head of State was on national radio and television assuring them for the umpteenth time that he lives only for them. The "*bourse*" of the majority of them had also been paid, leaving only the postgraduate students who, not being very many in number, are not expected to riot.

Eh students, is it that you no longer believe the Head of State when he tells you that you are his main concern in life, that your future is rosy and that you are the leaders of tomorrow? Have you now started caring about one another's interests so that you are venting your anger on behalf of the minority graduate students? Can you please tell the Cameroonian public what you really want? Are you not just an odd moribund collection of civilian adults flattered with the euphuism "youths" but completely lacking a sense of who you are, where you are and where you are going?

The world over, university students shape the future of their countries because they know it's their future. They watch over the resources of their countries like sentinels over a treasure chest. But for thirty years you have watched with complacency and complicity the rape and spoliation, the sapping and draining of your own country. Of course, you received your part of the loot in the form of 30.000 FRS monthly bribe, naively believing that it was only your illiterate mothers and fathers who were being exploited while you saw yourselves as "future leaders" soon to join the wreckers and squanderers. Now that the dregs have been drained and the coffers are empty, what are you going to loot as future leaders? Do you ever reason at all? For thirty years the same clique of people has been leading you while assuring you that you are future leaders. When will your turn come since there must be thirty sets of "future leaders" waiting on the queue?

You people burnt one car saying the owner must have come to chase girls. Well, are you sure your female counterparts were happy about this or that it was in fact in their interest? This is an underhand method of dealing with rivals in a free competition. You burnt another car belonging to one of your own fellow students saying you did not see how he could have bought a car from the proceeds of a 30.000 monthly allowance. What if he got it as a gift or won the lottery?

You see, what is worrying is that none of the things you did show that you were motivated by sympathy for your dead colleague. Or else one would have expected you to impose immediate order on the chaotic traffic situation on the campus, especially at the Cité and CRADAT junctions, caused by incredibly bad roads and the irrationality of taxi drivers, reinforced by your own very irrationality. But, of course, you are not an organized group and cannot be expected to do things which presuppose a high level of conceptual discipline and organization. Yours must be the only university in the world without any students' union. Of course, you are not permitted to organize yourselves into a students' union, which shows your mumuishness. Do you think if Ni John Fru Ndi had been waiting for permission to form the SDF this country would already be so close to enjoying multi-party democracy?

Please, let the toiling masses of this country, whose sweat and tears ensure your 30.000 Frs. monthly allowance, know what you really want. When your counterparts the world over want to move on a point of principle, the so-called forces of law and order take to their heels and ruling juntas crumble. If you are incapable of organizing yourselves into a force that can be reckoned with, at least spare us your occasional collective idiocies. When you do it they move in to block roads for several days to hem you in like young wild beasts thereby inconveniencing everybody else with a right of innocent passage through your campus.

And how are we expected to pity you when very soon we will see some of you playing cards and draughts with the very red caps sent to terrorize you and some of your female counterparts getting on the back seats of their motor cycles to be carried to we know not where?

8

The Two Faces of Mongo Beti
(Published March 21-28 1991)

In the ancient mythology of the white races, there is a deity named "Janus" who had two faces, one in front, the other behind, which were as diametrically different as they were opposite. The expression "The two faces of Janus" has thus been frequently used for depicting any ambivalent issue that can be looked at from two different perspectives or points of view. This is how I wish to look at Alexandre Biyidi alias Mongo Beti today.

After more than 30 years of self-imposed exile in France, Mongo Beti finally braved a visit to Cameroon recently. Like many other Cameroonians, he must have been carried along on the wings of unfounded euphoria generated by the democratic rhetoric and talk-shop of his countryman, Biya Bi Mvondo.

Two eminent intellectual, societies *Club de Recherche et Action* (CRAC) and *Conference National Cheick Anta Diop* (CNCA), showed their own political naivety by planning, without official clearance, a series of symposia in honour of this prophet who, so far, has gone without honour in his own country. Predictably, our ubiquitous security forces stepped in and prevented the Mongo Beti Round tables from taking place. Of course, Caesar himself had tactfully just checked out, ostensibly for routine inspection of his stables. So in point of fact, this rape on the democratic rights of people who should be leaders of thought, shapers of destiny and custodians of the country's democratic values, occurred in his absence.

But anybody who has followed carefully the political history of this country and particularly the relationship between the two giants

23

would certainly know that the check-out was a veritable alibi: well, suppose that X spent the whole night on which Father Fontegh was murdered between the warm arms and legs of Y, could X have been the one who committed the murder? See the point? Now when two elephants wrestle, the surrounding vegetation should be very careful!

Now, Mr Biyidi's front face is the literary face. If you have never read : *MISSION TO KALA, KING LAZURUS, THE POOR CHRIST OF BOMBA, PERPETUA AND THE HABIT OF UNHAPPINESS, REMEMBER REUBEN*, then you should scarcely consider yourself literate, let alone a member of the intelligentsia. These are the works which have made Mongo Beti a literary giant. As the Canadian, Professor Stephen H. Arnold, remarked recently in the course of an interview with Martin Kongnyuy Jumban (*Cameroon Life*, Vol. I, No.7, Jan, 1991):

"... the day is coming soon when Beti will be recognised as Cameroon's greatest writer of the 20th century, and probably the greatest African writer of the post-colonial period known as neo-colonialism."

This expert opinion is incontrovertible. The way Mongo Beti is "worshipped" in places like Nigeria, attests to this. If this were the only Mongo Beti that there is, he should surely have received a triumphant entry into Cameroon any day.

But there is a second Mongo Beti, or rather the second face of the same person: the overtly political face. Apart from his novels, Mongo Beti has also published a considerable amount of non-fiction. Professor Arnold believes that "…. It is on his non-fiction…..that his long term reputation will rest." A lot of this non-fiction demonstrates a perceptive and inclusive understanding of the political evolution and actual situation of Cameroon. Sample for instance, the following excerpts from an address by Mongo Beti read before the 7th annual conference of the Association of Nigerian Authors (ANA) in December 1989.

"….the truth is that on the first of January 1960….as they were made to believe that they obtained independence, Cameroonians allowed to be imposed on them a dictatorship from which they have not been freed, even if it

has as its leader a colourless person who has succeeded another equally dull person, thanks to neo-colonialism which enjoys the endless use of servants of the same ilk... Cameroon is perhaps the only country where the writing in the colonial era of a novel which shook the confidence of the colonizer and did honour to Africa, far from winning for its author the moral compensation that he deserves thirty years later, would to the contrary make him the special target of diabolic plans of the so-called emancipated African leaders. I am speaking from a privileged position because I am the author in question and the novel concerned is THE POOR CHRIST OF BOMBA *for which Paul Biya, the docile disciple of the Catholic Missionaries, has forgiven me less than his predecessor, Ahmadou Ahidjo, who was a moslem... The struggle will be particularly stubborn on two fronts which are vital: the first is the press front. The eager desire of Cameroonians to have a true press, a press that is free, that is pluralist and independent of government, which will be in the first instance simply returning to the situation on the eve of independence.*

".... Today, three newspapers appear most regularly in Cameroon, a country with ten million inhabitants; they all belong to the state, that is the dictator, precisely to Paul Biya and are of course used to promote his personality cult, in the truest way of totalitarian regimes; they publish his portrait in the appropriate place every morning in addition to some flat aphorism that is quoted from his fatuous eloquence...

"... the Anglophones are, as I speak to you now, victims of Paul Biya. An insidious Frenchification of the Anglophones is already in progress in Cameroon, and here lies the second front in the war Cameroonian intellectuals and writers have resolved to wage against neocolonial dictatorship. It started in 1972 with the coup d'état that allowed Ahmadou Ahidjo...to abolish the federation and to turn Cameroon to a unitary state in violation of agreements signed in 1961 at Foumban with the mandated leaders of the Anglophones.... The Anglophone province was then invaded by Francophone civil servants who filled up the educational institutions. Little by little, the French language became the only language in use even in examinations where the questions were first written in French and then translated into an approximate English. Paul Biya announced his arrival with an attempt to cancel the Anglophone Advanced Level examination to be replaced with the francophone equivalent..... it had to be abandoned temporarily following bloody riots in which some pupils were killed. These facts are documented in a public write up, which appeared in the form of a

25

tract entitled "Open Letter (From Anglophone Students) to Our Parents" published in October 1985. Instructed by the situation, the students who come from the Anglophone zone have asked for an Anglophone university knowing well that they have no place in the Francophone university in Yaounde, the only one in the country. It was a just and legitimate demand; it has not been met up till now, and nobody expects it to be.

".... Here we are at war with... the zombie-dictators; here we are again empty-handed seers, fighting the new incarnation of the African evil. As for me, I don't doubt for a moment that the hour of the zombie-dictators is at hand, that their reign will soon end."

Mongo Beti evidently knows the Achilles' heel of our incumbent "Leviathan." This, and not his authorship of *THE POOR CHRIST OF BOMBA* or *REMEMBER REUBEN*, is his unforgivable crime. It is for this "crime" that the Mongo Beti symposia billed for the Yaounde Hilton Hotel were proscribed. After all, has the UPC not already been recognized as a party?

To Mongo Beti, this column would like to say the following: you've come back 30 years too late, brother! The sack and rape of home is all but complete. But, as they say, better late than never. You may not realize that the visa for your present visit was paid for by the blood of seven innocent souls gunned down at Bamenda on May 26th 1990. Please don't run back to the comfort of your life in exile. Home is right here and the battle ground is at home.

To the organisers of the Mongo Beti Round Tables that never were, the column says this: Hope you have learnt the correct lessons! From the sidelines we are watching to see how much longer you will continue to be unwilling to be separated from your illusions and delusions. Whenever you part with them, you will realize what we have tried, so far unsuccessfully to impress on you, namely, that no formula works like the Ntarikon formula.

9

Now That the Opposition Is Really Here
(Published March 27-April 4, 1991)

With the legalisation of the Social Democratic Front (SDF), there is no longer any doubt that there is a credible opposition party in our political system, signalling the end of a quarter century of one party dictatorship. The SDF was legalized, not legitimized. The party legitimized itself.

Now, one very instructive fact is that although seven parties (as of this moment of writing) have already been legalized, you generally hear Cameroonians only talking about Ni John Fru Ndi and the SDF. I for one, for example, know that seven parties (excluding the DMCP or whatever they call it, whose legal status is very unclear) have so far been registered and legalized. But somehow, I remember only the SDF and UPC, the latter probably on account of its historical importance, since I don't remember the name of its leader. I know that Mr Ndam Njoya, a remarkable minister of the Ahidjo regime, has formed a party but I don't just remember the name of his party. I remember that one of the legalized parties is called DIC but I neither know what DIC means nor its founder.

Compared to the SDF, all the other legalized parties seem to be either armchair creations or paper tigers or both. The SDF by contrast, seems to be a mass party for the rank and file of common people, led by a common man - a book seller. Some ignorant opponents of the SDF have never stopped shouting that a bookseller cannot lead a country. This shows that they don't know anything about charismatic leaders throughout history and what it is that make them tick. Among the countless disciples of Jesus Christ, there were intellectuals, political theorists, economists, literary geniuses etc. But Christ chose a fisherman to be their leader. The Catholic Church is the most intellectualized of all world religions, and yet its leader is always selected and installed against a background of the ragged shoes of a fisherman. What have we in Cameroon got out of more than thirty years of post-independence rule? Wreck and rape. It is about time we tried a bookseller. Let us try a bookseller.

Any Cameroonian who really sweats for his/her daily bread cannot but feel identified with the SDF and its daringly bold challenge of the status quo. Martyrs got made in the process; a historic day - 26th May, 1990 - got indelibly marked on our national time-calendar, and a lazy Rip van Winklian giant awoke from 25 years of autocratic slumber. We have all benefited from that daring and doing, including those who now rush to form paper parties with the evident sole hope of bargaining for a foothold in the eventual new scheme of things or even merely of collecting and pocketing the subvention that the state will dole out to all registered political parties.

With the daily announcement of newly legalized parties, one wonders where now are all those 3.000 signatories per province which the regime in one of its tactical moves intended to demand of the SDF? The new ploy would seem to be to proliferate the parties in the hope that the SDF might thus be divided and routed. This, of course, is as mistaken as someone who, having contracted gonorrhoea, hopes to get rid of it by taking multiple baths a day.

Of all the tactical ploys, the most recent one of forging a letter in Ni John Fru Ndi's name, purportedly asking General James Tataw to single-handedly carry out a bloody coup d'état and impose the SDF on Cameroonians, is the most diabolical in conception and the most moronic in execution. If the authors of this diabolism are not publicly brought to book, this will be conclusive proof of the complicity of the highest authority of the incumbent regime.

Now that the opposition is really here, there are several aspects of our national life that need urgent and immediate adjustments to bring them in line with the reality of the present moment. Let's mention only two here - the national security and the national television. Since it is the national security which presented the forged seditious letter purported to have been written by the leader of the SDF, they have the moral duty to tell Cameroonians how they came about the letter, who wrote it and what was meant to be achieved by it.

When we talk of national security agents, the question to be asked is: whose security? The only defensible answer to this question is that the security in question is that of the state as distinguished from any particular regime, the security of citizen X, meaning any citizen, the nameless citizen, the unknown citizen, or the common man as they say in common parlance. But so far our security services have been deployed in the interest of a select group of individuals or even of one single individual. For Citizen X, the word "security" in our context has paradoxically usually meant gross violation of privacy, arbitrary arrest and detention, torture and death. All this will have to change in the new scheme of things. Protecting the common man against predators of all types, against night prowlers, marauders, armed robbers, even common thieves; preventing calamities, rescuing or saving people from natural and artificial catastrophes - these are the proper functions of a security organization, of any security agent. Let all those who wear dark glasses and swagger around as security agents only hoping to fabricate falsehoods against innocent people and get them nailed on the cross remember that they are also Cameroonians and that their compatriots know the vulnerable characters hidden behind the dark glasses. A day of reckoning will surely dawn along linear space-time.

Regarding television, every Cameroonian tax payer contributes a compulsory monthly levy towards financing radio and television. He who pays the piper cannot be indifferent to the tune. Yet out television, just like our black gold, has been shamelessly appropriated and arrogantly turned into a family business. Experts keep telling us that our television house at Mballa II has the best facilities in all of Africa. But consider the monotonous rubbish and idiotic programmes dished out daily from there. Most of the journalists with a gift for the job have been sent on punitive transfers to the remote provinces, frustrated out of the job or simply completely marginalized within the house.

How many of the new party leaders have we yet seen on our television explaining the policies, aims and objectives of their parties? Would it not have been the most natural thing for TV journalists to rush out to these leaders, as the parties are registered, so as to present them and their parties so that Cameroonians may be able to form an unprejudiced opinion of those bidding to take control of their destiny in their hands? The CRTV is talking of planning to create a special channel for politics. Why should politics be discussed only on a special channel?

On behalf of all Cameroonian tax payers, this column protests vehemently over the insults that the CRTV arranges to be added onto the injuries that have been inflicted on us. May we not see another puffy face on screens again assuming the posture of the only son of the Shah of Iran before the Ayatollah's emergence, telling us with reckless insolence and arrogance that it is none of our business to know how our black gold is exploited or what happens to the proceeds of its sale.

We demand to have a say on how CRTV is run and on the programmes dished out to us. We reject the genealogical considerations which seem to be the only basis for the appointment of a of General Managers of CRTV. We demand the immediate appointment of a credible G.M. for this important parastatal, who should be competent, accountable, fair and even handsome. We have spoken.

10

Is Mr. Paul Out Of Touch Or What?
(Published April 18-25, 1991)

It is now established tradition that for serious policy statements of stupendous import, we have to wait until our Head of State a takes trip to France and then listen to his answers to questions posed to him by French journalists. Of course, back home here, no journalists will dare pose questions to His Excellency. Be that as it may, Mr Biya's recent declarations to French journalists regarding the issue of a "National Conference," *inter alia* give cause for very grave concern.

Before his recent trip to France, Paul Biya had, during the anniversary celebrations of his party, declared that a National Conference was not necessary. This could not but be taken as the point of view of a party leader vis-à-vis other party leaders. The same declaration made in France is an *ex cathedra* pronouncement in his capacity as Head of State. At the very moment that Mr Biya was making his declaration in France, thousands of Cameroonians were defying police tear gas bombs, water cannon and truncheons in Douala and Yaounde to demonstrate in favour of a National Conference.

Mr Biya's pronouncement is extremely dilemmic, in that it cannot easily be withdrawn without considerable loss of face, and yet it is evident that it cannot obtain, given the realities and circumstances of the present moment. There are now 14 political parties in Cameroon. What system of logic would approve one of these parties imposing its wishes on the other thirteen? Cameroon intellectuals, collectively and individually, have repeatedly emphasized the importance of a National Conference; students, traders, workers and the jobless have demonstrated in favour of it. So why would a government which is responsive to the wishes of the governed (which is what is meant by "Democracy") not heed these demands? Is all the talk about democracy and liberalization really so much gimmick for the attention of international donors and money lenders?

31

Mr Biya seems to be thinking of democracy as something that he is giving to Cameroonians out of the magnanimity of his political wisdom. It is he who decides what amounts to give and at what times. He sees himself as a permanent factor in the whole process, no matter what else may change. That is why he could declare that he hopes to meet with all the leaders of the opposition parties "after the elections." You couldn't help laughing through you tears at that, could you? In other words, he is not only hoping to win but is quite certain to win! As for the time of elections, it is, no doubt, his personal secret. However, certainty, cock-sureness and overweening confidence are all subjective categories which may not necessarily be related to the reality, to the stubborn facts.

Why does is not occur to Mr Biya that the most fundamental issue for every Cameroonian at the present moment is whether or not he and his regime should continue in power? There are, of course, other issues such as the economic crisis, the politico-administrative system, etc. But all these, in my view, are subordinate to the question of who rules. Cameroonians will have to decide this fundamental question through the ballot box. Such decision confers a mandate to govern which, in turn, assures the cooperation of the governed. Within this scheme of things, a National Conference is a *desideratum,* to re-examine and reformulate the foundation charter of our society. Equally important will be a credible electoral commission.

One gets the impression that Mr Biya is not fully aware of the situation on the ground and would be shocked if he knew, just as one is sure he will be shocked if he took a trip by car from Mokolo via Elig-Effa to Biyem-assi, to realize that this is, in fact, part of the capital city in which he resides.

The spontaneous reaction of nearly all human beings before any source of power is flattery. All the lackeys on the corridors of power who have access to the presidential ears must be inundating them with assurances of how everything is under perfect control. No one will dare tell him about his descent from grace to grass in most parts of this country. In fact, it is with considerable wonderment that, I myself noticed this mutation in consciousness, first in Garoua and Maroua last December, and quite recently in Bui and Donga Mantung Divisions. The Holy Family Choir of Tabenken, which only five years ago showered eulogies on a "gentleman of gentility" may be embarrassed if their recorded voices are played back to them today. As a stranger in Donga Mantung, at the present moment, it is necessary to give the "power to the people" sign wherever you go. In Bui, the situation is no different. Their capital, Kumbo, once a bustling town with four banks and several night clubs is today a ramshackle town with not a single bank and with impossible urban roads. Last year, they accused their Mayor of corruption and passed a vote of no confidence on him. He came to Yaounde, saw his political godfathers and was told to go back to his post without fear because 4 million Frs. was too meagre a sum to have been accused of embezzling. Any wonder then that the name of the incumbent regime sounds like a plague in this area?

In the South West Province, even parliamentarians of the regime are openly resigning from the ruling party. The Littoral and Centre provinces are hotbeds of political opposition. The people of the West province are swearing by their most sacred *ngombas* against the regime.

Mr Biya does not seem to be aware of the extent of damage done to his regime by the recklessly arrogant utterances and actions of people he must consider diehard supporters of his regime: the Emah Basiles, Melinguis, Mendo-Zes, Ntsamas, Assoumous etc. These are the people who have completely destroyed the regime.

This column advised Mr Biya before (see *Cameroon Post* of Monday Nov. 19-26 page 6) to immortalize himself in the annals of our political history by not seeking another term in office. This highly professional strategic advice was given free of charge in all honesty and sincerity. But, like most things that come freely, it has been under-rated and ignored. Well, here is another piece of strategic advice offered him in the same sprit as the previous one: Your previous declarations in France are no more than a bit of procedural *shakara*. A National Conference is inevitable. Please, convene it immediately. Simply say, as President Ronald Reagan once did, that what you said before is now "inoperative."

11

The Past Tense of Shit*
(Published April 25- May 2, 1991)

Children fascinate me. A growing child must be one of the most fascinating mysteries in life. There is plenty of evidence to sustain the view that human life is one interminable series of pain and anguish, punctuated by fleeting moments of ecstatic joy. The pranks of a growing child must be numbered among these fleeting intervals which make life seem worth living in spite of everything else. Most attentive parents will agree, I believe.

Personally, I will put the "magic period" of the growing child at between 2-7 years. The innocence, the sudden flashes of insight, the unforced humour, the impeccable reasoning, as yet untainted by experience - these are the elements out of which the said magic is compounded. I have been a devotee in the temple where kids perform their magic. That is why, when some years ago, Mr Paul Biya asked us to seriously consider the type of Cameroon we would like to bequeath to our children, I was very touched.

I have an exercise book full of true anecdotes concerning children. On Thursday, 11th April, 1991, I was once more caught up in a mess while in the process of trying to exercise my "right of innocent passage" through Ngoa-Ekelle. On that day, I had a very important engagement down town but innocently ran into a trap in the university area where Mr Emah Basile had brought out the whole army to impose a 4 hour curfew so that the CPDM could carry out a demonstration down town. Thus stranded, I brought out my children's book of anecdotes and relived some of the best moments on the walls of my memory.

Here are a few excerpts for your delight:

Kiven is four years old and perfectly trilingual in English, French and Lamnso'. One day I accompanied some Banso man who wanted to see someone living in Kiven's house. We met Kiven playing in the garden outside. My companion demanded: "Kiven, is Payur in the house?" Kiven ignored the question and remarked, "His name is not

Payur; his name is Pius!" We roared with laughter. In a bold attempt to save his face, my companion answered: "Well, Kiven, you know I'm a Banso man. That's how we Banso people call it." To which Kiven retorted devastatingly: "I am also a Banso man!" And like someone who knew he had given a technical knockout, he immediately ran away after some butterfly.

When later I narrated this story to some friends, a university lecturer among them recalled an equally amusing experience he had had with the same kid. Hearing everybody addressing him "Doctor," Kiven calmly came up to him and demanded: "Uncle, where is your hospital?" Not quite seizing the import of such a question, he managed, "Who told you I have a hospital, Kiven, I don't have me any hospital." "So you don't you have a hospital?" pursued Kiven, "then why are they calling you doctor, doctor?" At a loss to explain to the child what an academic doctor is, our friend found himself saying "I am not a medical doctor, I am a doctor of book." "A doctor of book?" Kiven queried incredulously. "Do books also get ill? Do you give them injections?" "Yes, Kiven, yes," was all our friend could say.

Quite recently, I was discussing our economic situation with a friend, little knowing that his 7-year old daughter, who was all the while playing with her younger sister, was following our discussion keenly. We were lamenting the fact that all the money stolen from public coffers has not even been invested in any useful enterprises from where the public could benefit indirectly. When I said "all the stolen billions have just gone down the drain because these people only know how to eat and shit," the little girl immediately interrupted and jolted me with the following question: "Please uncle, what is the past tense of shit?" Like a shrewd teacher caught unawares, I demanded to know first what she was doing with the past tense of shit. She did not hesitate a moment. Said she: "When you said they eat and shit, I was thinking that in the future we shall say they ate and what?" Cornered, I asked her to make a guess while I thought rapidly. She suggested "shitted." Honestly, I wasn't sure. So I played safe: "You can also say 'shat'. They ate and shitted or they ate and shat. Why not ask your teacher in school tomorrow?"

At the time Mr Paul Biya posed the question of what future we desired for our children, most of us still had illusions of peculiarly Cameroonian peaceful revolutions and all that. But recent events have cleared the scales from our eyes. Mr Biya's one man "press conference" with a timid (or is it intimidated?) and worshipful Eric Chinje, shows clearly that what he means by "democracy" is very different from what we have wishfully thought he meant all along. Sitting through out on the edge of the chair, Eric aptly personified the whole of Cameroon as he cut the picture of a penitent reciting the act of contrition before the deity. So it is after all quite true that democracy cannot be given on a platter of gold. It has to be taken and there is a price to be paid for the taking.

It is also quite clear now what the regime would bequeath to posterity: huge mound of shit. Bate Besong is one Cameroonian who has shown great sensitivity to this reality. BB's shock-therapy is entitled *Beasts of No Nation* with the subtitle "*a docu drama.*" He should simply have said: "a shitological drama." He is the shitologian *par excellence* x-raying the shitters. When the play was performed recently in Yaounde, some people could not stand the image of themselves they saw by reflection on the mirror on stage and fled in terror from the hall.

Which clearly shows what task we have bequeathed to our children. They will first have to clear the mess and then disinfect and sanitize the environment. But whether they will be saying they "shitted" or they "shat" is quite unimportant. We anxiously and hopefully await the past tense of "shit."

12

The Questions Eric Did Not or Could Not Ask
(Published on May 2-9, 1991)

It cannot be said that Eric did not do his best during his 11th April 1991 chit-chat with the Head of State. He did his best, just as His Excellency, the interviewee also did his best. The point, however, is that their bests, individually and collectively, were simply not good enough. Following are some of the questions and issues that any such interview, to have even a semblance of credibility, could not fail to broach:

Q: Excellency, you are always so bold when you go to France that you can face the press and answer a barrage of questions on sensitive issues. Why does your boldness and self-confidence seem to desert you immediately you get back here (your own proper kingdom) so that you dare not face the Cameroonian press in like manner? Don't you think this arrangement whereby you sit down alone with me while I pretend to ask you genuine questions might be suspected of being a stage-managed show?

A....

Q: Your Excellency, you declared in France that you'll be quite prepared to meet and discuss with the opposition leaders "after" the elections. Does that mean that you are already sure to win the elections, and do you consider it wise to decide on the time of these elections without consulting your opponents?

A.....

Q: Your Excellency, you also said in France that you saw no point for a National Conference. Suppose the people insist, as they are likely to, what would you do then? Well, you probably think that the majority of Cameroonians don't know what a national conference is, just as your oil minister thinks that they don't know what oil money is. But since you have not been known to tour the country to meet the people at the grass roots, how do you know this and if you are right, why then do you think they are agitating?

A....

Q: Another thing, your Excellency. You seem to think that demonstrations are part and parcel of democracy. But don't you think that people take to demonstrating only when they don't have adequate avenues for dialogue?

A....

Q: At the time you said the army brought out to repress the demonstrations of the university students was already back to their barracks, they were not yet back, but, on the contrary, were committing havoc in the students' residential area. Excellency, I don't know whether you have a daughter, but just imagine that you had one and that the room where she was timidly hiding during all the trouble was broken into and she was dragged out from under the bed where she was hiding, beaten on the breasts and buttocks and then raped by five hefty men, one after the other, in turns. Would you send a motion of support to the perpetrators of such acts?

A....

Q: And now the rumours. You would agree with me, Excellency, that rumours can ruin a nation. The truth is always more decent than rumours. So, please do cough and clear your throat very well before separating the smoke from the fire of the following rumours which have been making the rounds throughout the length and breadth of the national territory. First of all, when talking about capital flight a while ago, you disapproved of Cameroonians going to set up businesses and enterprises abroad in the already developed countries. Can we infer from this remark that the rumour that you have a wine press in France and are building a hospital in Germany is false? Or should we rather assume that the law-maker is not necessarily bound by the law he himself makes? What about the one that Her Royal Highness owns a luxury transport company and a modern super market and that her goods, on which she pays not a franc of duty, are usually escorted by members of the armed forces from the port right into her warehouses?

A....

Q: Cameroon students in the USA, who have recently been giving Mr Pondi a hell of a time, have alleged that your son lives in a castle which you bought for him and that he has twenty billion U.S

Dollars in his personal account. Is he one of the cocaine barons or how did the kid come by such a fortune?

A...

Q: Your Excellency, do you own any shares in any enterprise?

A....

Q: Your Excellency, is it true that your regime has hired the services of a squad of professional murderers to eliminate your political opponents and any other person who might be a torn in your flesh?

A....

Q: Your Excellency, clear your throat again before answering this one. Polygamy is our African way of life. However, the rumour circulating in some Catholic circles is that, in 1984, you deceived the Pope that you were a monogamist, thereby causing him to give you the Holy Communion with his own hands and also drinking the blood of Christ from the sacred chalice whereas it is alleged that you are a well-known polygamist. Any comment?

A....

Q: Your Excellency, we are running out of time; so one last question. Some ignorant Cameroonians think that you are a dictator, not knowing that you had dictatorship handed over to you on a platter of gold by your predecessor. But as someone who would like to be remembered as having brought democracy to Cameroon, have you started practicing to think of some of your political opponents, such as Fru Ndi, as your Head of State in the likely event where he beats you in the next presidential elections? Or is it true that your regime has resolved to allow the whole ship to sink instead of losing power?

A....

13

Mitterrand Must Be a Mediocre Teacher
(Published May 9-16, 1991)

If Mr Paul Biya is a pupil of Francois Mitterrand, then the latter must be a mediocre teacher. So, since the former has openly declared himself the latter's best pupil, it can be safely concluded that Mitterrand is a mediocre teacher. To buttress this reasoning, we need not go outside of Biya's recent declarations in Paris and his address to the nation delivered under the guise of a prepared question and answer session with Eric Chinje.

A sovereign Head of State who on a state visit to another state openly declares himself a pupil of the host cuts a very sorry picture indeed. Even a French lady here in Yaounde, confessed that she was shocked by Mr Biya's declaration but quickly added that she is quite sure Mr Mitterrand does not consider his African counterparts as pupils. Well, our Head of State was in France to beg for loans and probably thought it wise to assume the humble posture of a good mendicant. For nearly Five years now, Mr Biya has been spending nearly as much time abroad as at home begging to borrow money to revive an economy which has refused to be revived.

The first thing a bright pupil should realize is that it is not logical to beg to borrow. The money lenders search all over the world for reliable customers to whom to lend their money, because money lending is a most profitable business. For this reason, most of the so-called developed countries get on very well simply by lending out money. If the borrower nations unanimously decided not to borrow again, the economies of the lender nations would get into very serious trouble. The thing is quite elementary. When you go to your *njangi* house you don't beg for a loan, you simply ask. As long as there is reasonable assurance that you will pay back, the *njangi* is quite happy to lend you the money because, in that way, it increases the collective revenue. The use to which you put the money is nobody's business, so long as you pay it back with the interest. So, Biya's begging expedition could not but be "very successful."

The next catalogue of questions are: for what purpose are we taking all these loans? What has happened to the money of the loans taken before? Who shall repay all these loans? Credible rumours have it that those who run all around the world borrowing monies on our behalf without our knowledge and/or consent simply bank the money in private accounts at home and abroad. It may be true that there is an economic crisis. But the solution to this economic crisis will not come from abroad and certainly not in the form of loans. The solution must come from within the country itself. This is the lesson that Ghana and Nigeria both learned in good time. Their own economic crises were much worse than ours on account of their large populations and consequent lack of food sufficiency. Their applied solutions were mainly inward-looking and their economies are picking up at an unbelievably accelerated rate in spite of the fact that neither the *naira* nor the *cedi* has any foreign backing.

The main resources for any country are its land, people, natural resources and agricultural produce. Cameroon is not at all lacking in any of these. Given these alone and a credible and efficient government, Cameroon has no reason for an economic crisis. President Mitterrand is reported to have advised his Cameroonian pupil to pump the oil money into the economy. (See *Cameroon Post* No. 65 of Thursday April 11-18, 1991). Our oil revenue has remained the greatest secret over the years since we joined the enviable club of oil nations. It is reasonable to believe that these revenues are banked in private accounts as alleged by rumours.

One indicator: when the catholic educational establishment which has not paid its teachers for nearly six months threatened to go on strike over government non-payment of subventions, the government reacted very promptly and signed a substantial cheque for them. Well, the cheque is said to have been signed by the oil chief and head of the SNH. So there must be an accumulated bulk somewhere into which the power brokers can delve in times of real trouble.

It is imbecilic for us to expect that French people would help us to solve our economic problems to their own detriment. It is foolish to hand over our strategic corporations and parastatals to French people to manage, under the misguided notion that they will manage

41

them more efficiently and thus necessarily to our benefit. Take CAMAIR, for instance. What improvements has it seen since it was handed over to French management? Instead, CAMAIR's French manager immediately demonstrated his bias by cancelling flights to London, thereby forcing CAMAIR passengers to use Air France between Paris and London. And yet economic, political and cultural considerations argue instead for direct non-stop flights to London.

Mr Biya's chit-chat with Eric Chinje, previously recorded, and broadcast over national television on Thursday April 11, 1991, is a bundle of incoherent contradictions and reckless gaffs. Mr Mitterrand's best pupil is evidently not good enough. This column had previously bemoaned the fact that Mr Biya did not seem to be aware of the extent of damage that has been inflicted on his regime by the silly arrogance and recklessness of some of his right-hand men. But after listening to him on 11th April, it seems both lucky and wise that he has not been addressing the nation more often. His own pronouncements seem not only likely to destroy the regime but the entire nation along with it.

14

Tribalism
(Published May 15-22, 1991)

Second to kleptocracy, tribalism is one of the problems that has bedevilled post-independent African countries. Tribalism, however, is essentially an artificial problem, a problem at the level of false consciousness, created and sustained by false politicians who are destitute of the sterling qualities of leadership or who want to cover up a hideous path of personal corruption. To say that tribalism is a false problem is not to under-rate its effects. It is only to say that if people reason or reflect before acting or reacting, tribalism would have no place in their lives.

Were it not of the crippling effects of tribalism, a country like Nigeria would, no doubt, have risen into a world power in all spheres of human activity in less than two decades after independence. But tribalism has dogged this potentially great nation since independence; the only black nation on earth where it can easily be demonstrated that the pigmentation of the skin is an irrelevant accident in human affairs. The most ruinous experience after the slave trade that Nigeria has gone through was the civil war of the late sixties which pitched Biafra against the rest of Nigeria. The catastrophic fratricidal conflict was a direct consequence of tribalism, generated and sustained by misgovernment and unrestrained kleptocracy. From the moment some Nigerians rose up, under the influence of mass hysteria, against other Nigerians, not for any crime committed but simply for being Hausas, Igbos, Northerners, Southerners, Nigeria's doom was sealed. Today in Nigeria the same folly manifests itself under the guise of religious conflict between Moslems and Christians.

Recently here in Cameroon, several incendiary tracts have been circulated calling on the *Beti* to rise up like one man against the *Bamilike* and the Anglophones, accused of seizing *Beti* land and causing all the political troubles with the sole aim of getting the *Beti* out of power. Reports have it that for some time now, well-placed *Beti* have been clandestinely issued permits to buy guns in preparation

43

for an impending tribal war. University of Yaounde students arrested and detained after their demonstrations, claim the *Beti* were separated from the non-Beti like sheep from goats; the sheep were released or fed while the goats were starved and/or tortured.

The fanning of tribal embers is extremely silly but also potentially quite dangerous. How is it silly? Among the *Bamis* and *Anglos,* against whom the present tribal war cries are raised, are some diehard supporters of the present *Beti* regime: people who have benefited or are benefiting immensely personally, from the present configuration of things or people who are indeed convinced that the regime is divinely ordained. In any case, the *Anglos* are not a single tribe but belong to over 200 distinct tribal groupings. Some of these Anglo-tribes are closer to the *Beti* in their traditional cultures than to the *Bami* or other *Anglo* groups. The *Bamis* could pass for a single tribe. But, if it came to tribal war-fare, I doubt if the *Beti* could stand up against the *Bamis*, let alone the *Bamis* and *Anglos* combined.

Now, why do I say that the present fanning of tribal embers is also potentially dangerous? It is potentially dangerous in the reaction it might elicit. I know some people who were so scared on reading some of these tracts that they dared not go out of their houses and remained in-doors awaiting the attack. Now this is a very dangerous psychological disposition to be in. Personally, I took these tracts just for a little bit of *shakara*. Remember the Afro-Beat king, Fela Anikulapo Kuti? *"Shakara Man. He go say: I go beat you, I go nearly kill you. You no know me, I go beat you ih go be like say you get accident. Wait make I commout my dress. Na shakara man. He no fit do nothing."* The danger in the threat "I will punch your nose" is that the addressee might react in a flash and deal a devastating retaliatory punch on your own nose. And he would be justified by your threat as acting in self-defence. In some parts of the North, uprisings (not preceded by tracts) have been reported against southerners, including not only *Beti* but *Bamis* and *Anglos*.

The reason I have not been overly scared about the tribal war cries of the tracts is that I believe the tracts were written and circulated by the small minority of *Beti* which has emptied our national treasury and which is now so nervous in dread of impending repercussions. These are the people who would prefer an outbreak of

44

total civil war to a change in the *status quo* because, in fact, if general civil war breaks out, they stand a good chance of surviving; as all issues will get confounded and mixed up and, in any case, they have considerable personal fortifications as well as stupendous financial reserves. I believe that the ordinary rank-and-file *Beti* are peace loving people and that, if they perceive the situation clearly and reason correctly, they would join the hounds to chase out that handful of their tribesmen who have wrecked our country and jeopardized seriously our collective well-being and existence. After all, does a goat eat into the stomach of another goat? But, even if I am wrong in believing that the generality of *Beti* are a peace loving people, they are, in any case, certainly, not a war like or bellicose people. This can be deduced from their culture. All cultures which move mainly the waist in their dancing, eat domestic animals including cats and dogs, and enjoy strong alcoholic drinks, have abandoned the art of warfare. To be dreaded are those who move the legs and/or arms in their dances or those who do not dance at all but jump on top of a horse as a form of amusement. This is a sociological thesis that I would love to see contradicted. But, if my thesis is plausible, then the tribal war cries of the *Beti* are potentially more dangerous for the *Beti* themselves.

Tribalism is perhaps a tendency in human nature. This tendency is essentially irrational and when carried to its psychological limits, ends in solipsism where the individual considers himself and his interests as the only thing that counts or that even exists. Every human being is born somewhere at some time. It is senseless but harmless to be proud of such ineradicable facts. Surely the most important things about any human being in interaction with other human beings is not *when* or *where* s/he was born but rather whether s/he is honest or dishonest, competent or incompetent, qualified or unqualified, fair or unfair, reliable or unreliable, kind or unkind, courageous or cowardly, diligent or careless, hardworking or lazy, intelligent or otherwise etc.

These sorts of attributes are not conferred by tribe and are not limited to any tribe and are the sort of criteria that would be used in a purely meritocratic system. These are the qualities that can be acquired or cultivated, and which are therefore fairly accessible to all human beings without discrimination.

Given the history and development of our country, we surely cannot limit ourselves to such criteria in, say, giving appointments. Some amount of geographical balance would still be called-for as well as redress of past injustices. But even if we did limit ourselves to such criteria, the point is that 37 out of 50 divisional administrators would not be *Beti* nor members of any single tribal group; 17 out of 25 parastatals would not be headed by members of a single tribal group; Assoumou would surely not be our oil chief and Mendo Ze would not be heading the CRTV. The prevailing situation is, indeed, one of the disasters of the so-called New Deal regime. But again, if we can learn the correct lessons, from the fact, it has done more harm to the regime itself which now is evidently in its last throes before death. There is really no strength like that founded on justice, fair-play and uprightness! Dr. Biya and his flagrantly unjust and corrupt regime will learn this by the end of the day.

On my part, I can confidently declare that I, Rotcod, son of Gobata, am one of the completely detribalized Cameroonians. I cherish my father's name and my place of birth, but tribalism cuts no ice with me. I have never asked anybody for a favour simply on the grounds of my place of origin and I would not grant any simply on those grounds. If my own twin-brother becomes a thief, I will beat him and rub his mouth in the dust.

15

The Foxes of Loo
(Published May 26-30, 1991)

A relation or friend of yours is arrested (without warrant), detained (without charges) and finally locked up in prison (without any conviction). A detainee or prisoner has the right to eat. But, no, this is Cameroon. Word reaches you that your relative (friend) has been starving for so many days. You don't have to presume that you have the right to take food to him. Wisely (wisely?) you first go to ask his armed captors, on your knees, if they would kindly allow you to bring some food for your friend (relative). "No objection at all, go right ahead and bring it. Very thoughtful of you!" you are told. You hurry to the nearest provision store and you buy some loaves of bread and tins of sardine. We all look down on bread except early in the morning. But if you have never really been famished then you have never really known the value of a loaf of bread and tin of sardine. You come back with your food parcel and proffer it to the officer who had so kindly (kindly?) granted you the permission to bring it for your starving friend (relation). But the same fellow now orders you to put your parcel by the side and pass behind the counter. You hesitate, showing total incomprehension. You are quickly saved from your quandary. You are roughly pushed with a gun and led to a cell where you are told to take off your shoes, wrist watch, and all clothing except your underpants and leave outside. You are pushed inside the cell and the iron door clangs behind you!

Well, if you think you have been reading a novel or something like that, then go and ask Dr. Siga Asanga or anyone else who has come close enough to these fellows dressed and armed through our sweat, ostensibly for our individual and collective protection. In Dr. Asanga's case, he was released within 24 hours, thanks to diplomatic pressure and pathological fear of the possible reaction of the no-nonsense political party of which he is Secretary General. But if it were you or me, we would still be in that cell, waiting for the second coming of the messiah. Hence, I say, these fellows are foxes.

The expression "forces of law and order" which always sounds so sweet in the mouths of our Francophone brothers; "*forces de l'ordre*" is one that always makes me want to laugh. How can people who always bring so much disorder and destruction wherever they are be termed "forces of order?" The irony in this expression is simply intolerable. A more realistic expression is that which dubs them "harm forces" since they inflict harm and havoc wherever they go. Their morality is also evidently morality of the loo or latrine.

Ask the university students. When the forces of law and order finished maintaining law and order in the university campus, what was the result? Fractured limbs, broken doors, looted property, raped girls and alleged corpses. One of the greatest scandals of these perilous times is that, in the face of all these atrocities, not even a supposed paternal instinct has moved our "*Père de la Nation*" to bate an eyelid. In like manner, the Minister of Computer Studies, Higher Services and Scientific Defects, whose direct concern one should have thought the university is, has maintained an undignified silence that is more eloquent in its significance than a siren.

The glaring contradiction in the official accounts of why and what happened at the university campus are a cause for grave concern. These conflicting accounts cannot be reconciled without exposing the Chancellor, the Minister of Information and Culture or that of the Armed Forces as blatant liars. Both the university students and lecturers have called for a judicial commission of enquiry to look into the whole sordid affair.

This column supports that call with the additional specification that such a judicial enquiry be also public. If past experience and present indications are anything to go by, it would certainly not be enough that such an enquiry be only independent while its findings are made public. The reason here is that the results declared may not necessarily be the results actually obtained or, in fact, the conclusions drawn may not necessarily follow from the premises or evidence adduced. But in a public enquiry, we will all hear the evidence for ourselves. Such a public enquiry would not, of course, prevent the judge sitting on it to rule that certain sensitive evidence, such as that of girls who were raped, be taken in secret. But all other witnesses should testify and be cross-examined in public. This will greatly enhance the results and recommendations of such an enquiry. As a very concerned citizen, I would gladly submit a memorandum to such commission of enquiry if and when it is set-up.

This is the sort of thing that the university students should be pressing for as a condition for returning to campus instead of getting bogged down with such minutiae as allowances, course coefficients, polycops, decongestion etc. These are matters that any responsible administration would automatically address itself to and matters that the envisaged public judicial commission of enquiry would have to consider, anyway.

It may also be necessary to institute a special commission of enquiry into the actions and activities of our "foxes of loo and udder" since April 1990. Why, for instance, is it that nearly all demonstrations where they did not intervene have been orderly and free of incidents? Or why is it that whenever they do intervene most of the things they do are unrelated to the declared purpose of their intervention? In Bui Division, for instance, we are told that they passed the scene of the riots they ostensibly went there to quell and went five kilometres to some Catholic convent where they scaled the walls and broke into Reverend Sisters' rooms. Well, if university female students, who openly line up under the lamp posts every evening, are reluctant to confess what they did to them after breaking into their rooms, do you expect the holy women to tell it? One shudders at the abominable atrocities here committed by people whose counterparts in other countries maintain peace and order and are considered protectors by the honest common man. Until our own situation changes, we should call them what they are; "foxes of loo" or members of the" harm forces"

16

Jean Zoa's Conceptual Problems
(Published May 30ᵗʰ-June 6, 1991)

His Lordship, Archbishop Jean Zoa, of the Metropolitan See of Yaounde, does not support the idea of a National Conference. This is no interesting piece of news. No one would have expected Jean Zoa to support the idea of a National Conference, in spite of the very clear and unequivocal stand of the Cameroon Episcopal Conference of which he is a member. As one of the greatest apologists of the incumbent regime, many people take the Archbishop to be a fanatical militant of the CPDM party, masquerading around in a soutane. But some of the Bishop's declared reasons for not supporting the National Conference are most interesting indeed.

According to his Lordship, the expression "national conference" is not to be found in any dictionary. He has carefully checked in the most authoritative French and English dictionaries. But all he can find is the word "conference" and the word "national," but nowhere can he find "national conference." Therefore, reasons our divine, the call for a national conference does not make any sense! The thing does not exist in the dictionary, you see!

This should make Gilbert Ryle, author of *The Concept of Mind*, who first analysed a conceptual deficiency which he termed "category mistake" to despair of the powers of human reasoning.

Suppose that someone, visiting Yaounde for the first time, was taken on a sight-seeing tour around the city. He is shown Etoudi, Bastos, Nlongkak, Tsinga, Mokolo, Messa, Melen, Obili, Etug-Ebe, Biyem-assi, Nsimeyong, Olezoa, Mvog-mbi, Nkoldongo, Central Town, Essos, etc. Suppose that, at the end of this tour our visitor then asks his host/guide: But where is Yaounde itself? It is really Yaounde I came to see and not all these other places you have taken me to. Please take me to Yaounde!" If he completely failed to grasp the fact that it is all that he had seen, taken together, which is called Yaoundé, we should say that he was indeed more than slow-witted.

If his Lordship found the word "conference" and also the word "national" in the dictionary, how could he still complain that he had not found "national conference"? Or is it a case of "When I learn one I forget two, and when I learn two I forget one? But even if neither "national" nor "conference" nor "national conference" could be found in a dictionary, is that a reason why we should not hold a National Conference? What is a dictionary after all?! It is only a record of the usage of words. The use comes before the recording and that is why there are always many words in use which cannot be found in the dictionary; the reason why dictionaries have to be updated from time to time.

Verbal/conceptual escapism is indeed one of the distinguishing characteristics of the present regime. Dr. (*honoris causa*) Biya himself had wondered aloud when the idea of a National Conference was first mooted, how 12 million Cameroonians could hold a conference. Crazy idea! Imagine it yourself. The conference table would have to stretch from Nkambe via Mamfe to Limbe via Douala to Kribi through Yaounde to Ebolowa, Ngaoundere, Garoua and Maroua. And when the Chairman clears his throat from Yaounde to declare the meeting open…how many days do you think it will take for word to go round the table of 12 million participants, from mouth to ear, that the honourable chairman had cleared his throat and was about to declare the conference open? What with all the children making noise and the newly born babies screaming! So, please, just forget about this crazy idea of a national conference. *Shogbo!*

The verbal sterility of the New Deal Regime is glaringly evident. No other regime has been so full of rhetoric about rigour and moralization; responsibility and accountability, efficiency and national integration etc. And yet, no other regime has been so wide off the mark in these matters. The most pernicious effect of this is that it has been made to appear as if the chief function of a government is to write good speeches and to formulate good slogans, no matter how unrelated to actual practice.

Since independence, three integral elements have fluctuated in varying proportions in the governments we have had: democracy, autocracy and kleptocracy. Any West Cameroonian who was already at the age of reason at the time of Reunification can easily distinguish

51

three distinct political regimes in his/her experience. Before and immediately after independence, we had a system that was basically democratic with negligible elements of autocracy and kleptocracy. The Ahidjo regime was basically a monolithic dictatorship, an autocracy with significant elements of kleptocracy and negligible elements of democracy. The Biya regime has almost achieved a perfect harmony between the three elements, but there is no doubt that it is, first and foremost, a kleptocracy in harmonious polygamous marriage with autocracy and democracy. In other words, autocracy and democracy are like wives of a powerful polygamist named kelptocracy. Either has been used according to time and circumstances to serve the kleptocratic practices of the regime. Verbal equivocations and conceptual mirages and gerrymandering are only a game within this framework, a supporting structure, as it were. If not, we may have to reappraise the full effects of iodine deficiency or something of that sort on the mental development of some of our compatriots.

17

The New Universities
(Published June 6-13, 1991)

I am writing this piece on the 26th of May, 1991 - the first anniversary of the struggle for genuine democracy in Cameroon. It was on Saturday, May 26th, 1990, that the Social Democratic Front (SDF) was launched in Bamenda, the political Mecca of Cameroon, against a backdrop of serious Government repression, resulting in the murder of six innocent citizens. Cameroon has never been the same again. The "Ntarikon Formula" as I once described this daringly bold venture of the SDF and the mammoth populations of the Bamenda metropolis, seems to have roused all Cameroonians from nearly 30 years of political slumber.

Looking back, it is hard to believe that so much progress could be achieved within the span of a single year. We are not through with repression, and so today, most Cameroonians will only toast in silence to the memory of the martyrs of May 26th, 1990, and the other martyrs who have since joined them, as statistical victims on our rugged path to democracy, social justice and responsible government. This column predicts that May 26th will eventually replace May 20th as our National Day.

There are some people who continue to clap their hands for Paul Biya and the CPDM, for magnanimously giving democracy to Cameroonians. Well, there is a fallacy which jurists and logicians call *"causa pro causa"* which consists in taking the non-cause of an event for the real cause. The same fallacy has been exhibited by those who have been sending messages of congratulations to the Government for creating the Universities of Buea and Ngaoundere. In fact, some mediocre teachers at the University of Yaounde, probably already imagining themselves power brokers in one of the new universities, have exhibited unbelievable naivety in their noisy euphoria over the Government's "omniscient magnanimity." The true creators of the universities of Buea and Ngaoundere are the striking students of Yaounde University and the opposition parties who together put the

Government in such a tight spot that it had to announce the new universities as a way of diffusing tension. But everything is still at the rhetorical level and, if care is not taken, it may, like many other fantastic announcements we have heard before, remain right there. The simple truth is that you don't create a university by word of mouth, and unless appropriate pressure is mounted and sustained, the new universities will remain only in the airwaves.

The first thing in the process of creating a university is to design viable academic programmes in line with a certain blueprint that must be clearly stated in the law or edict establishing the university. A course system is chosen in which the relationship envisaged between the various disciplines or faculties is rendered easily viable. An administrative structure is then set up. Physical facilities are provided. Staff, both academic and non-academic are recruited. Rules governing admissions, studies, graduation, appointments, service, promotions, retirements etc, are laid down. Feasibility studies, which, among other things, determine exploitable facilities and expertise must, of course, precede all the above.

Thus, creating a university is not at all a day's job. It is not an easy task. Anglophones, who have a thousand and one complaints about the University of Yaounde, should thank the students for making it possible for their dream to have a university in the pure Anglophone tradition to come true. They should put all hands on deck and maintain pressure on the appropriate authorities, until the idea is translated into concrete reality.

Some disturbing indications are that a dispute is reportedly already raging between South Westerners and North Westerners as to which faculties of the university would be established in Buea and which in Bambili. This is a silly dispute. Operational pragmatism should be the guiding principle. Let them remember, however, the story of the two hunters who once cornered a game and, while they were busy disputing over the formula for sharing it after killing it, the animal escaped into safety.

The senate of the University of Yaounde has already offered its services in helping to get the new universities off the ground. This offer should be politely but firmly turned down. As people who for over thirty years have been running an embarrassment which we call the University of Yaounde, they should not be given the chance to mess up another university. The senate of the University of Yaounde is mainly a political arena where pseudo-intellectuals hustle for political appointments. All appointments in all faculties of the university, beginning from Deans through Heads of Departments down to cleaners, are political appointments. The first thing that the new universities should try to establish from the word "go" is a separation between academics and politics. The present impasse at the University of Yaounde is a salutary lesson about the dangers of doing politics under the guise of academics. If the new universities cannot break clean from this ruinous tradition, they would not be worth the tax-payer's sweat.

18

Memo to the Endeley Commision
(Published June 13-20, 1991)

In an earlier edition of *"No Trifling Matter,"* this column had added its mellow voice to that of university students and lecturers who were calling for a judicial commission of enquiry into the university crisis (see *CAMEROON POST*, May 26-30, 1991). On that occasion, I did promise to submit a memorandum to such a commission of enquiry, if and when it was set up. The commission has been set up and here am I to fulfil my promise.

The Endeley commission as constituted falls short of expectations, but that is not sufficient reason to reject it. We must learn to accept things we cannot change, use what we have and make the best even out of a bad situation. I had in my own suggestion insisted that such a commission, apart from being judicial and independent, should also be "public," taking all the evidence, except that judged to be extremely sensitive, under the glare of the public eye. Otherwise, the danger of proceeding like some people who solve problems in mathematics by first looking at the answer is very real.

The students who made the call for the setting up of the commission are rejecting it, on the ground that it is a CPDM commission. The commission is rightly so described in as much as no Human Rights organization or opposition party is represented on it. Nevertheless, this does not necessarily mean that the work of the commission is vitiated from the onset. All members of the commission may be very loyal members of the CPDM party. The chairman of the commission, in spite of being recognized as a notable legal luminary, is by no means a radical. He sees no reason, for instance, why his province of origin should agitate for a fairer share of the national cake, on the grounds that it is the province which produces our petroleum. He also believes that it is the Biya-led CPDM which has "given" democracy to Cameroonians.

But I believe that this commission can still carry out its assignment very objectively, if it is conscious of the historical importance of the task. We should therefore forebear prejudging its work. From their fruits we shall know. If at the end of the day they declare a verdict of "zero mort" and "zero raped" or if they prescribe punishment for the small flies and tell us that the camels successfully passed through the eye of their needle, then, and only then, shall we learn another lesson. But for now, let us cooperate as much as possible with the commission and give it the benefit of our well-founded doubts. This column calls on the students, especially those raped, robbed or brutalized, to immediately report before this commission. Well, those killed cannot plead their cause before the commission. The commission itself must go out where there is the slightest lead to find out for itself.

On my part, I have the following brief submission relative to some of the structural adjustments which are absolutely necessary at the university, if it is to avoid similar crises in the future.

The University of Yaounde is an antiquarian and authoritarian institution which, if care is not taken, may resist democratic change more stoutly than the state at large. All appointments at the university, beginning from that of the Chancellor right down to messengers and cleaners, are all done in the guise of political favours. The university urgently needs autonomy and democratization. I would suggest the following structures, drawing on common sense

56

and experience from other universities around the world. Heads of Departments should be elected by the teaching staff of each department, for a period of two years, renewable only once. Deans of faculties or directors of institutes should be elected by the teaching staff of the given faculty or institute for a term of two years, renewable only once. The chief function of deans/directors and heads of departments should be to give intellectual and professional leadership.

The Chancellor and Vice Chancellor of the university should be elected by members of the University Senate and confirmed by the Government, for a two year term, renewable once. In this case, the senate should submit to the Government for each post, 3 names in order of preference. The Government will, in turn, select from the names submitted, without necessarily respecting the senate's order of preference. The senate should be composed as follows: all deans of faculties, all academic staff with the rank of Professor or Associate Professor, four representatives of each grade of lecturers, two representatives of the academic staff union, two representatives of the students' representative council, two representatives of the Government.

At the student's level, all students of each faculty or institute should elect their own students' union executive. The executives of the students unions for all the faculties will then come together to form the student's representative council, which should be the supreme governing body for the students. Each union at the faculty level should have credible secretarial and recreational facilities. To this end, the university must have budgetary allocation for the students' unions and students' representative council. This should be supplemented by compulsory contributions from all students (say 1000 FCFA per student) to be paid as part of registration formalities at the start of every session.

At the other levels, the academic staff, on the one hand, and the non-academic staff, on the other, should have their own unions to cater for their peculiar interests and to enhance probity, efficiency and professionalism.

If this sort of structure is adopted, I am more than certain that the sort of dangerous crisis the university is now going through would never repeat itself.

19

Where We Went Wrong
(Published June 20-27th, 1991)

I once described Cameroon in this column as a potential paradise. But in the last few months we have wandered to the very edge of a precipice and looked down below and seen a veritable hell, the hell that our potential paradise could easily become unless we recover our common sense.

I remember some Nigerian who visited Cameroon in 1981. He was extremely impressed by the general peace and security that reigned in Cameroon and by the extreme friendliness and helpfulness of Cameroonians. First of all, he had arrived Douala with a lot of apprehension, because all he knew was the name and occupation of his would be host. But to his pleasant surprise, with that scanty information, every Cameroonian he encountered was so helpful that in no time he had discovered his host. There is no Nigerian town or city where you would find anybody, let alone several people, ready to walk two kilometres with you, just to help you locate someone else you are looking for.

Our Nigerian friend was further "shocked" to notice that, in Cameroon, people could go to a night club, leave their cars by the roadside unlocked, drink and dance themselves out (and oh! what music and drinks!) and stagger back home in the wee hours of the morning, without any incident. In Nigeria, about the same time, you had to go to bed with nightfall, for fear of marauding armed robbers and, if you stopped your car by the roadside even just to urinate, you had to demobilise and lock it, or else, half way through your toilet ritual, you might see someone else zooming off with your car. So it is not surprising that our Nigerian friend, at the end of his visit, declared that Cameroon was the country he would most like to live in, in spite of the dust. But that was ten years ago.

A decade seems to be quite enough to turn heaven into hell. If our Nigerian friend revisited Cameroon this year, he would probably have been stopped at a road block mounted by hooligans in Douala and stripped of his clothes and money. He would also discover that he can no longer enjoy life for fear of being mistaken for a *Bami* or *Anglo* or for fear of a gun-shot or matchet-strike missing its target and landing on him.

Indeed we've never had it so bad and, what is more, there seems to be no end in sight to our tribulations and the continuing deterioration of the situation.

The frauds and embezzlements that have brought us to our knees economically have only intensified and the regime that, in less than a decade, has turned our potential heaven into a potential hell, has continued to be stubbornly arrogant against the expressed wishes of the overwhelming majority of Cameroonians.

Repression has intensified, coercion, intimidation and blackmail are the order of the day, blatant lies have taken the place of information and propaganda has replaced argument. The country is evidently in a state of permanent siege and it is clear that the people are being governed by dint of sheer physical force. For how long can this state of things be sustained?

Now, where did we go wrong? It appears to me that the first fatal error was committed when the Biya regime pretentiously accepted democracy merely as a tactic for perpetuating itself in power. Dictatorship is a viable form of government as can be witnessed by the last three decades of our political history. Democracy is also a viable form of government and the only one that is theoretically and philosophically justifiable. What cannot be done is attempting to combine dictatorship with democracy. For instance, it should be clear even to a child that the overwhelming majority of Cameroonians want a National Conference to sort out the mess that we have made of ourselves as a nation since independence and to chart out a new path from the vantage position of retrospective hindsight. For the Government to say a firm "no" to this collective wish of the people and yet continue in power is extremely dictatorial. It indicates clearly that there will be no means within the democratic set up envisaged in their conception, to remove such a government from power. It is thus meaningless to proceed to have elections because the collective will of the people would even be more easily raped in that process.

If Dr. Biya had continued with the dictatorship that he inherited from Mr Ahidjo, we should be living in peace, even if such peace is closer to that of the graveyard. But by dishonestly toying with the idea of democracy and at the same tightening his grip on the instruments of dictatorship, he has brought our security and collective existence seriously into jeopardy.

Had Dr. Biya been really sincere when he announced multiparty democracy a year ago, the first thing he should have done would have been to dismantle the CNU/CPDM party. This would have left a party-less interim government in place to supervise the formation of new parties and ensuing elections. Remember that the CPDM/CNU was a coalition of all the political parties which were existing at a certain point in time. This coalition should thus, naturally, have been dissolved before the formation of new parties since the coalition was viable within a single party framework. To have left it in place as a competitor to the newly formed parties, is certainly to give it what Lord Russell once described as "the advantages of theft over honest toil." This is the source and genesis of our present predicament.

There is no doubt that the Mandenge syndrome is what is still keeping some people in the CPDM.

20

Gobata on Gobata
(Published July 16-23, 1991)

My first name is "Rotcod" and not "Rodcod" or "Rodcot" as some people who talk as though with water in the mouth like calling me. Even *CAMEROON POST* was sometimes printing my name wrongly as "Rodcod." Was this due to what newspaper editors call the "printer's devil" or do they also have water in the mouth? The answer is blowing in the wind. But my name is very straight-forward and should be pronounced without *samsamness* in the mouth, but with alacrity (thanks to Zebrudaya) like a peal of thunder or an Iroko tree falling - ROTCOD GOBATA!

From today, anybody who calls me again with water in the mouth, I will not answer, I will just continue going, without looking back, even if the fellow is inviting me to have a beer at my favourite off-license in Djongolo.

"What's in a name?" you may be asking. Well, did you read the story of the boy whose parents named him "Mensah Paul Biya" when he was born in 1982, but who now wants to change his name to Mensah John Foncha?" I know another kid who was named "Ahidjo" in the early seventies. By the mid-eighties the name had become an unbearable embarrassment.

The only heroes on whom you can confidently hang your cap are the departed ones who have joined the communion of saints. Today, however, I wish to defend, not only my name, but what I stand for.

Every week I always hear some people saying: "I didn't like GOBATA's *No Trifling Matter* this week; too strong for my stomach! Undue radicalism can spoil things." Others will be saying: "I didn't like GOBATA's *No Trifling Matter* this week; too weak, very much unlike him. Maybe he has been Lapiroed. Do you think any Cameroonian can resist 22 million frs. cash?" Whenever I hear these diametrically opposed verdicts, I always say to myself: "Too strong for some, too weak for others, just fine for the rest." Just like a meal set before many people. Some would taste the soup and impatiently shout for salt, declaring that the cook forgot to put any salt. Others would taste the same soup and wriggle the nose and declare it over-salted. And yet others would relish the meal without any complaints. Which may suggest that the taste may be more in the palate than in the meal. No serious-minded columnist can set himself the objective of satisfying the whimsical reading palate of his readers.

Human beings are like pilgrims on earth, plodding along the straight and narrow path that lead to enduring human values, spiritual stardom and moral immortality. That path is characterized by fallibility and ineradicable subjectivity which together militate against the accurate perception and the attainment of perfection. And so it is that at the end of the day, when all's said and done, and the chips are all down, we often discover that the "good" were not so good and the "bad" not so bad. He who truly desires perfection must be willing and ready to change; for to live is to change and to be perfect is to have changed often.

Now, the one single activity which is indispensable for positive change is "criticism." People who have achieved a high level of self-criticism are those most firmly on the way to perfection in whatever sphere. But the habit of self-criticism though essential for self-development and even for survival, is not easy to cultivate. Those who know the value and scarcity of the practice of self-criticism, would value criticism no matter where it comes from. The critic does for us, what, in our own interest, we ought to do for ourselves. The societal critic is the most valuable member of the society, even if s/he is, more often than not, considered in the light rather of an irritating nuisance.

Such, in a nutshell, is the scaffolding of the philosophy underlying *No Trifling Matter*. We are guided by no other manifesto. We are moved by persuasive arguments or demonstrations but we are no respecter of persons. We look all individuals straight in the eye and we call them by their names, because we know that all human beings are basically the same, in spite of cosmetic differences due to accidental particularizing data. We know that no human being can become a god and those who have tried or pretended to be God have always ended as devils.

Of all the divine attributes, the ones most sought or pretended are omnipotence and *omniscience*. It is very significant that very few human beings aspire towards the third divine attribute: *omnibenevolence*. And yet this is the only one among the divine attributes which is, to a great extent, attainable under human conditions. For all that is needed to attain it is a perfectly good will, which, as some German philosopher discovered, is the only thing in the world or anywhere else which is good in itself, without any qualification.

Many readers of this column have tried pigeonholing the author. The editor of *CAMEROON POST*, Chief Bisong Etahoben, once described me in an article: "Anglophones And The Search For A New Hurrah" (*CAMEROON POST* April 4-11, 1991) as "undoubtedly a very strong militant of the SDF." This hasty categorization was based on a slight misreading of the *No Trifling Matter* of March 27-April 11, 1991) entitled "Now That The Opposition Is Really Here." The Chief substituted "is" for my "seems" in the article to obtain his categoric statements. My article had for its theme the immunizing tactics or ploys of the regime while the chief's article was on one of his pet worries, the North West/South West problem - issues on which I am sure, in the main, the chief and I would be in perfect agreement. Now, other people, reading the chief's article obviously without having read mine, have improved on the chief's remarks by claiming that I want Cameroonians to believe that the SDF is "the party" west of the Mungo. (See Tande Dibussi, "The Anglophone Opposition and Us" in *Cameroon Life,* Vol. 1 No. 10, June 1991). This would make of me not just a "very strong militant of the SDF" but its campaign manager. The bizarre twist here is the assimilation of my positive highlighting of the SDF to the North West/South West problem, a problem which, like the problem of tribalism, I consider to be a problem at the level of false consciousness.

In considering the SDF at the time, I was not at all viewing it as a party "West of the Mungo." My main concern was the bold and successful challenge of those who believe that the present move towards pluralism and democracy are a magnanimous gift of the one party CPDM regime.

Criticism being the central concern of this column, the column itself is open to and welcomes criticisms, including both negative and positive appraisal. If you feel strongly about it, just put it down on a piece of paper and send it to the Editor-in-Chief of *CAMEROON POST*. No use running a private verbal commentary to me when you meet me in a bar or *njangi* house. That way we would all be helping to bring about the free, open and just society that we all long for. On my part, I pledge that neither blackmail nor bribe can move me to change my convictions, but good arguments always move me.

21

From "La Democratie" To Democracy
(Published July 30 –August 6, 1991)

President Paul Biya's recent address to the nation, from the podium of the National Assembly, is so far the greatest psychological blow that the democratic struggle in the country has received since inception early last year.

I once remarked, while alluding to Eric Chinje's last "press conference" with Biya (see *CAMEROON POST,* May 9-16, 1991 p.4) that it was both lucky and wise that the President does not address the nation often, because his utterances seem to be dangerous not only for the regime but the nation as a whole. It is thanks to God alone and to the general docile nature and peace-loving disposition of all Cameroonians that this whole country did not go up in flames the day the President made his speech at the National Assembly. Of course, some places, notably in Douala, did go up in flames and some people reportedly smashed their own television sets in rage. But these isolated incidents can be considered quite mild compared to the intensity of the provocation.

In all of contemporary Africa, it is perhaps only in Cameroon that a Head of State could make a speech like that one and get away with it. Even the most ardent supporters of Biya's regime must have been disappointed.

For quite some time now, nearly all Cameroonians have been swearing by the National Conference. Everyone expected the President to concede, no matter in how reluctant or qualified a manner, to this overwhelming wish of the Cameroonian people. But what did we get? The flat statement: "I say it again, and I repeat that the National Conference is pointless in Cameroon." And then the threats that peace would reign at all cost, over the entire national territory! A declaration of war if ever there was one.

How could anybody be politically really so tactless? I think someone should urgently advise Dr Biya, in his own interest and that of the nation, never to address the nation again. He evidently just doesn't have the gift for this type of thing. His fidgety nervousness, erratic outbursts and general lack of composure, always give the impression of someone who is trying unsuccessfully to cover up something. Just contrast this with the calm confidence, composure and persuasive coherence of people like Dicka Akwa and Samuel Eboua when they passed on TV, even in the face of the naughty and very provocative questions, which any politician should expect anyway. But we should not blame Biya. It is said that some people are born dictators, some acquire dictatorship, and others have dictatorship thrust on them. Biya is one of those who had dictatorship thrust on him. And, in his candid moments, he comes out extremely clearly with insights into his own actual situation, as when he described himself as a pupil in Mitterrand's democracy school. He is likely to remain in that pedagogic institution for long, because what the French call "la democratie" is very different from what we understand by "democracy" in English.

"La democratie" is really nothing more than a bit of "*tricherie*," "*tracasserie*" and "*demogogie*" all mixed together. With enough determination, will-power, and appropriate sacrifices, the Cameroonian people will surely transcend "*la democratie*" and at last attain democracy. For, let us face it, Cameroon is not yet independent and none of the former French colonies in Africa seems yet to have attained independence, although the struggle is fiercely on at the moment.

Some people would consider what I have just said as an exaggeration. But consider the following: why is it that the Cameroon

Head of State never makes an important policy statement except from France or at least after a visit to France? What is the French army still doing in Cameroon more than thirty years after "independence"? Or maybe you don't know this fact. I myself discovered it only lately. The French army is here in full force. They even have an exclusive officer's mess, where Cameroonian officers are apparently not allowed to go, their own mess being situated about 250 meters down the same road. Well, as everyone knows, officers' messes, the world over, are the places where army officers discuss politics and strategic matters, form opinions and generally get a bit civilised. So the fellows are not only here, but practice apartheid which is fast crumbling even in South Africa. Or, tell me why the Central Bank of Cameroon is headed by a French man. If you don't know this, then maybe you don't also know that the two most important colleges of the University of Yaounde, namely the Medical School and the Polytechnique are headed by French men. So are all the so-called liquidators of defunct banks and parastatals French men. Is it that there are no Cameroonians capable and qualified enough to do these strategic jobs? The answer is blowing in the wind.

Of course, if your orientation is wholly or mainly Francophone, you may not be impressed by the partial scenario I have just pointed out. It does require a mutation in consciousness to think in this "subversive" manner, which would seem to be part and parcel of the Anglo-Saxon tradition of education. Ask yourself, for instance, why most Anglophone journalists and media persons have such a completely different attitude to their work from that of their Francophone counterparts. The latter clearly consider Government propaganda and praise singing as their bounden duty, whereas the former, whenever possible, tell things as they are, no matter whose ox is gored, except in those instances when some of them have succumbed to what I once described as the "Mandenge syndrome." Well, if your daughter needs a job and you yourself need 15 million francs, you can exchange nearly three decades of a highly credible journalistic career for these needs and become a Government apologist and sophisticated rationaliser at the dimitial hours of an otherwise meritorious career. But, on the other bench, are the Charlie Ndi Chias, Anembom Monjus, Shifu Ngallas etc., whom, even though we know them only by their voices, we are sure can neither be bribed nor bullied into proclaiming that the King is robed in purple, when all the evidence shows that the King is parading in the nude.

"*La democratie*" will surely catch up with democracy one of these days. Has Dr. President not already decided to meet the opposition leaders individually? (The radio and TV have since been hinting that Dr. Biya is ready to receive "even groups of persons"). But why individually? Does he think it would be easier to convince them singly of what he has failed to convince them collectively? Or is it that, individually, each of them can easily be Lapiroed out of the idea of a national conference? Well, I don't see any of the opposition leaders of the banned coalition of opposition parties who can easily be Lapiroed. And even if any or all of them are, it doesn't change much, as the Lapiro experience has shown. The people to convince are the Cameroonian masses. As long as they think that a national conference is the only way forward, little would be achieved without the said conference. If Dr. Biya has changed his stand on the issue of the national conference, let him just say so, pump and plain, without circumventions or circumlocutions. The proposed individual meetings with opposition leaders are really "*sans objet*" at this point in time.

22

Nigeria-Cameroon: No Problem?
(Published August 26-September 2, 1991)

President Paul Biya's recent hurried "state visit" to Abuja, Nigeria, was most surprising. Coming so shortly after Biya was in Abuja, Nigeria, for the OAU summit, there is no doubt that it was occasioned by something both serious and urgent. The visit itself lasted only half a day - a most unusual state visit. And yet, at the end of the visit, President Babangida of Nigeria and Biya of Cameroon issued a joint communiqué to the effect that there was no problem at all between Cameroon and Nigeria and that even if there were it would be solved amicably – a most unusual declaration which should worry thinking citizens of both countries.

Who can really believe that Biya had to jet all the way to Abuja and spend half a day with Babaginda only for the purpose of reaffirming that there is no problem between Nigeria and Cameroon? These leaders must really take those they are supposed to be leading for fools. They gamble with the future and security of people without the courtesy of even letting the people know what secret pacts have been made in their name.

It is a fact that the boundary between Cameroon and Nigeria has never been precisely defined. At many points, it is not clear where Cameroon ends and Nigeria begins. This is not surprising. First of all, the colonial nations which quartered up Africa at the Berlin conference in 1884 did so in the manner of any gang of robbers. Their only concern was fairness between themselves. The convenience of the booty did not cross their minds. That is why; with their robbers' pens they split some African nations and tribes and forced the resultant parts into different new entities. Secondly, the colonial entities called "Nigeria" and "Btritish Cameroons" were for a long time administered as a single entity, thereby obliterating any lines of demarcation. Again, with independence in 1960/1961, when the boundary should have been more precisely determined, a part of Cameroon opted to join Nigeria. It must be noted that in spite of the imprecise boundary, there had never been any problem between Nigeria and Cameroon until the late seventies/early eighties. Is it an accident that the commencement of border problems coincided with the discovery of petroleum and other minerals in the border zone?

By the early eighties, the border problem had become so bad that five Nigerian soldiers were allegedly killed by Cameroonian gendarmes in one of the border areas. Fuelled by the ultra-dynamic Nigerian press which described the incident variously as "cold blooded murder right inside Nigerian territory," "a dirty slap by a mosquito on the face of a giant" etc., indignation mounted high all over Nigeria and there were calls for a retaliatory strike. Some even called for the forceful annexation of Cameroon. The Cameroon embassy in Lagos came under physical attack. In Ilesha, Oyo State of Nigeria, a Cameroonian narrowly escaped being lynched. But when he returned to Cameroon, he was shocked to realize that Cameroonians were generally completely ignorant of what had happened. People were drinking their beer, dancing Makossa and discussing local football as usual. And yet, were it not for President Shehu Shagari's restraint in the face of the promptings of radical Nigerians, Nigeria would have attacked Cameroon even if only to satisfy a popular outcry. In an interview with Peter Enahoro for *Africa Now*, Chief Obafemi Awolowo declared that, if he had been in Shagari's place, he would have occupied Cameroon within the twinkling of an eye. A few Nigerian war planes did in fact fly over Limbe, although its inhabitants could not have been aware of what they were.

There are two plausible theories to explain Dr. Biya's hurried visit to Abuja. The first is that he rushed there to enlist Nigeria's sympathy and help in his determined effort to hang on to power, even if that means from a single finger of one hand. This possibility cannot be ruled out. But it is unlikely that President Babangida, who is firmly committed to the democratic process in Nigeria, would be supporting a tottering dictatorship abroad. The second theory is that Babangida "summoned" Biya over border problems between Nigeria and Cameroon. The Nigerian press has recently been alive again on these problems.

A persistent rumour that has gained wide currency in Nigeria is that General Yakubu Gowon once "dashed" Cameroon a strip of Nigerian land in appreciation of Ahmadou Ahidjo's support of Nigeria in the Biafra-Nigerian civil war. At the time, some young Nigerian army officers, including the Late General Murtala Ramat Muhammed and the incumbent President of Nigeria, are said to have seriously opposed Gowon's gesture and sworn they would never stand by it.

If there is any truth in this scenario, the second theory may be more plausible than the first. Babangida is a strategist of the first order. All observers of the development of the Nigerian political scene would agree with this. Since 1966, when Nigeria had its first coup d'état, Babangida's strategic genius has never failed him. He has never yet lost out in any dogged struggle. In 1975, he single-handedly disarmed someone who had already carried out a "successful" coup d'état and completely reversed the latter's fortunes in a manner that remains a mystery. Ten years later, he himself carried out a coup to end all coups, and subsequently survived two serious coup attempts against him. His creation of two political parties and transition to civil rule programme in 1992, are nothing short of a magician's hat tricks, considering the highly politicized and unruly nature of Nigerians. Both projects are firmly on course with only minimal problems.

Might such a strategic genius not have chosen a moment he noticed his eastern neighbour was facing a hydra-headed problem at home to force the best concessions out of him? Given the additional fact that Biya is stone-deaf in English and seems to lack both style and strategy, it is most dangerous if he signed any pacts on our behalf. No citizen can claim the right to know everything that their Head of State discusses with other Heads of State. But the citizens of any country have the right to know the full details of any agreement or pacts that are concluded on their behalf by whoever, since such are binding in perpetuity on the country and not just a regime.

The details of what Biya and Babangida agreed on in Abuja recently, beneath the fraternal rhetoric and diplomatic jargon, should be made known to us. It is very doubtful that those who cannot protect our long and short term interest at home would do so abroad.

23

Anti-Democracy Fails in Russia, Succeeds in Cameroon
(Published September 6-13, 1991)

The same day that the anti-democratic coup d'état failed in Russia, the anti-democratic forces in Cameroon fired on the leader of the Social Democratic Front (SDF) party, Mr John Fru Ndi, and a crowd of demonstrators in Bafoussam. That day, one really felt like singing with one eye for Russia while crying with the other for Cameroon.

Those who attempted to topple Mr Mikhail Gorbachev were irked by his democratic reforms and general opening up of Russian society to the rest of the world. And yet, there are other Russians who thought that Gorbachev's reforms were too slow and who might have tried to over throw him for that reason, if they had the chance. But, on balance, there is no doubt that Mr Gorbachev is the most remarkable political leader at the global level so far, of the last two decades of the twentieth century. In one masterly stroke, he ended the "cold war" between super powers, demolished the iron curtain and removed from the global horizon the spectre of communism, which for decades had haunted the so-called Western world, particularly the United State of America.

It must, however, be remarked here parenthetically that those who take the mass rejection of communist party dictatorship to be equivalent to the end of communism are having an optical illusion. This identification can only be made by those who fail to see the difference between communisms as such and Stalinism. The failure of "scientific socialism" does not mean the failure of socialism. Marxism and socialism are having a bad day because of the accidental historical linkage with intolerant monolithism, dictatorship and repression. But, as people all over the world continue their struggle against the evils of the so-called liberal economies, which depends purely on "market forces" resulting in private ownership of vast wealth by a small minority, and the consequent impoverishment of

71

the majority, the advantages of planned economies within a democratic set up, the advantages of socialism and even of communalism would soon be rediscovered.

At a point, Gorbachev was deservedly more popular in the United States than the American President himself. The political effects of what we can call the Gorbachevian miracle were first felt in Eastern Europe, where democratic revolutions sprouted like mushrooms from the ground. It did not take time before the democratic wind of change, blowing from the East, reached the African continent and caught all the monolithic regime dictators taking their prolonged siesta.

It is on historical record that, with the sole exception of Julius Nyerere of Tanzania, no African dictator has ever voluntarily and honestly given up power. Some, like Master Sergeant Samuel Doe of Liberia, have even preferred to have their manhood slashed off in an outrageous public ceremony than voluntarily give up power.

In Cameroon, the incumbent autocrat, who has always practiced what he dares not openly preach while preaching what he does not practice, caught the ill wind from the East quite early and thought that he could ward it off easily with palliative medicaments. Hence, the anti-democracy marches of March 1990, in which we saw clownish ministers and traditional chiefs leading crowds of clowns, dancing to the tune of "No to Precipitate Democracy!" But it soon became clear that more subtle and potent antidotes were needed, as Cameroonians gradually awakened from their long apathetic slumber.

Since May 1990, the struggle has continued fiercely and unabated, now openly now secretly. Democratic rhetoric has continued side by side with the most savage repression. The death toll has already exceeded 150! Can such waste ever be justified? Pro-democracy groups have been subjected to discriminatory bannings, physical obstruction and proscriptions.

Now, people who look on these things from narrow perspectives have been preaching the need for compromise. What compromise can there be between democracy and dictatorship? What middle ground is there between the two on which we can firmly stand with confidence? If Boris Yeltsin, the Russian masses and the three statistical martyrs of their collective will, had opted for compromise, would Russia not have headed back towards Stalinism today?

The Biya regime has become like a stubborn jigger in the foot. Shall Cameroonians endure the pain and trauma of removing it or give up and limp along with it as best as possible? That is the critical choice.

Last line: Do you remember Rene Philombe? He is a cripple, a writer and an intellectual. When this whole business first started, when many of us did not yet even know what a national conference is, Rene Philombe sat down on his wheel chair one day and cold-bloodedly declared over CRTV that those opposed to the national conference are "criminals." Looking back now, who would deny that "what a sage can see from his wheel chair a non-sage would not see even standing"?

24

To Hell with Culture
(Published September 20-27, 1991)

Yes you heard me quite alright. Your ears are not deceiving you. I say, "To hell with culture!"

What is culture? It is the total way of life of an identifiable group of people. The elements of a people's culture are: their food and manner of eating, their clothes and manner of dressing, their songs, dances and musical instruments, their ceremonies, the manner and content of their education, their belief systems, their customs, taboos and morality, their technology, art, architecture etc. Now, do you need a national propaganda campaign to "promote" any of these things? The answer is blowing in the wind.

Culture is something that manifests itself naturally, unobtrusively. If there is such a thing as "promoting culture," the best way to do it would be to promote general welfare and well-being at all levels - material, intellectual, spiritual. The view of culture as something separate and distinguishable from the way of life of a people, as something that can be put on display and admired *per se*, a spectacle that you go to watch in some hall during leisure time, something that can be bought and sold, is completely erroneous. This erroneous idea is one of the legacies of colonialism. Colonialists created ministries of culture and departments of anthropology to help them collect the "curiosities of the natives." These curiosities they exported to the *Metropoles* where their exoticness generated great interest and speculation, and market forces raised their value. But, as Okot p'Bitek once asked, what is the meaning and significance of an African religious mask, for instance, hanging on a concrete wall of an apartment in Paris or Los Angeles, a room reeking with unbelief and aimlessness in life? What is the use of a drum on display? Drums are for drumming and dancing, not for being hung on the wall and merely gazed at.

But, of course, when the colonialists departed, they left their successors. These are those who descend from the aircrafts at our airports, in their three-piece stripped suits with tie to match, and stop for a while to be entertained by "traditional dancers" lustily chanting, on command, songs they do not believe in. It is the successors of the colonials, who, in fact, are strangers to and among their own people, who have continued to maintain ministries of culture. What use is a ministry of culture in a country like Cameroon? It is by no accident that the native colonial masters usually pick some uncultured fellow from among their ranks to head this superfluous institution.

The recent hullabaloo about a national cultural forum on the general state of culture (whatever that means) is just diversionary tactics from people who don't want to admit that they can no longer deal with a socio-political situation over which they insist on presiding. What is the use of culture, let alone a cultural forum, to the more that 50% of Cameroonians who are completely jobless? Or those who have jobs and yet go without pay, while over 250 million francs are spent in "organizing" the cultural forum? What is the use vaunting the "bottle dance" over the mass media when people can no longer go out of their houses to enjoy the bottle dance in its natural setting?

All talk about culture, especially within our present circumstances, can only be calculated as a dope, an opium. I agree with Eric Bill who once declared: "… culture is a dope, a worse dope than religion: for if it were true that religion is the opium of the people, it is worse to poison yourself than to be poisoned… To hell with culture, culture as a thing added like sauce to otherwise unpalatable stale fish."

The recent national cultural forum on "the general state of culture" forcefully reminded me of a story I first heard from the novelist, Chinua Achebe. According to the story, someone whose house was on fire saw a rabbit escaping from the flames. He left the house flaming and went in pursuit of the rabbit. He so much loved rabbit meat, you see! Ah, Cameroonians!

President Biya's recent visit to the northern states was clearly calculated to remind the people of those states of his multifarious acts of magnanimity to them, which do not seem to have been sufficiently appreciated. What paternalism! "I created this state and built the road from X through Y to Z." Nobody retorted: "Haba, Mr

President, was the creation of the state a special favour, and did you construct the road out of your pocket?" "I permitted the first President of this country to come from here." No one enjoined: "Aaah, is that why you further permitted him to die in exile and refused him burial here, bah?" "I did this, I did that, so let's forgive and forget." Nobody asked: "How are we to forgive, let alone forget, sins which have not yet been admitted and confessed, let alone of repented?" I repeat that nobody reacted in this way to speeches which elsewhere would surely have been answered with rotten eggs and tomatoes. No one did that. Instead, we saw the Alhadjis nodding their heads, making one wonder whether their long caps are not, in fact, an extension of a vacuum that begins at the upper extremity of the neck.

25

What Will He Say at Limbe and Bamenda
(Published September 27- October 4, 1991)

The son of GOBATA is not a prophet or an astrologer, not a ball or star gazer, not a dreamer or seer, not a four-eyed wizard, nor a gifted futurologist of any other kind. This genre of gifts has never manifested itself in the family line, going back as far as it can be traced. The "predictions" contained in this piece are to be considered as purely "scientific" predictions based on causes and effects, action and possible reaction, in human affairs. This type of predictions requires no special gift or calling. It requires neither genetic endowment nor even audacity. It is open to all human beings who observe and reflect, and falsifications can be taken without undue loss of face.

Thanks to the time lag between the time of writing and the time of reading, you yourself can assess the truth coefficient of the non-prophetic predictions in the piece, since they would all have come to pass by the time you are reading this on Wednesday September 4, 1991, as President Biya is reading his campaign speech in Bertoua, the Eastern Provincial capital. The speech itself has not changed from the "sound and fury signifying nothing" that we heard in the northern states where, incidentally and ironically, we hear "operation ghost towns" has intensified after the President's departure. The Eastern speech is, however, bolder in tone, with a clearer hint that he is determined to stand by his verdict of "*sans objet*" concerning the Sovereign National Conference.

The angelic clarity and naïve innocence of the little girl who welcomed the President to the East in perfect English and French, symbol of hope for the Cameroon of our dreams, contrasted sharply with the latter's own verbal chicanery and demagogy. The little girl's face was never shown on the screen and we can from that fact predict that she must be a bilingual Anglophone rather than a bilingual Francophone.

From the East, we predict that the President will go to the south province, rather than to the South West province as is being widely speculated. Part of the ground for this prediction can be deduced from what must have been an inadvertent slip in the speech of the Eastern provincial host, thanking the crowds which had come from the Centre and South to support the visit. For logistical reasons, it would be necessary for the mobile crowds of this circus show to be moved to the South province immediately, to leave more time for working on the modalities for moving them to the remaining provinces, which have been under a state of emergency. The Chadian refugees used in the North cannot easily be brought down from the north. Going to the South province immediately would also give the President more time to revel in his own self-deception. No one wants to be roused too soon from a sweet dream, and the chances are that Dr. Biya might be shaken up from his induced sweet dreams in the remaining provinces.

What will transpire in Douala and Bafoussam is an open guesser's game. As for Bamenda and Limbe, we predict that he would first visit Limbe before Bamenda. This caution would be dictated by the need to pick his way gingerly, carefully taking the pressure and temperature of the people before advancing. The "*kwifon*" and "*ngwerong*" factor makes a direct frontal approach to the North West inadvisable. Remember that "*kwifon*" is no respecter of fons or fons of fons, but moves decisively without fear, favour or prejudice, on behalf of justice, morality and fair-play.

In Limbe, he will repeat the same clap-trap with which all Cameroonians are by now so familiar with only slight changes in phraseology. Given that his English has not improved since his beautiful nursery rhyme in Buea more than eight years ago ("I am a Cameroonian, I was a born a Cameroonian and I will die a Cameroonian!") it is doubtful that he would risk the comparison of his bilingualism with that of the unknown little girl who welcomed him to the East. On his way to the Municipal stadium in Limbe, he will pass Ombe without looking left, pass Mile Two without looking right, and the rest of the journey without looking left. In his speech, he will enumerate his magnanimity to the province: roads, tar factory, university, agric research centre, etc. He will try to make the people feel proud by saying in general terms that the province is economically important to the country, but without elaborating lest he be forced to mention the dangerous word "oil."

In Bamenda, he will stand facing the east with his back firmly to the west (Nyos you know). His speech will, however, be delivered with great self-confidence, thanks to the inspiration of the ever smiling Nkwain (who declared to have achieved his life's ambition by accompanying the President to his Eastern Shore *honoris causa* doctorate trip last Fall). He will not attempt to enumerate his acts of magnanimity to the province, since the only possible item under that rubric would be his famous "soon to be constructed" Bambui-Fundong road. He will recall that he is the Fon of Fons in the province and that this is why he appointed another fon as his second in command in his great party. But he will not add that this was after the dramatic resignation, in protest, of Mr John Ngu Foncha. He will strongly commend certain sons of the soil, especially Mr Nkwain – who, during Mr Biya's 27th April speech, showed that he was capable of laughing excitedly in a funeral-hall, for his child-like cheerfulness and alacrity, and Mr John Niba Ngu for his general hard work and truly heroic attempts in bilingualism. He will flatter North Westerners who always seem to cherish their independence, virile bellicosity and dare-devil chivalry and adventurism above all else, by saying that Bamenda is the political Mecca of Cameroon and the birth place of his own party. But it cannot be predicted whether he would add that he hopes the birth place of the party would not also be its burial ground.

At the end of the presidential speech, several hands will shoot up in the air, but it cannot be predicted if questions would be allowed. In the usual consultations to follow, he will depart from tradition and insist on meeting all the "leaders of thought" in one big group, so as to avoid sitting face to face alone with Ni John Fru Ndi.

26

Me Voici A Douala
(Published October 4-11, 1991)

Even Anglophones who are completely dumb in French and those who have a strong psychological aversion towards it have recently learnt a beautiful French expression: "Me Voici." Yesterday (Wednesday, 25 September, 1991), I went into a shop called SHO in down-town Yaounde to look for some spare parts for an appliance. As I was coming out of the shop, I noticed an excited crowd in *"Marché des Femmes"* just opposite and was compulsively drawn to the spot. The centre of attraction turned out to be a toddler (Francophone) of about 3 or 4, I would say, trailing the mother and shouting very articulately: *"Maman, me voice, me voice donc au Marché des femmes!"* The lady was explaining, with a touch of exasperation, that that was all her kid had been saying since President Paul Biya's speech at Douala on Friday 20th September. He would, for instance, rush into the kitchen as she was cooking and announce *"Maman, me voice dans la cuisine."* She would ignore him but he would insist: *"Maman, me voice donc dans la cuisine."* No sooner had she finished her explanation than the mischievous toddler obliged the crowd with his compulsive song, drawing, once more, thunderous hilarious laughter from all around, including yours truly.

Indeed, if anybody wanted an appropriate caption for Biya's Douala speech and, in fact, for his entire provincial safari, this would take the prize: *"Me voici…Me Voici donc a Douala"* Translation: *Na me this for Douala! Whetti una fit do me? Wuna be say I no fit put foot for here. Na me this. Make wuna do whetti whe wuna fit do make I see. Wuna think say I de fear? Wetin wuna fit do me?!*

I don't know why, but quite curiously, President Biya's speech in Douala conjured up from the sub-consciousness walls of my childhood memory, the image of a long forgotten childhood contemporary. This fellow was a terrible weakling. Even girls younger than himself could give him a thorough trashing. But he had three unequalled gifts: a bitingly provocative tongue, unbelievably swift legs and a real brute of a father. If his father cracked you on the head, you could never forget the experience. He would beat a kid exactly the same way he could have beaten an adult his own age. He was quite aware of his son's physical weakness and always immediately went to war on his behalf, without ever bothering to find out the cause of the dispute. Now, whenever his weakling of a son provoked anybody and was being pursued, he would fly until he got within hearing range from wherever his brute of a father was. He would then stop and turn round to face his pursuer and say in a voice loud enough for his father to hear: *"Na me this!"* beat me now. *Na me this.* Why are you going away again. Beat me. *Na me this!"*

Biya loves Douala so much. Why didn't he go to take a walk alone in Bepanda, Diedo or New Bell? I mean alone, without taking the entire army with him, preceding, accompanying and following, with all the guns, machine guns, tanks and what have you? Then he could truly and justifiably have beaten his chest: *Me voice donc a Douala!* By boasting otherwise, he has only shown himself to be *"Wanyetoh"* (Well, if you don't know who Wanyetoh was, go and ask that man of Letters and Science, Professor of Community Health, Daniel N. Lantum, alias Fai wo Bastos, to relate to you some of his collected folk tales). When cornered, Wanyetoh could successfully feign great humility, friendliness and helpfulness. When concerned, Wanyetoh could feign great humility, friendliness and helpfulness. But once safely across the uncrossable river, he would beat his chest most arrogantly: this is me, Wanyetoh!

How do you explain the fact that, so far, the President's speech in Bamenda has been the most conciliatory, the most reasonable, of all the eight provinces he has so far visited as I am writing this? My own answer to this question is simple: he didn't understand what he was reading, being in English. Whoever wrote the speech must be a secret sympathizer with the cause of the people as championed by the opposition parties. Be that as it may, history will not fail to mention the welcome speech of Mr Jomia Pefok. It is the first welcome address to a Cameroonian Head of State in the past thirty years that was transparently honest, straight from the heart, and void of exaggerated flattery and a catalogue of silly demands.

Optimism has again started mounting among the populations that "Wanyetoh" would announce the convening of a national conference after completing his provincial visits, just as it mounted before the June 27th address to the National Assembly. There is nothing to justify this hopeful optimism. If it happens, it would be truly miraculous. If his name is really "Wanyetoh," then he has no intention of ever giving in to the demand for a national conference. What can he possibly learn from his provincial jamborees that he did not already know even before Prime Minister Hayatou, started his smiling "consultations," that he did not already know before his own "consultations" in Yaounde, that he did not already know before setting out on the present provincial tours?

The money wasted in the present pointless exercise could have conducted ten national conferences. The people's act of self-flagellation and immolation through "operation this and that" cannot move Wanyetoh. It is not today that he agreed with his mentor to put the famous French paratroopers on full alert, just in case. ... Wanyetoh, like Toonga, will quit only when God, in his infinite mercy, decides to send him the way of all flesh.

27

A Basket Full Of... Promises
(Published October 11-17, 1991)

Just for one moment, imagine the following hypothetical situation. Suppose all the baskets in Cameroon were one single basket! What a big basket it would be! But, if we put all the promises that President Biya has made, since inscrutable historical circumstances catapulted him to the summit of political power in this country, they would fill our imaginary basket to over flowing. However, a basket full of promises is a basket full of air, an empty basket.

If there is one art that Biya has mastered, it is the art of promising, complimented by the art of enumerating apparent achievements. The art is charmingly simple. Make the most extravagant promise and swear that you will personally ensure its execution (*"Je m'engage personnellement....."* By the time it becomes clear that the supposed promise was the equivalent of a dud cheque, you simply make a more extravagant promise with more solemn assurances of its implementation. Apparently, human beings have such short memories that what matters is always the promise of today, not the failed promise of yesterday.

I still remember the excitement and euphoria all over the national territory that greeted Biya's promise, sometime in 1986 or so, that the "chasing of files" to Yaounde would be abolished. As usual, he swore to see to it "personally." Well, everyone knows or should know how far that promise has been fulfilled. As for the enumeration of apparent achievements, how could a whole Head of State, after ten years in power, name as some of his achievements, the tarring of "some" streets in Buea and Limbe and the establishment of a Technical School in Kumba? If that declaration in Buea, Southwest province, on Friday 27 September, 1991, did not make you laugh, then what I am writing here cannot make any sense to you. Dr. Biya certainly has some achievements to his credit, such as the Nsimalen international airport, Yaounde, the Hilton Hotel, Yaounde, the Yaounde-Mbalmayo highway, the Edea-Kribi express road etc., etc.

But it is significant to note that, none of these projects were preceded by a glamorous promise. In fact, I dare say that, if he promises anything, it is a sure indication that he has no intention of ever doing it. Promising for him is simply a political strategy that has been working wonders to him. Even the noisy students of the Yaounde University have completely forgotten that, nearly two years ago, they were promised a decongestion of the university. A university village was to be constructed somewhere at Nkolbisson and the land, we were told then, had already been acquired, surveyed, and all marked out. What of the promised universities of Ngaoundere and Buea? Is this not the month of October? If Biya is not a "merchant of illusions" then, Cameroonians are certainly buyers of illusionary promises. This is what makes the South West provincial edition of Biya's recent tours so thought-provoking. As I am writing this *"Cameroon Calling"* of Sunday 6th October, 1991, is on-air and three "executive members of the South West Elite Association" are on the programme.

I honestly don't know who an elite is, although every province now seems to have an association of "elites." But whoever these so-called elites are, if the three fellows blasting away on "Cameroon Calling" as I am writing, are really representatives of the South West elite, then it must be an association of very confused people. They think that Biya's visit to the South West was very special and unique in comparison to the other provinces. They highlight the legendary peacefulness, hospitality and patience of the people of the Southwest. (Sure? Hear! Hear! No violence in Kumba, Ombe, Limbe?). They think their catalogue of reasonable demands is a very effective and sagacious political strategy. Yet, they all express disappointments at the President's failure to make any promises in the South West. Nevertheless, they don't intend to abandon their policy of patience, because it is part and parcel of their culture, although they are quite aware that a patient dog eats the fattest bone only after the impatient ones have finished all the meat. On the other hand, the President did make promises. When they met him for over forty minutes, ever before they said it, the President had said that he knew all their aspirations, which include a deep sea port in Limbe; that it would be done when funding is available (is that not a promise?) but that he thought the question of dis-enclaving by constructing roads to all parts of the province was of more immediate importance (not a promise?).

The South West elite, who say they are un-conditionally committed to national unity, point out that the Limbe sea port had been into used before and, even now, when the Douala port is congested, it is used. Hence, it does not need to be constructed, but only revived. In the meantime, they have adopted a "wait and see attitude." Wait and see what? Are they implying that there is something which might make them reconsider their much trumpeted culturally grounded legendary patience.

As the province which presently supplies nearly 70% of the country's revenue, it is quite amusing that the people of the South West are begging the Cameroon government for favours. At no moment during the president's visit to the South West, was there as much as a hint that the people would like to fully participate in the policy and decision-making processes resulting in the sort of things they are begging for. In other words, they fully accept the Divine Right of the regime to monopolise these vital processes, provided they are granted favours and privileges by comparison to the other provinces. That is why they had no opinion, let alone demands, regarding problems at the national level.

Kwame Nkrumah was quite right when he advised that we should first seek the political kingdom and all other things would be added thereto. Did the people of the Centre and South provinces beg for a road from Yaounde to Kribi?

Well, Biya did promise a deep "sheport" in Limbe. But the "heport" at Batanga, Kribi, is already under construction, with money from the African Development Bank. The same bank is financing the Yaoundé - Kribi road, the Edea-Kribi highway notwithstanding. By all means, let South Westerners maintain their legendary patience and peacefulness. But let them not expect any fat bones in the end. The bones are already being devoured by members of their elite, who worked so hard to ensure the "huge success" of the President's visit to the South West province.

28

The Does of Africa
(Published October 24-31, 1991)

Remember Samuel Doe? Yes, Master Sergeant Doe! He was a Master Sergeant when he felt the call to save his people from tyrannous dictatorship. It is quite probable that, at that point in its historical time, Liberia really needed a messiah. Doe answered the call to messiah-ship. However, when the task of deliverance was accomplished, he no longer felt like quitting. He forgot the example of the prototype of all messiahs, Jesus Christ, whose messiah-ship lasted only three years and then he simply ascended into heaven, in spite of the noisy protests of his apostles, disciples, fans and supporters.

Samuel Doe slowly transformed himself into an intolerable yoke for Liberia, much worse than that from which he had "saved" them. He held tenaciously to power, in spite of numerous opportunities for a graceful exit. Only death could separate him from his beloved spouse - power. The combined forces of Johnson and Taylor ensured that separation in a most gruesome manner. But, at what cost to Liberians? Hundreds of deaths, displacement, destruction, starvation, disorganisation, etc. etc.

There are many Does in Africa; tragic heroes, whose fatal fault is simply not knowing when to quit the stage of this marvellous thing called power, which tends to corrupt and corrupts absolutely when wielded absolutely.

There is a legion of African Does. Quite curiously, they include the leaders of all French former colonies and trust territories. One simple way to recognize this is to take a look at the currency used in the particular territory. If the indomitable face of an incumbent Head of State stares at you from the currency, don't waste your time looking for further evidence. The fellow is undoubtedly a Doe. It really beats me why anybody should imagine that his austere face is necessary on every currency note minted for his country. I strongly suspect that this silly practice is one reason why these fellows invariably consider the national territory as their private property. For as long as this practice persists, for that long shall we be sure that the Does are still with us. All African Does are equal but some are evidently equaller than others.

If we were to compose a litany of the frontline Does, Africa's sit-tight dictators, it would run something like this: Houphouet Boigny, have mercy on your people and quit. Eyadema, have mercy on your people and quit. Sese Seko Mobutu, have mercy on your people and quit. Paul Biya, have mercy on your people and quit. Omar Bongo, have mercy on your people and quit. Abdou Diouf, have mercy on your people and quit. J. J Rawlings, have mercy on Ghanaians and quit. Arap Moi, have mercy on Kenyans and quit, etc.

In this satanic litany, Daniel Arap Moi of Kenya deserves special mention. Arap Moi is an intolerable dictator who evidently has no intention of ever quitting power while the slightest breath remains in him. He doesn't even pretend democracy at the rhetorical level as the others do. He has consistently declared that all is well in Kenya, that Kenyans are as happy as Adam and Eve in Paradise before the Fall and that they do not therefore need multi-partyism, which would usher in tribalism, nepotism, disunity, instability and general confusion.

Beneath the rhetoric, however, the sordid reality is that of secret murders, disappearances, proscriptions, obstructions, banning, coercion, intimidations etc. Would you believe the fact that the world's famous scholar, Professor Ali Mazrui, who is a Kenyan, was recently prevented, just like Mungo Beti in Yaounde, from giving a lecture in his home town, Mombassa, after he had read the same lecture, more than four times in Nigeria and elsewhere? Mazrui's remarkable 12-hour movie *"The Africans"* has been serialized in many countries all over the world, including all African countries except racist South Africa and Kenya. The sin of this prophet who has so far gone without honour in his home country, is simply that he has consistently called on Kenya, which was in the forefront of the liberation struggle against colonial rule, to assume a comparable vanguard position in the new liberation struggle for indigenous democracy.

86

There is something very instructive about the Kenyan situation and this concerns the erstwhile colonial master, Britain. Like the USA, Britain prides itself in being a champion of Liberalism and democratic values. But just like the USA, Britain does not hesitate to support autocratic dictatorship in other countries, if that is in its interest. Of all African ex-colonies, Britain has its best stakes in Kenya - a military base, economic investments etc. The climate in Kenya is extremely agreeable to white people and Nairobi is nothing if not an African London. Britain thus prefers to support dictatorship in Kenya, rather than risk its interests by supporting democracy. What all this means is that the English are in no way different from the French nor both from the Americans. For all of them, their interests and privileges are primordial and non-negotiable and, when they talk of democracy and liberal values, they mean them for their own people. What can be said for the English as against the French is only that their style of colonialism made it easier for the colonized to struggle for more meaningful independence. Every people must struggle for their own freedom. This is one thing that has never and will never be gotten as a free gift.

29

The Exorcist
(Published November 6-13, 1991)

A magician who conjures up ghosts from the nether world should also be able to send them back to the nether world - their proper abode. For several months now, seventy per cent of our country has been occupied by ghosts, originally conjured by the Coordination of Opposition Parties. It is becoming increasingly clear that these ghosts are unwilling unceremoniously to be ordered back to the nether world. The magician seems to have lost control.

One indication: Mr Ni John Fru Ndi, who brought democracy to Cameroon and who, in spite of what some people like to believe, is a level-headed moderate, was recently unable, in spite of his charisma, to convince the crowd at a rally in Bamenda, to partially bury the ghost, specifically as concerns the *"rentree scolaire."* In fact, Ni John seems to have had to use one of his disappearing tricks to get away from the ill-tempered crowd which would not hear of any other exorcist except the "sovereign national conference." Fru Ndi and Bi Mvondo seem to have at least one thing in common - the belief that school should be left to scholars and politics to politicians - a view yours truly, the son of Gobata, does not share. Why should politics be left to politicians? We left politics to politicians and see the mess we are in today.

As for schooling, many of our politicians need it badly, beginning with our almighty head of state, Wanyetoh II, who must be credited for realising at least that much. He has openly declared himself a pupil in Mr Mitterand's democratic nursery. The problem, however, is that Mr Biya has enrolled in the wrong school. The French, whose well-being depends on exploitation of third world countries, especially Cameroon, cannot be expected willingly to commit economic suicide by supporting real democracy in Cameroon. The art they have thought our Biya is that of democratic theory and rhetoric combined with the most ruthless autocratic practice.

Those who think that our problems of schooling are different from political problems are very myopic in their thinking. The question every intelligent Cameroonian school child should be asking is: "Schooling for what?" The number of certificated idlers and street roamers, from first school leavers to PhD holders in our country today calls for a completely new rethinking of our situation, objectives and strategies. A national conference or whatever, whether sovereign or not, could conceivably have ensured this, among other things. Perceptive parents and even school children cannot be indifferent to this. A traveller who has lost his way and bearings would be wiser spending time to consult people, maps, etc. instead of rushing randomly in just any direction.

In any case, it is very clear that our long sleeping monster has been roused from slumber. No opposition leader and no member of the present power-tenacious regime goes without three good square meals a day. Some of them even have enough in foreign and domestic banks to assure a comfortable life till death many times over. This cannot be said of the majority of those clamouring for a sovereign national conference. These are mostly people who have nothing, nothing to hope for, and nothing to lose except their wretchedness. If guns and hand grenades (in Cameroon we disperse peaceful demonstrations with hand grenades!) cannot deter them, what else would?

It is to be feared that, if Mr Biya keeps dancing like Lakayana, his two spears, courtesy of the Centre Province in hand, around the issue of the national conference, we are in for an indefinite continuation of our day-time nightmare. The worst in human nature has already manifested itself in the several past months. And things are poised to worsen, since evil has no intrinsic maximum. We may never be able to fully recover from the psychological wounds that have been inflicted on our body politic. We urgently need an exorcist.

The meeting of the Opposition with the Prime Minister is a ray of hope in the horizon. If good results are achieved, it would be clear to everybody. When things return to normal, no one would need to be told. For yours truly, one indicator would be when the terrorists we euphemistically call "forces of law and order" pack their bags and baggage, guns and grenades, from our pavements and street corners, to return to their barracks to face their proper civic duties.

But, given Mr Biya's track record, one has to be a sceptic. It was rather amusing to listen to Dr. Simon Munzu, a self-confessed member of the progressive wing of the CPDM, on "*Cameroon Calling*" the other day. Simon Munzu was charmingly eloquent. If his unavowed aim was to improve his personal political fortunes, he certainly is on the right track. But his claims on "CC" were manifestly contradictory. By implication, the progressive wing of the CPDM is inconsistent with itself. Munzu insists on presenting Biya as a democratic super star from whom the progressive wing draws inspiration and to whom it assures its loyalty. But, in the same breath, he laments the absence of democracy within the CPDM, exemplified by the refusal (Biya's refusal) to convene a meeting of the Central Committee in violation of the party's constitution. If Biya is so afraid of democracy even within his own party, what logic permits us to believe that he would tolerate it at the national level? This is one of the questions Munzu should have been asked in his one-man show on "CC." If a member of the opposition had been facing him, his concealed contradictions would have been brought out. But his claims should equally have been tested against those of a representative of the non-progressive wing of his party. *"Cameroon Calling"* of old would certainly have ensured this. But the "CC" of nowadays is no longer distinguishable from most of the rap trap the CRTV inflicts on us daily.

30

Beyond Elitism (Including a Reply to Tande Dibussi)
(Published November 13-20, 1991)

My piece entitled "A Basket Full of Promises" (CAMEROON POST Oct. 11-17, 1991) was not an attack on SWELA, let alone a "vicious" attack, as alleged by Tande Dibussi, in his piece: "SWELA and Gobata's Vicious Piece" (CAMEROON POST Nov. 6-13, 1991). I am not a "detractor" of SWELA nor of anything else and certainly have no hatred for South Westerners as alleged by Dibussi. Are these allegations deduced from my piece or is Tande Dibussi drawing on some privileged knowledge not available to me and my readers? The answer is blowing in the wind.

Anybody who wants to know me and what I stand for, should reread, *No Trifling Matter* of July 16-23, 1991 entitled "GOBATA ON GOBATA." I strongly recommend that piece for the careful reading of Tande Dibussi. I am first and foremost a critic who has openly pledged that "neither blackmail nor bribe can move me to change my convictions, but good arguments always move me." Where people come from is the very last thing that interests me. To put it another way, in carrying out my project of criticism, I don't care where anybody comes from or what relationship holds between us. If my twin brother, or even myself were a member of SWELA, that would not have in any way mitigated my criticism.

I must admit, however, that I didn't understand fully what SWELA is, at the time I wrote "A Basket Full of Promises." Tande

Dibussi's piece (attack?) has really enlightened me in this regard. Had I known at the time of writing that SWELA is a mere "interest group - a collection of people who try to realize their narrow and particular interests," the colour of my article would certainly have been different, although the matter, pace and tempo would have remained pretty much the same.

Now, given that SWELA is a lobby or pressure group, which is "not concerned at all with national issues," I should have queried why the producer of *"Cameroon Calling"* would give so much public time to it in a national programme. Is it because he is possibly a member of the "pressure group"? Next, I should have been pointing out that it is more in SWELA's "narrow particular interests," at this particular point in time, to be concerned rather with larger national issues. Lobbying cannot work within a one-man dictatorship. Yes, there may be more than 17, 500 interest groups in the U.S.A. But that is because the USA is an open, pluralist democratic society. To be able to have a comparable situation in Cameroon, the first indispensable condition is to have a truly democratic society, and this is a "national issue." In my "vicious piece," I did prove that both lobbying and promises do not work in our system. Dibussi came close to disproving this when he claims that "as a pressure and lobby group, SWELA is succeeding. The disproof could be completed by enumerating the purported successes.

It is likely that Tande Dibussi was just using me as a rider to advertise SWELA. On re-reading "GOBATA ON GOBATA" in which he came in for mention, it is also clear that he is rather obsessed with the so-called North West/South West problem - a problem which I maintain is a problem only at the level of false consciousness. I must return to this theme in future.

There is a certain" fallacy of provincialism" that needs careful debunking. Members of the "Eleventh Province" association should be aware of this fallacy. Consider the following true story: there is a young Cameroonian named Weledji Donald Nkamayi. He was born and brought up in Kumba, South West Province. Two years ago, Donald made his GCE O/ Levels in 10 papers with flying colours. This year he made his GCE A/Levels in the same manner in 5 subjects, two A's, one B and two C's. Three universities abroad have offered him admission. But he cannot go to university because he has been refused Government scholarship, the underlying reason being that his parents, who teach in Catholic Primary Schools in the South West Province are not "authentic South Westerners" (to use Dibussi's phrase) nor are they authentic citizens of any other province. The parents have, of course, written an appeal to the Prime Minister, which by now is already in some waste paper basket. Can SWELA help a fellow like Donald? Can its philosophy allow it to use its art of lobbying to help him?

This is a scandal and I believe we urgently need to find a way of getting away from this way of thinking. We must find a way of getting away from our obsession with this business of *where* people come from and start installing MERITOCRACY as our national philosophy. I must return to the idea of meritocracy in future.

I still don't know who an "elite" is nor do I really care. But the recent memorandum of "Anglophone Elites Resident in Littoral Province" addressed to the "Fons, Chiefs, Political Leaders and People of former West Cameroon," seems to me completely in the right direction. It addresses "national issues"! I recommend it for the perusal of every West Cameroonian.

It is very consoling that the legal case, as pointed out by the Anglophone "elites" of Littoral Province, for the return to the *status quo ante* 1972, is both clear and highly persuasive. What is left is the political will. Given the palpable fact that our Francophone brothers don't seem in any hurry to learn democracy, I would suggest that West Cameroon leaders of thought should come together and hold a national conference to save this country. In the meantime, we must again start calling, without stammering, such names as "West Cameroon" and "Victoria" (three cheers to Victoria United!). I sincerely thank Tande Dibussi for his provocations.

31

Professor Obenson Was Right
(Published November 20-27, 1991)

I would not allow Prof. Gabriel Obenson's article "Lake Nyos, Neutron Bomb, Alarm Bells, Boundaries And All That" (*CAMEROON POST*, Oct. 24-31, 1991, page 6) to be filed away without an appreciative comment. I enjoyed the article immensely, no less for its tinge of mature humour than for being a subtle but veritable synthesis of "the trouble with Cameroon" (thanks to Chinua Achebe). Some of what Prof. Obenson is saying in this article may need a little unpacking for the benefit of those who find it hard to read between the lines or those who see no more in a joke than the laughter that it illicits.

In my own interpretative understanding, Obenson perceives the main problem with Cameroon to be the enthronement of mediocrity. The other problems, such as "our toilet paper system" which has left us with no role models, no heroes, the fact that we view our problems through the eyes of foreigners etc., are only derivatives of the underlying problem of mediocrity at the leadership and policy-making levels.

In Cameroon, we have raised up mediocrity on a pedestal as a god of whom we are faithful devotees. This is an inevitable thing within an intolerable dictatorship of the type under which, for decades, we have been suffering in silence; a dictatorship which controls tightly all aspects of public life. Under such a yoke, even the findings and discoveries of experts cannot be publicized without clearance from the regime which effectively means from the fellow at the summit of power. In such a system, something good can only be achieved, if and only if, the man at the pinnacle of power is an all-round genius. The majority of people under such a system cannot help becoming professional praise-singers, eternally chanting the omniscience, omnibenevolence and absolute indispensability of their God-sent leader. That is, understandably, rational self-interest. We cannot all be Charlie Ndi Chias, Bate Besongs or Christian Tumis.

But no human being can be an all-round genius, let alone of a possessor of all divine attributes.

If we leave the dead alone for the time being, it could be asserted that, if Paul Biya is both author and writer of *"Communal Liberalism,"* then he certainly cannot be an intellectual mediocre. He could certainly teach Social Science at Ecole Normale or even the University. But to go by his political pronouncements and practices, he is palpably a political mediocre. Cameroon is a plural multi-ethnic country, a veritable patchwork of linguistic and cultural groups. How could any leader with political tact, let alone wisdom, in such a context, in nearly a decade, concentrate all major development projects in his own area of origin or stand up at a time of serious national tension and declare that "if Yaoundé is breathing, Cameroon is alive" and that "those who want peace should prepare for war"?

To get back to the Nyos disaster, which Obenson uses as his rider, what the scientific spirit, if not method, demanded in the circumstances was to carefully collect all plausible hypotheses, ruling out none *a priori* and then use rational arguments to eliminate some of them. The hypothesis that the disaster was a surreptitious test of the neutron bomb by the American CIA and Israel, using local collaborators, originated in America itself. Knowing the CIA and what it has done, should we have ruled out the hypothesis *a priori* as a monstrous impossible suggestion? As for the local collaborators in this hypothesis, is it impossible that people who throw hand grenades to disperse a civilian crowd would collaborate in such a project for substantial financial gains?

As for the scientific conference on the disaster, it is perfectly understandable that, if a scientist of Obenson's calibre was involved, it could only be as a consultant to some foreign interest. Even if he had applied to the Cameroon government, stating that he felt strongly that he could unravel the mystery, some "commission" would have sat over his application and returned a verdict of *"profil non conforme."* How would the "profil" "conforme," when large sums of money are involved and he is not a member of the cartel of national kleptocrats?

Shortly after the Nyos disaster, a writer in *Cameroon Tribune* (Tuesday October 28, 1986) opined: "The Lake Nyos disaster is a great challenge to Cameroonian scholars, researchers and policy makers. It offers both an opportunity and incentive for relevant research and patriotic commitment. It can only be hoped that they would prove equal to this challenge." This writer did not realize that there was nothing any researcher, no matter how motivated and willing, could do if the powers-that-be were unwilling to cooperate. Was Dr. Michel Belombe not there all the time? Was he invited? And yet, this is a man who has gained considerable international reputation for his work in solid state chemistry and the invention of novel chemical compounds to the extent that Nigerians once co-opted him into their nuclear power commission, in spite of his being a foreigner.

Obenson is perfectly right regarding what needs to be done. "Forward ever, backward never. Let us change our SYSTEM of governance first, not just persons..." It is really an astounding fact that many Cameroonians don't yet seem to realize this.

32

From the Fruits We Shall Know
(Published December 2-9, 1991)

The tripartite talks, or what some people have preferred to call "Non-Sovereign National Conference," have come and gone. It is too early to say with complete confidence whether these talks have been a miraculous success as claimed by some people or simply another squandered opportunity to put this country on a firm unshakable foundation. What we can affirm with more confidence is the truth of the common adage that whoever fights and runs away from the fight lives to fight another day. If someone shits in the living room and the members of the family decide to cover the shit with banana leaves and go to sleep, the shit will surely be waiting for them when they wake up again.

On balance, my own intuitive assessment tends more towards the verdict that the talks swept a lot of cockroaches under the carpet rather than the one that Our Lady of Nsimalen might have performed another miracle among us.

The "accord" signed by the ruling oligarchy and the so-called hard-core opposition at the end of the talks understandably generated a lot of optimistic euphoria among Cameroonians. Anyone who has experienced the phenomenon of "ghost towns" or who has been tear-gassed and hand-grenaded for no justifiable reason, could not but jump for joy at the prospect of ending the terror under which we have been living and partly living during the past several months. But the indications that the euphoria might not have been justified and that the accord might have been just one more gigantic fraud by the ruling oligarchy, were not long in coming.

The first of these was the dramatic speed with which the talks were brought to an end, at a time many of us expected the real talks to begin. The other is the retrospective realisation that the government worked hard behind the scenes and made the concessions it did to secure the signatures of the opposition leaders so that Biya could take them to the Francophone summit in Paris, prove that he is a hard-working pupil in Mitterrand's democratic school and, of course, secure more loans to add to the burden of debts that our children will surely have to sell themselves into slavery to repay.

There is not enough evidence to prove the contention of some people that opposition leaders who signed the "accord" were bribed to sell out the cause of the people. We should give them the benefit of the doubt and say that, if the "accord" turns out to be a hoax, they were only being politically naive. It is very significant in this regard that the two fathers of Cameroon democracy, the initiators of the present wind of democratic change, namely, Yondo Black and Fru Ndi, both expressed serious reservations about signing the "accord." Whatever the case, only the unfolding of events will confirm or disconfirm either hypothesis. Until then, we must avoid both naive euphoria and extreme pessimism. From the tangible fruits we shall be left in no doubt.

There is one very instructive lesson to be learned from the reactions of the populations to the "accord" in particular and the tripartite talks in general. Those aspiring to the supreme magistracy had better learn this lesson. And it is this: gone are the days when the masses of this country could tolerate broken promises and commitments and allow the Head of State to behave like the lord of the manor in the manor of the lord. The next Head of State, whoever he will happen to be, would be sadly mistaken to think that he too can go ahead and appoint his relatives, friends, classmates and tribesmen into lucrative positions; that he too can sell our petroleum without saying for how much or what happens to the proceeds; that he too can at any time telephone the Minister of Finance and simply instruct him to transfer so many billions into his bank account in Switzerland or the Bahamas; that he too can seize any piece of land he fancies anywhere and direct the authorities concerned to prepare a land title in his name, etc. He would be sadly mistaken because those days are fast marching out and would be completely gone by the time we swear in a new President. From all indications, the people, who are the real custodians of power in a democratic setting, are going to insist on transparency and accountability.

I don't know whether the tripartite talks were a fraud or not. Whether at these talks we ran away from the fight or stumbled on a political Aladin's lamp, is something that we will know as events continue to unfold. I am, however, worried about important issues that were carefully swept under the carpet whenever they raised their ugly heads. One of these is the "Anglophone Problem" which, I would assert, holds the key to the solution of our present problems as a nation.

Whether we like it or not, we will have to address ourselves to the nasty task of uncovering frauds, sooner or later. One of these frauds has been the surreptitious but persistent attempt to assimilate the Anglophones. The surreptitious changes of the name of our country from the " Federal Republic of Cameroon" in 1961 through the "United Republic of Cameroon" to the "Republic of Cameroon" today; changes which have no *fundamentum* in law, are only outward signs of this fraud. But no identifiable group of people can be assimilated against their own will and better judgement. Just look at Canada. After decades, the French Canadians of Quebec Region, who are smaller than Anglophones in our own country, will be having a referendum next year to decide whether to continue the union with the rest of Canada or to declare sovereignty.

33

Democracy, Kakistocracy and Meritocracy
(Published December 12-19, 1991)

The most fundamental assumption of democracy is the equality of all human persons. To say that all human persons are equal is not to say that they all possess exactly the same descriptive attributes. It is not to say that all human beings were born at the same time and place, are of the same gender, height, weight, complexion, strength, intelligence, etc. These are particularising attributes which individuate humans. These are accidental elements. If all human beings had all these in common, they would be one single person.

We may state the common and defining characteristic of human persons as rational animality. That is to say that all human beings are, first and foremost, animals endowed with reason. All human beings are also limited in their capabilities, especially with respect to their knowledge, power and goodness. All human beings also possess the capacity to suffer, to inflict suffering on others and also to act altruistically. If this is true, it goes without saying that each human being is autonomous, a master of himself/herself and may not be subjected to another's power and control without sufficient justification.

A democracy, then, is not only the most rational but also the most justifiable form of government. It is, of course, quite evident that the individual's right to autonomy cannot be directly exercised, outside of small and rather elementary initial groupings. Hence, the need for periodic delegation of the prerogative. And once this idea is entertained, a certain amount of division of labour and specialisation becomes imperative in society.

This is where meritocracy comes in. A meritocratic system is one in which every individual does what s/he is best suited for by his/her natural and acquired endowments and receives in compensation a reward commensurate to the overall value of such contribution to the collectivity. Of course, in every society, there will always be individuals who cannot contribute anything to collective well-being on account of infirmity, extreme age or youth etc. But the moral sensibilities of human beings should ensure that such people are also adequately catered for. But, apart from these, every other individual must contribute something to the common good in exchange for which s/he also gets some personal rewards. And it is only rational that each individual should contribute what s/he is best suited for contributing. A physical weakling may be quite clever with his/her hands or mind. It would be irrational to assign such a weakling to be a soldier or to dig trenches or break rocks while someone with muscles and an empty head wears a suit and sits in an office making a mess of conceptual and paper work. There is a widespread and dangerous misconception that some jobs are "better" than others. This misconception comes about because of widespread parasitism and exploitation. In a meritocratic system, which goes hand in glove with democracy, there can be no exploiters or parasites, that is, people who live (sometimes in opulent luxury) out of the toil and sweat of others.

Within any system, such parasites would usually be people in positions of power, authority or responsibility. That is why their presence can be taken as the unfailing indicator, the litmus test, as it were, that the system under operation is a kakistocracy.

That we have been operating a kakistocracy in Cameroon in the past several decades, is a palpable fact. It could not have been otherwise given our one-man autocratic dictatorship. No matter how benevolent a dictator may want to be, his human limitations will force him to make disastrous mistakes in the absence of severe criticism.

Mongo Beti once remarked that Mr Biya is someone whose endowments should, at the very best, have led him to be the Assistant D.O. of his area of origin. I don't know whether Mongo Beti was right or wrong. But if we ask how Biya became our Head of State, we can answer correctly by saying that it was through his "loyalty" to one man, a dictator, Alhaji Ahmadou Ahidjo. A good dictator would always seek to dictate his own successor, and his choice cannot but be guided by considerations of personal loyalty, apparent or real. Now, loyalty to persons is something that can be completely dispensed with in a democratic and meritocratic system. Within such a system, all individuals are equally dispensable. We may therefore be loyal to principles and institutions, but not to persons as such.

Some people express reservations about meritocracy because of the pluralistic nature of our society. But, barring past injustices which should be compensated, there is no group of human beings without its own geniuses, muscle men etc. A meritocratic system would not only be fair, it is liable to satisfy all.

34

The Pre-Conditions of Meritocracy
(Published January 6-13, 1992)

The last time, I talked about meritocracy within the context of democracy and kakistocracy. This time around, I wish to touch on what I consider to be the pre-conditions, the indispensable requirements of a meritocratic system.

Based on the postulate that all human beings, as human beings, are absolutely equal, meritocracy recommends itself as the fairest and most rational system.

But to treat people on the basis of merit rather than on the basis of their place of origin, tribe, family or linguistic affiliation, etc., requires a method of assessing merit that is objective and transparently fair. In the modern world, the most important *prima facie* criterion of merit is, no doubt, formal education. It is therefore crucially important that our system of formal education should have methods of assessment and certification that are objective and absolutely fair. A teacher, at whatever level, who awards marks or grades to a student/pupil which are not objectively related to performance, commits a crime whose gravity has so far been greatly under-estimated. An action like that subverts a meritocratic system from its very foundations.

In West Cameroon, at least, we can say that the First School Leaving and GCE examination systems are objective and fair methods of academic assessment. Teachers and pupils/students may engage in fraud during the years leading to these examinations, but the examinations themselves are usually fair because of the blind system of marking. A pupil/student who had got promoted from class to class as a favour rather than on merit would usually meet his/her "waterloo" at these examinations. If we check the details of performance at these exams, we would learn a lot of lessons regarding meritocracy. There has never been an occasion when only members of one single tribe performed well or even predominantly well in these examinations. There would, of course, be schools which outshine all others. But this is usually due to their local organisation and effectiveness of teaching. The individual students themselves who perform well will always be a veritable mixed bag of families, tribes, of all religious and social backgrounds.

It is a very significant fact that, when the First School Leaving and GCE results are released, no one is ever heard to complain of discrimination on any grounds. Those who fail in the examinations look inward to themselves for the cause of their failure. The objectivity and fairness of these exams can be improved upon and extended to all levels of the academic enterprise.

In this country, the objectivity and fairness of assessment at the primary and secondary school levels, at least in West Cameroon, is completely lost at the tertiary level. What reigns supreme at this level are fraud, favouritism, bribery, corruption, calculative bargaining and sheer chance. I challenge anybody to refute these claims. Take the University of Yaounde and its various affiliates - the University Centres, ENS, CUSS, ESTI, IRIC, Polytechnic, etc. What reigns in all these institutions is fraud, pure and simple. Do you remember why Prof. Jacob Ngu's office was burnt last year? Well, like many other cans of worms accidentally opened, we firmly closed that can and have continued as if nothing ever happened. The frauds and rackets must not only continue but must be carefully covered to protect the sacred cows who practice them.

I know a student who was unable to register at the University five years ago, because of age limit, but who has successfully registered this year. I can never understand why anybody thought that people above 25 should not enter the University. But that is the rule at UNIYAO anyway; on paper, that is. Now, the student just mentioned was unable to register five years ago because of his/her moral scruples. S/he had been clearly told at the time what was required to enable successful passage through the needle's eye. Five years later, during which time s/he saw people almost twice his/her age register and graduate, and still jobless, s/he finally dumped his/her moral scruples on the rubbish heap and was able to register this session.

This little fraud from which, under situation ethics, the student might be completely exculpable, had to involve not only university administrators but also police commissioners and secondary school principals who had, each within his own functions, to certify false documents knowingly and willingly.

In 1988, someone went to a *njangi* house to borrow 500.000 francs, because he badly wanted his son admitted into ENS Bambili. This year, the admission exercise into both cycles of ENS has come and gone. It is hard to dismiss the claim that the Government used the exercise this year mainly to raise money for its empty coffers. How the selection was done in both cycles is an open guesser's game. A story is still circulating among young ladies who were involved in the competition about a gentleman connected with the admission exercise who developed bruises on his "*wetincall*," thanks to the number of female aspirants he "horizontalized" in the process.

All candidates for admission into ENS and all the other public schools firmly believe that the easiest way to get in there is through the string-pulling favour of some Minister or Director. Are they wrong? Of course, the authorities concerned would have us believe that they make admissions on the basis of a most rigorous and objective study of "*dossiers*." Let them tell us what it is they study in the *dossiers*, since the final selection is never related to any conceivable set of criteria.

Recently, an alarm was raised that the admissions into the Douala University Centre were fraudulent. The Minister of Higher Education is reported to have said that it was a lie and that he would produce

102

proofs to the contrary. Who will he convinced with his proofs? Is it those who got in through the mediation of some big shot, those who passed envelopes under the table or those who traded their fine bodies for their places? The answer is blowing in the wind.

Two years ago, a scandalous story was circulating around town about a lecturer at UNIYAO (we will not name the faculty but we are sure that all faculties will justifiably feel accused) who made love to a female student in his office and changed her failure into a resounding pass. Now, the way people were telling the story, really worried me. Everybody seemed to be shocked at the fact that the man "did it" *to his student* or *in his office*. People were saying things like: "With so many hotels around, why should a man like that descend so low" etc. But, if two consenting adults decide to make love with full awareness of the possible consequences, where they do it is their bloody private affair. Nobody seemed to be shocked at what really looked scandalous to me in this case, namely, that a teacher could, with his own hand, fraudulently change a grade a student had earned in exchange for sex.

I could go on multiplying examples, but what is the use? Anybody who honestly takes a critical look at all our tertiary institutions of learning has to agree that the future of our country is founded on quick sand unless…we begin to install meritocracy now!

35

Meritocracy Continued
(Published January 15-22, 1992)

Today, I am constrained to continue with the theme of meritocracy for two reasons: (1) the issue is extremely important in our context, (2) I am not yet satisfied that I have demonstrated it sufficiently convincingly. The last time I identified formal education as the most important criterion of merit in the modern world. But I was careful enough to qualify it as a *prima facie* criterion. Education, whether formal or not, is not enough. It only gives good grounds for certain expectations. In this case, it is like a promise. Some promises are simply false while others, in spite of being genuine, fall short of fulfilment for several putative reasons. Thus, education, as such, must be combined with other criteria of assessment in any meritocratic system. Among such criteria are: <u>performance</u> and <u>character</u> or general moral integrity.

All education involves the teaching and acquisition of certain skills, whether these be manual (physical), mental or spiritual. Proof of education is therefore not to be found only in certificates and diplomas but on what their possessor can do. Recall the award of false certificates at the University of Yaounde which Prof. Jacob Ngu was attempting to investigate when his office was burnt and he (ironically) lost his job as Vice-Chancellor, probably so that the issue might be swept under the carpet - as it has - thereby protecting the sacred cows who have institutionalised the practice. This type of fraudulent practice has flourished because our system depends solely on certificates for employment. No one cares about performance thereafter. If performance were to be taken into consideration, the advantages of a forged certificate would be very short-lived indeed. Because, from the moment the possessor of such a fake document shows that s/he does not possess the skills which the certificate claims s/he possesses, that should be the end of road for him/her. But, as I have asserted before, our system is one big fraud and the future of this country is very bleak indeed if we do not, sooner than later, get down to the task of uncovering the numerous frauds, the quick sands, on which we have laid the foundation of our future.

Just consider an institution like our Centre for Health Sciences (CUSS). Medicine may be rightly considered as a very special, almost sacred, profession because of its close connection with life, health and death. But our CUSS has not been spared the general fraud that reigns in the country in its selecting and training of doctors and other paramedicals. The entrance examination into our CUSS is one of the most fiercely competitive. The reason is not (unfortunately) that hundreds of young Cameroonians are attracted to the ideal of service as medical practitioners, but simply that the prospects of a secure and lucrative job are most assured. Well, you may not know that well-connected candidates who fail to make it through the needle's eye into CUSS are usually permitted to "audit" courses freely and to participate in all tests and exams "as a formality." After a few terms of such free auditing, they are invariably smuggled in and the grades they received "as a formality" are quietly attributed to them substantively. In this way, they gain through the back door access into the same house whose front door had been firmly barred against them. The training which medical students receive in CUSS is thoroughly suffused with the same type of trickery and chicanery at all levels. Is it not a great tragedy for our country? Well, answer that yourself.

But, to get back to my main theme, I was saying that, while qualification is very important criterion of merit, it is not enough. Qualification must be combined with performance. Indeed, we should say that qualification can only be proved through performance. But that is not the end of the story. A person may be highly qualified and very efficient in his/her performance; but, if s/he is a crook, such knowledge and efficiency could be very dangerous. In fact, we should go as far as saying that knowledge and efficiency in an immoral person are much worse than if such a person were ignorant because such knowledge and efficiency are invariably used for immoral, egoistical and personal ends. Hence, I say that character or moral integrity must be added to education or qualification and performance as indispensable criteria of a meritocratic system. In other words, if two people are equally qualified and efficient on the basis of their qualification, a meritocratic system would argue for preference for the one with a better character. Of course, there are several ways of assessing character or moral integrity, but that is not our problem for now.

My main argument is that a meritocratic system in which due consideration is given to qualification, performance, with or without qualification; moral integrity, is a fair and rational system. Within such a system, such criteria of selection as tribe, province of origin, linguistic camp, favouritism, connections of all types, bribery and corruption of all types, even gender and age, have no place whatsoever. Our problem, of course, is that it is the latter considerations largely that have so far determined our selection and reward system. How are we to break through that immoral, vicious and rationally unjustifiable system to a more meritocratic system? In my view, the starting point must be the uncovering of past and on-going frauds. After that, there should be the righting of wrongs, compensation for those frauded, cheated or injured in the past. At that point, a pure meritocratic system can be installed. But can all this be done with a fraudulent Government on the seat of power? The answer is blowing in the wind.

36

The Panel Beaters of the Biya Regime
(Published January 29 – February 4, 1992)

The Biya regime can now be compared to an old battered car with thread-bare tyres, its suspension system and alignment out of order. It should long have had a police "OFF THE ROAD" sign plastered on it, but recklessly insists on tottering along, a danger to all other road users and to its own very occupants. A fatal crash seems only a matter of time. In the meantime, it receives nasty bashes left, right and centre, every passing day. But, every day, these bashes are panel-beaten, sand-papered, and a dash of left-over paint of any available colour, splattered on it. The result: a veritable patch-work of the most incongruous metals and paint colours.

Today, let us cast a glance at the panel beaters. These are the fellows appointed to straighten and to conceal the blunder of the regime through unconvincing rationalizations and bold-faced lying. They all operate from one indispensable and non-negotiable premise: the regime can never make any mistakes or do any wrong.

There are two master panel beaters in the garage: the Honourable Minister of Information and Culture, His Excellency Augustin Kontchou alias Zero Mort, and his equally Honourable counterpart in the Ministry of Higher Education, Joseph Owona alias Mike Tyson. These are the two pillars and twin engines which are sworn to keep the battered regime going against all odds. If care is not taken, these two fellows will continue going even after Biya himself would have heeded reason and capitulated. The recent case of the Moslem land in Tsinga shows that, even if Mr Biya is a common land speculator, he does yield to common good sense occasionally. Before he did the honourable thing in this case, the panel beaters had been all out telling us he was given the land as compensation for the hill on which Unity Palace is built. How did he acquire Unity Hill? However, we salute Biya's courage in this case and hope that it is a sign of many more repentances, reparations and restitutions to come.

Back to our master panel beaters. The former of the two is evidently the Cartesian "evil genius" of the regime; ready, willing and capable at all times of convincing us against our most hyperbolic doubts about the regime. Of his intelligence, no one can be in doubt. Only that intelligence employed in the service of evil or unjustifiable causes creates its own limits from within. His calm smoothness is a remarkable asset. But he must be one of those rare individuals on whom psychologists complain that lie detectors don't work.

The latter of the two is the indispensable "crown prince" of the regime. Like Hamlet, the other crown prince in Shakespeare's imagination, he knows how to keep mum and also how to feign madness, but there is always enough style and system in his madness. Even in his "madness" the prince of Denmark could tell the difference between a crow and a hand-saw. This one knows the difference between empty air waves and black marks on white paper, on the one hand, and a well-sharpened matchet, on the other; the difference between action and passion and the efficacy of action from a distance without a traceable causal chain.

Below these two masters, is an array of subordinate but equally efficient panel beaters. They are too many to treat individually but a few remarkable ones must be mentioned. John NIBA Ngu, for example. I have written his middle name in capital letters so that he may not be confused with his brother who, until fairly recently, was also a minister but who, from all indications, is a bird of completely different plumage, made of completely different stuff. This, incidentally, demonstrates what I have never tired of emphasizing, namely, that *where* a person comes from is absolutely of no consequence and that tribalism, provincialism etc., are problems only at the level of false consciousness. Here are two people from the very same womb. When we draw the contrasts between them, this has absolutely nothing to do with their coming from the North West, let alone with their being Baforchus. Sorry again for the digression.

A newspaper recently called for John NIBA Ngu to be sacked from his post as Minister of Agriculture, for shamelessly announcing for a record three times the postponement of the of the Ebolowa Agric-Show. "SACK THIS MAN" the paper screamed under the picture of the (Honourable?) Minister. But *"Le Messager"* was only displaying confused thinking on this issue. A call on Niba Ngu to resign would have been more logical. Who is to sack him? Is it those who hired him? Would they sack him for faithfully carrying out their instructions to the extent of losing his personal credibility completely? If he had been a man of honour and integrity would he not have resigned the very first time it became clear that, as Minister of Agriculture, he hadn't a free hand in organising the Ebolowa Agric Show? But, no! He is made to tell us one day that the magnanimous regime had resolved the farmers must have "their feast" and fixed a "firm date" this time around. "Sorry for the earlier two postponements. They were owing to this and that. The response from the farmers this time has been fantastic. We have even run out of exhibition stalls. We wanted to be sure that everything would be superb. We can never disappoint the farmers in whose interest all our efforts are engaged. The ultra-hospitable people of the South Province will display the very best of their legendary hospitality to all attending the Agric Show. So, please, start rushing down to Ebolowa immediately. Bla-bla-bla." Only to come back a few days later to give reasons which sound so good, so natural and so commonsensical for postponing the show once more (again!) for the third time! The word is CREDIBILITY. That is what this whole regime has lost, irretrievably, it seems.

The "anticipated legislative elections" seem poised to become another Ebolowa show. The Minister in charge of the elections, Gilbert Andze Tsoungui, is one of the best panel beaters in the regime. The opposition had long since signalled its opposition to these elections for various reasons, including the electoral code, proposed date etc. We had all been made to understand that an agreement was reached between the Government and the opposition during the "tripartite" talks resulting in the signing of an accord. Now the Minister is telling us that the electoral code was "inspired" by the tripartite. He assures us that the elections will be free and fair because of indelible ink and foreign observers. How on earth can indelible ink ensure free and fair elections? And who are the foreign observers and why would they want free and fair election in Cameroon? Please, let's start being serious. This costly joke is going too far.

37

Blueprint for University Studies
(Published February 7-14, 1992)

As I predicted before, we have already all forgotten that we were promised two new Universities - one at Buea ("on the Anglo-Saxon model," whatever that was supposed to mean!) and the other at Ngaoundere. We were all given the most convincing assurances that the new Universities would take off this academic year. As recently as six weeks ago, the Honourable Chancellor of UNIYAO, Dr. Peter Agbor Tabi, who is manifestly one of the most promising apprentices in Biya's advanced school of political panel beaters, was on the air, assuring twelve million Cameroonians that the new Universities of Buea and Ngaoundere would take off this academic year. Giving the impression that he was already the *de facto* Chancellor of these (newly created?) Universities, he even went as far as stating that the unit course system, as it operates in American Universities and under which it is impossible to have an *"année blanche"* would be adopted. Well, those of us who have never studied in America and those who never even went to school anywhere found it hard to follow how a unit course system or any system of studies for that matter could make it impossible to lose a year, if students decided to disrupt lectures for a year. Nevertheless, we were happy with the "firm promise" and repeated assurance that the Universities of Buea and Ngaoundere would start this academic year.

Credulity and credibility are next-door neighbours. The billion Dollar question is this: WILL THE UNIVERSITIES OF BUEA AND NGAOUNDERE STILL TAKE OFF THIS ACADEMIC YEAR? The answer may be blowing in the wind. By deduction or induction or intuition, you may arrive at yours. Here is mine: If the Universities of Ngaoundere and Buea (on the famous Anglo-Saxon model!!) take off this academic year, then my father's name is not GOBATA! Nor will they take off in any foreseeable near future. For the moment, they are mere theoretical entities, products of the art of the seeming, in which the Biya regime has truly distinguished itself.

110

But while we await the unlikely opening of the Ngaoundere and Buea Universities, here is my own blueprint relative to the hot and thorny issue of scholarships for University students. Eric Ngufor's letter to the Editor (*CAMEROON POST*, Jan. 29-Feb.4, 1992) and Ndek Ebaressi's earlier article (*CAMEROON POST*, Jan. 15-22, 1992) are in the right direction, if the details are correctly arranged. The scholarship programme in UNIYAO as it has operated up to the present is an extremely foolish policy which, all things carefully considered, is neither in the interest of the students nor that of the country at large. Such a policy could only have been designed to achieve short-term advantages both for the Government and the students. As one student put it recently, the so-called scholarship is really a bribe in exchange for freedom of thought and expression. The extreme savagery with which anything resembling a rebellion or protest has always been suppressed in UNIYAO supports this view. What is the use of receiving a monthly stipend of 30.000 francs in an educational institution where you learn little or nothing and from which you graduate into firm joblessness?

My suggestions here must be read in conjunction with my earlier write ups on "The Pre-Conditions of Meritocracy" (*CAMEROON POST*, Jan. 6-13, 1992). No serious University anywhere can really combine an open door admissions policy with free tuition and scholarship for all and sundry. But every serious country must ensure that its best talent receives the highest education and training and that none of its citizens is hampered from this objective for merely financial reasons. In other words, while a policy of generalized and indiscriminate scholarship is unjustifiable, some form of scholarship programme is indispensable. University education is not mass education. It should be reserved for the most talented tenth of the population. And only a further tenth of that tenth can be provided with scholarships. Now, how may this be done in a rationally justifiable manner? I don't have a sufficient understanding of Francophone secondary education. So I'll limit myself here to the Anglophone GCE system. If the same hustling, fraud and forgery that we have noted at the tertiary level also exists at the secondary level of Francophone education, then my recipe would not be applicable there without further preconditions. But, given the

Anglophone GCE system and limiting ourselves to the Advanced Level, let us assign the following points to various grades that a student may obtain: 5 for A, 4 for B, 3 for C, 2 for D and 1 for E. In this way, a student who obtains three papers with grades A-A-A and student who obtains four papers with grades A-A-C-D would each have a total of 15 points etc.

Now, my suggestion is that the minimum cut-off point for admission into the University should be 7 points. In other words, any student who makes seven points or above should automatically qualify for admission into any University of his or her choice within the country. A token tuition fee of 50.000 francs (25.000 francs per semester) should be charged every student. Students who score 12 points or above should automatically gain full Government scholarship for any University of their choice within the country. Those who score 15 points or above should automatically gain full Government scholarship for any University of their choice anywhere in the world. But those who accept scholarship should be bonded to serve the state for a certain number of years after graduation; failing which they should refund all the money enjoyed as scholarship, plus an appropriate interest. This should help to check brain drain out of the country.

For those unqualified for scholarships, refundable loans and work-aid should be provided on the basis of demonstrable need. Things such as sweeping, cleaning, clearing, garbage collection, etc. within the University, should be handled by students for substantial pay as work-aid.

38

Blueprint for University Studies (2)
(Published February 19-26, 1992)

A University is first and foremost a configuration of infrastructures and facilities: buildings, roads, housing, transport, restaurants, markets/supermarkets, banks, post offices, sporting and recreational facilities of all sorts, health facilities, secondary and primary education facilities, etc. In short, a good University would always be a veritable city, usually within a city. This configuration ensures that those who pass through the University receive a certain unique formation and orientation which remains with them for the rest of their lives. Such background is presupposed when someone proudly says: "I am an Oxfordian, a Havardian, a Lion" or "I graduated from Legon, UCLA, Ife, Manchester" etc. Such declarations tell a lot about the person in question, about what may be presupposed in his/her background, to the extent that accurate predictions could be made about his/her behaviour and general comportment, within certain limits. There are places and cases where someone could get a job without any further ado simply by declaring the University from which s/he graduated.

It is the absence of any particular orientation or formation that is largely responsible for the fact that the so-called University of Yaounde is the sorry affair that it is. From this respect, it cannot even be described as a "glorified secondary school." It is simply a conglomeration of civilian adults who come there for multifarious reasons. There, nothing really ticks.

The University cannot itself run all the facilities required in a University city. For some of them, such as banking, communication, marketing, supermarketing, restauranting, etc., it must invite professionals to establish these and run them according to agreed terms which must always seek to secure the greatest advantages for the University community. Others, such as housing (for both staff and students), health facilities, printing, book selling, etc., are so vitally important that any University worth its name must either run these itself or closely control in detail their running by others. One simple procedural rule can be laid down here: where the University depends on outsiders to provide any facilities on contractual basis, on no account should officials or staff of the University or members of their immediate families be allowed to tender for such contracts. Such an injunction would check the tendency to fraud, corruption and all sorts of *magu-magu*.

There obviously are gaps in my proposal. But these can easily be filled on a case by case basis.

This is how far I had gone with the second part of my "Blueprint" when I was distracted by seeing Mr Paul Biya's face again on our television screen. Since his very unfortunate address at the National Assembly on June 27th last year, I thought he might have accepted my free advice NEVER, in his own interest and that of all Cameroonians, to attempt addressing the nation again. Here was I again before his coughy voice, dancing eyes, and hands all over the place, frantically gesticulating, demonstrating, estimating and measuring, we-know-not what.

39

Biya Plays His Last Joker

The first thing that jolted me from my seat during this stage-managed "interview" with Charles Ndongo was the declaration: "I have given 500 million to be placed at the disposal of those parties which accept to participate in the elections on March 1st." If Cameroon had had a credible judicial system, I would immediately have rushed out to file a suit against the President for "calculated conspiracy to enrich certain lazy and dishonest individuals at public expense." With over sixty political parties on paper, the issue of financing political parties is one that must be very thoroughly debated and the details and modalities carefully worked out. So all those me-my-wife-and-driver parties in all combinations of P's and S's are going to share 500 million francs of public money, when thousands of slaving Cameroonians are going without their legitimate wages for months and months? We say: "NO

SIR," let every so-called political party finance its own campaigns. That way, those of them without any following would stop confusing and compounding our struggle. But, of course, Biya is offering the 500 million in characteristic style as a procedural bribe on the way to his March 1st dream. The further 5 billion to pay outstanding wages, scholarships, and to ease social tension etc., is no less a bribe, but why should anybody be grateful for being bribed with what rightly belongs to him in the first place? No thanks for the 5 billion, Sir, thank you!

But the real question is: From where has so much money suddenly surfaced, just when we had got used to the loudly trumpeted idea that the state coffers are empty? There are two competing theories in answer to this question. The first is that Cameroon is a much richer country than any of us suspects, but that the ruling clique is keeping this fact secret so that it can cart away as much of this wealth as possible before relinquishing power. The second theory is that the money is a little chip from Mr Biya's personal holdings in foreign banks. Rumours estimate such holdings to total about 25 times the country's entire budget in the boom days. That way, the man is perfectly capable of holding out for the next quarter of a century; because, with money, nothing is impossible. So, jigger tight for foot, Abi?

The most reassuring part of Mr Biya's interview is where he assured all of us that there is no religious problem in Cameroon and that only a handful of extremist Moslems, who are condemned by the majority of their brethren, want to march at Briqueterie over their land-coveted-by-His-Excellency affair. Well, if this be the case, why bring out the whole army to prevent this handful of misguided individuals from marching? After all, are they using your feet to march? When tired of marching, won't they return to their ghettos to die of epidemics and hunger? So, why go into so much trouble to prevent their march?

40

Our Beautiful Ones Are Not Yet Born
(Published February 29-March 6, 1992)

Recent political developments in Cameroon indicate that the idea of "CHOPPING" is still the basic motive force for most Cameroonians. Our politics, contrary to hopeful early signs, is being unmasked as being largely *garri* politics, politics of the belly or *"chop I chop palaver finish"* type of politics. In this type of politics, those who can equal, let alone beat, Mr, sorry, Dr. Biya and his CPDM are not yet born. Which means that those of us, the non-choppers, might as well prepare to continue suffering in silence (if they spare our lives) under his hegemony for at last another two decades, as I estimated before. I have noted it before somewhere that Biya's regime can aptly be described as being basically a kleptocracy with fascistic and democratic elements, which are brought in from time to time as the need arises, to serve the main *raison d'être* of the regime - thievery.

When Biya made his address to the nation, under the guise of an interview with Charles Ndongo, and offered 500 million francs to those parties willing to go the March 1st elections, I thought the tactic was so crude and so obscene that it would be roundly condemned by all the other parties. But it is now clear that even those opposition parties which signalled their intention to participate in the elections before the announcement of the bribe, unless they are CPDM-satellite parties, did so because they had already got wind of the impending inducement. That same night or thereabout, some group of jokers, with a diabolically good sense of humour said to themselves: "Why not let's go for a good cut of these millions? After all, it's our oil money of which we have never seen a franc! Let's form a political party! If we call it "conservative something-something," it will surely give the impression of being a zombie of the regime and will be registered in spite of the expiry of the registration period. Of course, we must announce, with our registration, our intention to take part in the elections with immediate effect and automatic alacrity." And they did. And the party was duly registered by the authorities. By now, they must be smiling over their millions, embracing and slapping one another on the back, and congratulating themselves for their cleverness which has turned them into millionaires overnight.

We have watched with total consternation as the UPC, which we thought was the most solid and formidable of opposition parties with a radical and revolutionary reputation going back to pre-independence days, cracked right up the middle. And Mr Bouba Bello Maigari, for whose return from exile we had waited like people waiting for a messiah, and whom many were already tipping as our next President also gets lapiroed and settles for power-sharing with the incumbent regime, after successive denials of rumours to this very effect.

One thing finally stands out clearly. Any Cameroonian who has shared power and its spoils at the centre at any time in the past three decades cannot be completely trusted. What all these people have learnt unforgettably is how to make things seem to be what they are not, how to manipulate people, facts and figures, and, above all, how to chop. Any of these fellows seems perfectly capable of selling Cameroon as a whole for one million pieces of silver. Many rank and file Cameroonians are not different. I know some people who consider Biya's regime as the greatest plague that ever afflicted this country but who, nevertheless, are, right now, out campaigning for the CPDM. They are doing what they hate and preaching what they don't believe, because they expect in reward, lucrative appointments and promotions, or are simply afraid to lose their jobs or be retired at the right time. It is equally unbelievable the number of ordinary Cameroonians who would happily jump up the back of an open lorry and wear a CPDM uniform and go anywhere in exchange for free food and beer.

Against the back drop of this scenario, there is no doubt that someone like John Fru Ndi will continue standing like a solitary and lonely tree on our political skyline. As for us, ordinary Cameroonians, we must admit that the beautiful ones are not yet born. At least, not in their numbers. We await still that calibre of Cameroonians, in sufficient numbers, who will decide to salvage this country without counting personal cost, without the readiness to exchange their birthright at any time for any mess of pottage. We await the birth of our beautiful ones.

41

Basically a Fraudulent Victory
(Published March 6-13, 1992)

Among the undesirable character traits of Cameroonians is the tendency to get carried away by deceptive appearances to the detriment of palpable reality. This trait has manifested itself in the world of sports, especially football, and in the practice of hero-worship. Many Cameroonians have got so carried away by the recent CPDM-organised parliamentary elections that they seem to have momentarily forgotten the very weighty reasons why these elections were inadvisable. People are now bemoaning the fact that, by boycotting the elections, the main opposition parties handed victory to the CPDM on a platter of gold. Some people are even going as far as talking about the "foolishness" of the boycotting parties. Some militants of the boycotting parties are even biting their fingers in regret. But all these are very superficial reactions and appraisal of this most recent development on our political chessboard.

The "victory" of the CPDM in the just-concluded elections was not only predictable but predicted, and was both known and expected by all Cameroonians. That is not to say that there been no surprises. But the surprises have been in the details, not in the overall game. It was certainly surprising to see the competition to which the CPDM was subjected in areas which we all considered CPDM strongholds, where going to the elections was not in question. Even in these areas, the CPDM got a good run for its money or rather our money which it dished out right, left and centre to lure people to participate in the elections. If, in spite of bribery and corruption, in spite of intimidation and blackmail, in spite of its huge propaganda machinery so efficiently handled and co-ordinated by the CRTV's so-called journalists, in all the provinces; if in spite of all these, the

CPDM did not win a landslide victory, then what would have happened if we had a fair electoral code, an independent electoral commission, and if every eligible voter had cast a vote in the elections? The CPDM would surely have had an earthquake failure.

Those who are now regretting the boycott of the elections are reasoning backwards. The "victory" of the CPDM in these elections is demonstrably a fraudulent victory and, in spite of the present moment, the best thing remains to have boycotted the elections. Parties and voters who boycotted these elections did not make any mistake. It is, of course, ironic that the CPDM could be declared winner in boycotting opposition strongholds, where less than 5% of eligible voters went to the polls. But what this demonstrates is the unacceptable nature of the rules of the game. It is these rules that the boycotting parties were challenging. If you disagree with the rules of a game, then you cannot at the same time take part in arguments as to whether the rules you have rejected are being correctly applied.

Anybody genuinely interested in democratic reforms in Cameroon, and not just in a cut of Dr. Biya's cake, could not have participated in the March 1st elections. To have done so on the ground that abstaining would give Biya's CPDM uncontested victory is to reason very poorly and to substitute expediency for principle. Expediency should never be substituted for principle, although, once the principles have been agreed, expedient methods could be used to achieve their goals. To do otherwise is to shift or run away from fundamental issues, and, as we all know, he who runs away from an inevitable fight lives to fight another day. In our struggle for a just and democratic Cameroon, the most fundamental requirement remains a constitution and an electoral code acceptable to all Cameroonians. Without these, there is no guarantee that fundamental human and democratic rights would be respected.

Some people believe that the March 1st elections were fairly conducted, albeit with an unacceptable electoral code. This belief is naive and unwarrantable. The CPDM electoral code was flagrantly violated before our very eyes several times, and the violations justified expediently. Who is quite sure that the results declared reflect the reality in all case? On what ground can we support credulity? Are these not the very people who shot six people before

119

our very eyes and nearly convinced us that they were trampled to death by our own feet? Some of us would prefer to remain sceptical.

For the time being, our political future remains very unpredictable. We look forward to the presidential elections which Bi Mvondo will surely not contest before completing the Batanga deep seaport, Yaounde-Kribi highway and shifting by decree the industrial and economic base of the country to the Centre-South. Meanwhile, the people of South West province, including the SWELANS, can await the year 2000 for a reactivation of their own natural deep sea port of Victoria and the North Westerners the Year 2001 for the construction of the Ring Road which their beloved and magnanimous President personally pledged to see constructed immediately in the unforeseeable future. I spit on their pyrrhic victory!

42

Shall They Make or Mar?
(Published March 13-20, 1992)

As the euphoria over the hasty legislative elections subsides, it is urgent to remind all Cameroonians that the main task facing our generation at this point in our history is that of placing our country on a firm and unshakable socio-political and economic foundation. The task is no mean task; for what is at stake is our collective survival. As I have remarked several times before, our country is, from all indications, a potential paradise, if only we can perform this task well – that is, thoroughly, objectively, disinterestedly and unselfishly, rationally. Before this task, SHALL WE MAKE OR MAR?

The 180 parliamentarians who should be sitting in the Ngoa-Ekele glass house in Yaounde by the time you are reading this, have a special responsibility before history in the execution of this task. Shall they make or mar? The son of GOBATA hereby solemnly calls on these assemblymen, irrespective of the party banner under which they

120

have been elected, to take this task seriously. Let them eschew *"garri politics,"* short-sighted egoism, political horse-trading, unprincipled compromises, and all forms of corruptibility and bribability.

Dear parliamentarians, your predecessors, whom you have just replaced, spent their time in that very house hand-clapping and sleeping, only to wake up and clap again. In exchange they got their Pajeros and stuffed brown envelops from an executive Government that had raised bribery and corruption to the status of a fine art. As a consequence, our constitution got trivially tampered with, indecently fingered and caressed, raped and mutilated, according to the momentary whims and caprices of the executive power. Your first and main task would be to give Cameroonians a credible and acceptable constitution that clearly recognizes the pluralistic nature of our society and that does not wantonly trample on the inalienable rights of any minorities. Such a constitution must also include an acceptable electoral law that makes it easy for Cameroonians to change any government that no longer seems to serve the general interests of all Cameroonians. It is a pity that, owing to the boycott of the elections in many parts of the country, some of you cannot really claim to be representing the majority of your own people. Nevertheless, this fact should not stop such from joining the bandwagon in executing the TASK OF THE DAY. Besides, there are several knowledgeable, upright and serious-minded Cameroonians who will gladly join you, within the context of an enlarged forum, to ensure that this task is executed thoroughly. Now that the CPDM is clearly poised to taking the back benches of the opposition, it will be easier for all of us to agree concerning the importance of just and fair laws and rules of procedure. Are we still scared of the expression "National Conference?"

It is not by accident that our National Assembly building is all in glass. What takes place there and what comes out of there should be solid and transparent. Please, take a good look at yourself everyday on the mirroring walls of the assembly building. The day you catch yourself beginning to resemble your predecessors, from that day, know that you have started failing us. You are REPRESENTATIVES and the interest of those you are representing must always be foremost in your consideration. The day you exchange for this sacred duty, blind support and propaganda for any regime, you have missed your calling and have no more justification to consider yourself a parliamentarian.

On February 23rd, just about a week before the parliamentary elections, I had the privilege of travelling together with a parliamentarian of the old dispensation, representing the Wum "constituency." I don't know what considerations made "the Honourable" to leave his personal Pajero, to be travelling by public transport from Bamenda to Yaounde. But I'll never forget some of the shocking things this fellow said in the course of arguments with some rather loquacious young ladies in the bus that day. According to him, the New Deal regime of Paul Biya had brought unbelievable prosperity to all Cameroonians. He invited his listeners to compare Cameroon with all her neighbours. In his view, the French system on which our Francophone administrative system is based, is more liberal than the English system! That was his justification for the abolition of the West Cameroon system of administration. Asked what he thought about the condition of roads in Menchum Division and the North West province in general, he replied that the New Deal was aware of the need, but that it was not a priority now. For him, the priority for now was the construction of the Batanga deep seaport and Yaounde-Kribi road. Paul Biya, he said, has ruled for only 10 years and still has 15 more years to go to equal Ahidjo's record before handing over power. Embezzlement, he declared, is not a problem, because whoever is there will embezzle. "Even if Fru Ndi becomes the President tomorrow, he will also embezzle," he concluded. Needless to say, that his interlocutors loudly disagreed with him. But he lets all the noise die down before calmly and clearly pontificating: "You people can talk as you like. We are going to win the elections. We have everything: the men, the army, the guns and munitions. Could you talk so freely before? We gave you democracy and if you joke we will withdraw it again."

It is more than likely that a fellow like this is back to the National Assembly to "represent" the people of Wum again. This would be one of the oddities of our present situation. But such possible oddities notwithstanding, the present members of the National

Assembly, collectively have a historic mission to accomplish. They cannot afford to fail in this mission.

43

Two Types of Cameroonians
(Published March 20-27, 1992)

As a diehard optimist, I believe that the struggle for democracy, liberalism, justice and fairness in Cameroon is now irreversible. This struggle which received a momentous impetus with the launching of the Social Democratic Front (SDF) in Bamenda on May 26th, 1990, has left a long list of martyrs in is trail. At this point in the struggle, we hope that the register of martyrs can now be closed. May there be no more martyrs! Amen!!

Our struggle did not begin on May 26th, 1990. That date is significant only because of the boldly defiant and public nature of the event that occurred, sending shock waves down the spine of one of the most repressive regimes in modern Africa, by its sheer daring. The struggle had been on long before 1990, and any future citation in honour of John Fru Ndi would not fail to make honourable mention of Albert Mukong, Yondo Black, Pius Njawe / Celestin Mongo, Charlie Ndi Chia, Bate Bisong, and many more like them. What all these people have in common is COURAGE, the courage to sustain their convictions, the courage of facing the inconveniences of one's convictions. "It was by daring and by doing that the Roman Empire prospered and not by the timid policies which cowards call caution."

Cameroonians as a whole can roughly be divided into two camps: those who would rather die than be slaves and those who would rather be slaves than suffer the slightest inconvenience. The Cameroonians I have mentioned above belong to the first camp which is yet scanty but rapidly growing. The second camp includes all those who find it possible to profess what they don't sincerely believe and those who believe what they dare not profess. In this camp are the fence-sitters, the double-dealers, the equivocators, the panel beaters. All those who boldly claim that they are seeing clearly in the dark, that white is black and vice versa, all those who run with the game and also pursue with the hunters.

The son of GOBATA would like to identify with the first camp, the camp of those who can neither be bullied nor lapiroed out of the straight and lonely path of their well-considered and firm convictions. *NO TRIFLING MATTER* has been the modest contribution of yours truly to the struggle for a more democratic, more liberal, just and stable Cameroon. Every Cameroonian convinced of the necessity for this struggle must contribute to it from his/her own resources using whatever tools are at his/her disposal. For yours truly, the main tool has been the bic biro and, since 1990, when *NO TRIFLING MATTER* started appearing on page 4 of *CAMEROON POST*, a lot of ink has flowed. Whether, as they say, the pen be mightier than the sword or not, there is no doubt that the task of waking Cameroonians from decades of dogmatic slumber and sensitizing and conscientizing them has been largely achieved. The struggle certainly continues, but I bet that no other regime will ever again take Cameroonians for a ride.

The Biya regime will be remembered in our history for its attempt to destroy this beautiful triangle called Cameroon; an attempt that cannot as yet be categorically said to have failed. The regime firmly installed kleptocracy as a system of government, backed by empty rhetoric and sterile and noisy sloganeering. It inscribed tribalism with indelible ink on the national agenda. The son of Mvondo is first and foremost a tribal chieftain and I recall again Mongo Beti's remark to the effect that left to his own endowments he would have reached the zenith of his career as the *Sous-Préfet* of his *arrondissement*. But the inscrutable vicissitudes of our political history catapulted him (with disastrous consequences alas!) to Unity Palace.

There are those who do not accept this analysis and who continue chanting that the Biya regime brought democracy and unparalleled prosperity to Cameroon. Only yesterday, Minister *"Zero Mort"* was insisting over the mass media that Cameroon performed a miracle by conducting the March 1st legislative elections. According to him, congratulatory messages have been pouring into Cameroon from foreign nations because, for the first time in human history, a peaceful and smooth transition had been effected from monolithism to democratic pluralism. This theory is diametrically antithetical to ours and we can all await the verdict of history.

In the meantime, we hope that no Cameroonian will again be gunned down so that the regime might survive. We hope that people can express their views and feelings without being tear-gassed, hand-grenaded, arrested, brutalized, locked up and starved. We hope that all these are things of the past. We hope that the mediocres who run our lives and those who (mis)manage important public institutions would be replaced immediately by more credible Cameroonians.

It is an incredible act of self-deception for the CPDM to think that it won the greatest number of seats in the March 1st elections. Let them just ask those who went campaigning for the CPDM in, say, the North-West province to honestly tell about the rejection of the regime publicly demonstrated everywhere they went. Only people like Mr John Niba Ngu who are perfectly capable of both believing and asserting a manifest contradiction can continue insisting on the "massive support" enjoyed by the CPDM in the North-West province. The Honourable Minister is being tipped as the next P.M. and, if his party is in control, he certainly deserves the post for his incredible efforts on behalf of the regime. His popularity is certainly on the rise, if one can take public attention as an accurate index of popularity. In a taxi a few days ago, someone said of the minister that even when he is quiet, his mouth always looks as if he is about to say something. Another enjoined that, for him, the minister's mouth always gives the impression of someone who has just finished eating fresh fish pepper soup. And yet another opined that, if there were a national prize to encourage Anglophones to speak French, the minister would win it every year. So everyone seems to have noticed something or other about the honourable minister. Is that not popularity? Let them make the man Prime Minister, boh! He can't be worse than Hayatou.

44

The Missing Links in Nfor Gwei's Programmes
(Published April 2-9, 1992)

One of the guests on the *"Cameroon Calling"* (CC) programme of Sunday 29th March 1992, was Honourable Solomon Nfor Gwei, the Chairman of the Government-created Human Rights Commission. This is the second time I've heard the erstwhile Minister over CC in his capacity as Chairman of the Human Rights Commission. Both times, he has really been at pains to convince sceptics and to prove the credibility of his commission. Listening to him this time around, one really has the impression that he might soon succeed, if a few missing links in his programme are put into place.

Scepticism against the commission was very well founded. How could any reasonable person be expected to take seriously the purported creation by a regime that is demonstrably one of greatest human rights violators in the modern world and that had only recently proscribed all associations concerned with Human Rights? How many other countries are there where people peacefully demonstrating for whatever reason are sprayed with tear gas and hand grenades from military helicopters? How many other countries are there where the peace of peasant villagers is disturbed in the wee hours of the morning by heavily armed soldiers who indiscriminately beat up and brutalize all and sundry, forcing them to roll in mud, drink dirty water, eat soil and stare continuously at the sun? Which other country is there where University students have their heads shaved with broken bottles for marching or throwing stones?

Against this background, one could not but consider the creation of the Human Rights Commission as a subterfuge, a smoke-screen to conceal Human Rights abuses. The sort of complete about-turn required in the contrary supposition does not seem possible in human nature, without sufficient antecedent causal factors. It is, however, quite possible that the master-trick, the subterfuge could back-fire and end up in the real thing, which was far from intended. In fact, this is what is happening to our democratization process.

After seriously resisting the on-set of the process, the regime suddenly came to the decision that, to effectively contain it, the best thing was to grant it in theory, take control of the process so as to carefully guide it away from its natural goal, while creating a different impression at the level of appearances. The regime reasoned as follows: "Let us allow them say whatever they like. That would give everyone the impression of how democratic and liberal we are. But what can mere words, whether spoken or written, do to us? We have the power and everything with it. What miracle will ever make us to lose it?" This reasoning did not bargain with the powers of a well-informed, sensitized and conscientized population. This is what has happened and our democratic process now looks quite irreversible. It has been a costly joke for the regime. Much like the story of the woman who, to stop her child who was crying at night, thrust the child through the open window and called: "Satan o! take your child." Whereupon an unseen mysterious hand seized the child and disappeared into the dark night and the child was never seen again.

It is quite possible that a similar thing might happen to the Human Rights Commission. Scepticism about the Chairman of the commission himself was grounded on the fact that he is one of the Anglophones who, in the last three decades, has been kissing the ground at the feet of our two successive dictatorships. But here again, radical change, a complete *METANOIA*, such as that experienced by Saul of Tarsus on the way to Damascus in the biblical story, are not impossible. And this is where the Chairman's earlier emphasis that he is first and foremost a Christian minister might just be relevant. Thus far, we can certainly give him the benefit of our doubts. By the tangible fruits of his work, we shall be left in no doubt.

Nevertheless, there are certain missing links in Reverend Nfor Gwei's programme as thus far unfolded. Had he answered Julius Wamey's question during the programme under consideration, he would have supplied these missing links. But he only rambled through the question. In other words, having discovered all the Human Rights abuses which he so well described, in Bamenda and Balikumbat, what next?

The Legion Commander of the Gendarmerie in Bamenda, who did everything to obstruct the investigations of the Commission and

127

the Minister of Armed Forces who used delaying tactics, what has been done to them? Are they not still holding their respective posts? What of those who directly committed the violations and brutalities? Has anything been done by form of sanction to any of them? What of the victims of these brutalities and violations? Has any of them received any compensation? What about the Government whose functionaries perpetrated such heinous crimes against human beings and went unpunished? Elsewhere, such a Government would be forced to resign, if such crimes are proved. Any possibility of that happening here?

If Rev. Nfor Gwei's Commission does not have satisfactory answers to such questions, it may turn out, in spite of our present optimism, to be one more enterprise that sells illusions to Cameroonians. The Commission should not wait for other Human Rights associations to come to it; it should seek them out and invite them. If the next investigations of the Commission are carried out with the assistance of, say, *"Cap Liberté,"* our lingering vestiges of scepticism might be completely banished.

45

The Anglophone Problem
(Published April 9-16, 1992)

If you have read the memorandum of Dr. Simon Munzu et al, submitted to the Technical Committee for the Drafting of the Constitution, concerning the "Anglophone Problem" (See *CAMEROON POST* of March 27-April 3, 1992, then you would not ask if there is an Anglophone problem or what that problem is. The memorandum of Dr Munzu and his other two colleagues, Dr. Carlson Anyangwe and Mr Sam Ekontang Elad, is so far the simplest, clearest, most direct and most powerful statement of the Anglophone problem or, to be more exact, the West Cameroon problem. The memorandum highlights the most significant historical, political and legal elements and considerations that circumscribe the problem and clearly points to the required solution thereto. The circumstances surrounding the writing of the memorandum - the fraudulent and dictatorial behaviour of the Chairman imposed on the committee, the threats, intimidation and cajoleries, as well as the betrayal of the 4th Anglophone member of the committee, are in themselves a miniature version of the macroscopic problem. The memorandum is a historic document and should be read by all West Cameroonians including those who betrayed and sold their own children into slavery and those who today are still ready to do same for thirty pieces of blood money in whatever form. We can draw a lot of instruction from the scenario.

Many things which we were seeing before, as if through a film darkly, are beginning to stand out in bold, clear relief. During Dr. Biya's meaningless provincial tours last year, he arrived West Cameroon with a basket full of promises. In this column. I tried to warn that the fellow was only signing dud cheques. When I took SWELA to task for apparently falling victim to these clearly illusory promises, I was nearly mistaken for a detractor of SWELA. I even revealed as far back as then that, while West Cameroonians were being promised, with tongue in cheek, the rehabilitation of the deep seaport in Victoria and construction of the Bamenda Ring Road, work was already advanced on the Batanga-Kribi deep seaport as well as an express road project from Yaounde, meandering through the entire Beti countryside, to Kribi – projects neither promised nor announced. Was I wrong?

In a later write-up, I again speculated that the main assignment the Biya regime seemed to have set itself was that of transferring the economic and industrial base of the country to the Centre-south. With the recent designation of the Nsimalen/Yaounde International Airport as the main gateway into the country, is anybody still doubting? The Biya junta is hypersensitive to the "Anglophone problem" because it is the exploitation of West Cameroon that has rendered possible the building of an eventual Fang Empire, which Owona has been brandishing like a *waachuchuu* against Anglophone demands for a return to Federalism, justice and legality. The demand for a return to Federalism is not, I repeat not, repeat not, a call for secession. If it were, many of us in the forefront of the struggle would not even support it. The idea of a Fang nation is clearly secessionist as well as treasonable. But that is not our problem. We are not Fangs. Let them put their own case if they have one.

I have never stopped emphasizing in this column that I consider the so-called North West/South West problem, a problem at the level of false consciousness. Ditto, for the problem of tribalism. I believe that I have demonstrated my position in this column sufficiently convincingly. It is now also clear that this problem has been mainly created and fuelled by the Biya regime to achieve its own unavowed aims. Suppose two orphans disagree over the sharing of their patrimony, including their father's powers and authority. Can they accept to submit themselves as slaves to a stranger because of their domestic quarrel?

Why did Honourable Benjamin Itoe refuse to append his signature to the memorandum of the Anglophone members of the Owona Technical Committee? The answer may not exactly be blowing in the wind. Note that both Itoe and Munzu are from the same constituency. Their "MY PEOPLE" is exactly the same people with the same problems, worries, aspirations and destiny. Note further that both Itoe and Munzu are members of the CPDM party.

So, why would one act like a cowardly traitor of his people while the other is championing their cause against all odds? Some would say that it is because one is a Minister and could not publicly demonstrate his support for a cause he knows his paymasters to be bitterly against. It is even suggested that he supports the memorandum "privately." This is nonsense. First of all, there is no private aspect to this problem at all. Secondly, is Dr. Munzu not a member of the Central Committee of the CPDM, the next step to being appointed a minister? Should he not have been more anxious to taste ministerhood than someone who has been minister for two decades and is afraid to lose that blessed state? The robust truth is that spinelessness and treachery can find no adequate alibis.

Many of older generation of West Cameroonians have shamelessly sold their own children into slavery in exchange for their personal material comfort and positions. It is in this light that Mr Achidi Achu's declaration to the effect that Federalism would bring nothing to the average Cameroonian must be taken. What has Unitarism brought to the average Cameroonian? On the contrary, it has brought indescribable material well-being to a select few of un-average Cameroonians, who are ready to equivocate on issues concerning the future and well-being, nay, the very survival of their own children, in exchange for even merely being considered for the Prime Ministerial position in Biya's regime. To all these un-average West Cameroonians, the message should be clear. Their children have totally rejected the slavery into which they have been sold and will not be kept in that condition except through sheer physical force.

46

A Ceremonial P.M. As We Totter Along
(Published April 16-23, 1992)

The recent appointment of Mr Simon Achidi Achu as Prime Minister (and Head of Government?) has not come as a surprise to anyone who has been carefully observing our political landscape. From the moment he made his now famous declaration that "Federalism would bring nothing to the average Cameroonian," it was quite clear that Mr Achidi Achu was under serious consideration for the post of P.M. and had either been directly consulted or somehow indirectly got wind of the fortune that was about to befall him. Rising Anglophone awareness, power and assertiveness is the greatest nightmare of the Biya regime. It therefore goes without saying that anyone being considered for an important position in that regime had at the very least to equivocate on a demand that the powerfully rising Cameroon Anglophone Movement (CAM) has described as "not negotiable."

Someone has aptly compared the new P.M. to a weak and timid student who is appointed prefect in a class full of rapacious and predatory bullies. For those used to the West Cameroon educational system, this simile needs no unpacking. Some people have been celebrating the appointment of the "first Anglophone Prime Minister." But in this situation, can you imagine Achidi Achu as Prime Minister disagreeing with, let alone calling to order or, most unlikely of all, sanctioning the likes of Joseph Owona, Andze Tsoungui, Augustin Kontchou Koumegni etc? The palpable truth is that these people remain the real power brokers of the regime. Why has the post of Secretary General at the Presidency been reintroduced? Evidently, Owona is the *de facto* Prime Minister of the present Government.

All this is in line with the phobias and concerns of the French, the real Masters of our political situation. I listened to Mr Achidi Achu's interview on *Cameroon Calling* (CC) of Palm Sunday, 12th April, 1992, and it is very significant that he describes himself as being "very lucky" to have been appointed, and he refers to Biya as the "Boss." Anything resembling a policy statement that he ventured to make had to be quotations and paraphrases of the Head of State. Insisting that he feels he has a leeway and freehand and is not in any way hemmed-in is simply part of the appropriate rhetoric in the game. How can the appointment of a Prime Minister, who is supposed to form a Government, be announced simultaneously with that of the Government he is supposed to form? In spite of our "advanced democracy" on paper and the airwaves, we all know that ours is still a dictatorship and no one is in doubt concerning the *locus* of real power. We have a ceremonial Prime Minister, a "king of the Jews," going to battle on the back of a donkey.

I don't know Mr Achidi Achu personally and it is possible that, within the circumstances and reality of the moment, he might spring a few pleasant surprises on all of us. He has our benefit of the doubt while we wait for time to tell.

I remember how some years ago, at the beginning of the life of the last monolithic parliament, it was strongly rumoured that Achidi Achu would be appointed President of the National Assembly. People were extremely excited over the impending appointment, because he was then being considered a radical of sorts. But the Biya regime, in its own political chess-board manipulations, surprised everybody by appointing a little-known dotard, sexagenarian, Lawrence Fonka Shang, as President of National Assembly. Fonka Shang, in spite of his obscure origins, might have immortalized himself in the annals of our political history had he shown firmness and independence of mind. There were at least two occasions when he should have resigned. But he chose to be a yes-man, re-echoing, zombie-like, sometimes quite unconvincingly, the voice and wishes of his real masters. That is why he could naively believe the false assurances that he would be reappointed. Credible rumours have it that, the day the new President of the National Assembly was announced, Fonka Shang's Presidential car was unceremoniously taken from him outside the Assembly Building, and he had to make it *cum pedibus* to the Presidential Residence to pack his stuff and vamoused by 03.00 a. m., thanks to public transport. Now, we hear he will not be drawing the benefits of an ex-President of the National

Assembly the way Pa Muna is doing, because he is still a parliamentarian. That is not fair, but it is the direct consequence of his own spinelessness.

Over the years, the dictatorship has reserved the harmless position of "President of the National Assembly" for Anglophones. But now that the advent of multipartyism, if not democracy, is likely to transform that post into a position of real power, the Biya regime, in its Machiavellian political wisdom, has moved fast to take over that position. By reinstating the post of Secretary General at the Presidency, the post of Prime Minister has been effectively castrated and rendered impotent. Now an Anglophone can safely be moved there. This creates the illusion that Anglophones are at last about to start sharing power at the centre. The regime and its French mentors certainly have mastered their game. But we are not deceived. We are anxiously awaiting the Municipal and Presidential elections, and we predict that the regime will develop cold feet and find excuses for postponing them. Whatever the case, the struggle intensifies and continues on all fronts.

47

This Celebration Mania
(Published April 23-30, 1992)

A contemporary Ghanaian philosopher once remarked that there are three deadly diseases that can afflict any society, namely, anachronism, authoritarianism and superstition. Today, Cameroon society is suffering from all three ailments and one of the best ways to realise this is to reflect on our mania for celebrations of all types. This mania is not, of course, unique to Cameroon. It is an African disease. Quite recently, the father of some fairly well-to-do Nigerian, died at the ripe old age of 97. The fellow wept uncontrollably, dashing himself several times unto the ground in his apparent distress. When some sympathiser tried to restrain him by encouraging him to bear his loss like a man and tried to reason with him that death at such a ripe old age calls more for celebration than anything else, the man retorted through his tears: "Exactly! It's not for him I'm crying. But where will I get the money to bury him!?"

In both Nigeria and Ghana today, if a close relation of a man dies, then, unless he happens to be very rich, he is surely in for very hard financial times. He would have to borrow very respectable sums of money and also spend several days to organize the burial ceremony. And after the burial, there are other ceremonies such as the "Memorial" and the "Second Burial" to look forward to. This state of affairs has led to a situation in these countries where a dead person is sometimes left in the mortuary freezer for nearly a whole year, while the family "prepares' for burial. Nor is this scenario limited to death and burial. A very similar thing happens in the case of weddings, births, promotions, appointments etc. These events have become the occasions for unbelievable squandermania. If this were limited to the rich it might be okay, but the truth is that the social pressures on everyone to do likewise are almost un-defy-able.

Cameroon is a late starter on this irrational and ruinous path; but, from all indications, it will soon overtake both Ghana and Nigeria. For quite some time now, this trend had caught my critical attention and I have all along had it in mind to comment on it, as you would realize if you check "NO TRIFLING MATER" of Wednesday, March 6-13, 1991. So this present piece is partly the fulfilment of a promise. You can bear me out that I always fulfil my promises unlike some people, like Bi Mvondo, whose empty basket, full of promises, has become an object of irritation and embarrassment to all of us.

The recent ministerial appointments are what have forced me to pick this issue of our celebration mania from the shelves of my memory. It has been simply scandalous to watch the intensity and feverish excitement that has accompanied these celebrations. For about five days, following these appointments, it has been continuous dancing, eating and drinking in the houses of those appointed or reappointed ministers. And the crowds! For people like yours truly who consider the Biya regime as a surely sinking ship, it is very hard to understand this particular aspect of the behaviour of Cameroonians. Why would anyone be so excited about being

135

appointed a cook or steward on board a ship which is sinking and whose captain is mad?

I actually visited one of those people recently appointed, and what I witnessed was very instructive. First of all, the lady of the house, who looked like someone who had just survived a very severe attack of malaria, confessed that they had not had any sleep for four consecutive days, following the appointments. There had been a continuous stream of congratulators and "well-wishers" for all the twenty-four hours of each of the four days. Many of these came from as far as the provinces and some of these had been thoughtful enough to bring along goats or fowls. But such thoughtful good gestures were neutralized by the fact that accommodation had to be provided for them, let alone feeding. "The Madame" confessed that even though they had done their best to prepare for the event, they had now practically run out of food and drinks. But how could they stop the people from coming? Talk of innocent victims of social expectations and pressures! Someone kindly suggested that, if they went to the Fonka Shangs, they might be able to buy cheaply supplies which the latter had stocked in preparation for celebrating his anticipated reappointment which never was. But another chipped in that the Fonka Shangs had already vamoosed to their village.

Now I recall that when Fonka Shang was appointed President of the National Assembly, the appointment took him completely by surprise. It is Achidi Achu at the time who was said to have stocked supplies and even brought dance troupes from the province in anticipation of being appointed.

The mystic of appointments will remain with us for quite some time and we are looking forward to the regime that will demystify the whole thing. But this may never be done successfully unless we also find a way of curing our mania for celebrations in general. One very significant fact is that nearly everybody considers these appointments as signs of divine intervention. And this is where the superstitious element comes in. I listened to some of the impromptu toasts and all of them thanked God and begged him again to prolong the longevity of the appointment. Does Mr Biya know that thanks which are rightly due to him are being misdirected to God? And why pray a prayer which you know or should know God would not answer?

We must all join hands together and find a way of combating our mania for celebrations. It does not augur well for the future well-being of our society. Individual deviations from the norm would be a good starting point. The son of GOBATA, for instance, has a wife but is apparently not married if you go by the complaints of those who know him. A manifest contradiction? Not if you consider that what they mean by "being married" is making an elaborate and lavish public ceremony. On those terms, Gobata's son will remain unmarried, in spite of his wife.

48

We Will Dedicate a Toilet to His Memory
(Published April 30-May 6, 1992)

As our 'doctor' (*honoris causa*) is dancing his last tango, historians and chroniclers would, no doubt, already be pondering how generally to assess and what summary title to give to his decade of (mis)rule. To faithful readers of this column, it would be no secret that the Son of Gobata considers the ten-year reign of Mvondo's son as the greatest catastrophic calamity or, if you prefer, calamitous catastrophe, that has ever befallen this country. But, even out of misfortune, human beings can learn useful lessons. It is extremely important that the lessons of history should not be lost on future generations. Where people do not learn from history, history tends to repeat itself.

Now, one of the easiest and best ways to record and preserve the lessons of history is through dedicatory monuments. It has often been remarked, and rightly with regret, that Cameroon is a country without past heroes or role models who can serve as inspiration for future generations. Not because these heroes and role models have been non-existent in our country but because we have so far collectively refused to immortalise them by means of dedicatory monuments. If Cameroon were not Cameroon, the so-called University of Yaounde, Yaounde, Cameroon, would since have

137

become THE BERNARD FONLON UNIVERSITY, Yaounde, Cameroon. But we have so far collectively resisted even the dedication of that institution's library to that remarkable Cameroonian.

The lessons that we can learn from history are both positive and negative and both should be captured and encapsulated in our dedicatory monuments. That is why when Alhaji Ahmadou Ahidjo died in exile, in Senegal, some of us were of the strong opinion that he should be brought back immediately and buried in Cameroon. But the Biya regime was so cowardly and/or so mean that it refused to publicly even admit the fact that the man had died. Today, Ahidjo has been 'rehabilitated' along with other historic figures, and this is a very good thing. Today, we again have the 'Ahmadou Ahidjo Stadium' and if we could have an 'Ahmadou Ahidjo Brewery' somewhere, that would complete the historical lessons that we need to retain concerning his life and times. Sport and beer-drinking are the two potent drugs with which Ahidjo stupefied Cameroonians and reigned over them for two decades as an absolute dictator.

So, in strongly arguing for appropriate monuments to be dedicated to our historical memory of Ahidjo, I am by no means saying that I consider him a hero. This is an issue on which opinions will surely differ. From hindsight, he certainly has some good points to his credit. But on the opposite side of the balance, must be considered the fact that he was an intolerable dictator who, having the exclusive and inalienable dictatorial right of choosing his own successor in absolute dictatorship from among 12 million Cameroonians, saddled us with someone like Paul Biya. If I were asked to propose an epitaph for Ahidjo's grave, I would propose the following: "HERE LIES HIS EX-EXCELLENCY, ALHAJI AHIDJO, A MORTAL, WHOM, FOR TWO DECADES, WE MISTOOK FOR GOD ALMIGHTY."

Mr Ahidjo's successor in dictatorship has never seemed to bother himself about having places and monuments named after him. During Ahidjo's heydays, we ran the risk of having every street named after him. But I don't know of any "Paul Biya something" anywhere. Presumably this is as a result of humility and I consider it a point to his credit, although, when I expressed this opinion some time ago, someone retorted that, if he too had a hospital, a brewery and a 10-figure bank account in *obodo-oyinbo,* he would have no need for dirty streets to be named after him back here in the jungle. In any case, we need a nail on the wall of our historical memory on which to hang the lessons of our historical experience of the Biya phenomenon. We need dedicatory monuments that would capture and encapsulate the lessons that we ought to carry with us from the Biya decade to future time.

I have a humble suggestion to make in this regard. This suggestion would surely no come as a surprise to faithful readers of *NO TRIFLING MATTER,* especially those who can still recall "The Past Tense Of Shit" (*CAMEROON POST,* April 25-May 2, 1991). I suggest that the public toilets at Ntarikon Park or some other such historic spot be named "THE BIYA (ANTICIPATED) MEMORIAL LATRINES." But I don't know if there are really any toilets in the park. If there is none, I would strongly suggest that they should be constructed with immediate effect and automatic alacrity. But while waiting for the construction, "the pissing corner" in the park should be dedicated (*en attendant, non?*) and conferred with the appropriate title: the Biya (Anticipated) Memorial Pissing Corner! The opinion of readers of *NO TRIFLING MATTER* to the above suggestion is highly solicited.

49

Misconceptions of Federalism
(Published may 6-13, 1992)

"Federalism" has become the battle cry of the Cameroon Anglophone Movement (CAM) and is only a little short of becoming a sacred hymn for all Anglophones. The demand for a return to the Federal system, that is, to the *status quo ante* 1972, is a simple, straightforward and reasonable demand. The arguments in favour of the demand are logically impeccable and overwhelmingly compelling. Unfortunately, however, a lot of confused thinking and woolly reasoning has been exhibited concerning the concept of "Federalism" both by opponents and supporters of the return to Federalism call. These misconceptions are very pernicious and, if care is not taken, they might subvert and vitiate what clearly is an excellent and powerful case. This again shows that conceptual clarity is extremely important in practical matters of import.

The "assimilationists" (those East Cameroonians who secretly planned and those who have covertly and surreptitiously been systematically executing the plan to assimilate West Cameroon) cannot be expected to carry banners in support of the call for a return to Federalism. Furthermore, there is something which we might call the "French Mentality" (for want of a better term) which seems to make it extremely difficult for any *bona fide* Francophone to really grasp the logic in a demand such as that for a return to the Federal structure. My guess is that this curious fact is to be explained by reference to the French-imposed Francophone educational and administrative system with its well-known attributes of authoritarianism, dogmatism, centricism and intolerance.

In February this year, I noted in my diary that Mr Jean-Jacques Ekindi was the very first Francophone political leader of note ever to have spoken in favour of the Anglophone demand for a return to Federalism. But today, I am reading in *CAMEROON POST* (April 23-30, 1992) that Mr Ekindi declared in Bamenda that he is strongly against Federalism because it would be more costly than a unitary system. That leaves Mr Samuel Eboua as the only Francophone political leader of note to have expressed sympathy with the Anglophone cause. And, would you be surprised if he too changes his mind tomorrow? We've witnessed this scenario in other contexts many times before - recall Dicka Akwa, Woungly Massaga, Bouba Bello, Frederick Kodock, Dakole Daissala, etc. Now, why are Francophones so flexible (not to say unreliable) in these matters? The answer is blowing in the wind.

If in the face of the demand for a return to Federalism, a return to legality and justice, some Francophones react like people who, having cornered a big game, don't want to take any chances lest it escapes to safety, that is understandable though unacceptable. It is such people who would create and try to sustain the spectre of secession. But any West Cameroonian who equivocates over the Federalism issue or who claims not to be in support of the call is either dishonest or is otherwise confusing it with several other issues. The very powerful case for a return to a Federal set-up is extremely simple, clear, and straight-forward. Those who are still confused about what is involved are once more encouraged to read carefully the Memorandum of Dr. Simon Munzu, Dr. Carlson Anyangwe and Mr Sam Ekontang Elad (*CAMEROON POST* March 27-April 3, 1992).

If this potentially great nation is to be put on a firm and unshakable foundation, it is time now carefully to uncover and redress certain important frauds. Those relating to a surreptitious annexation and assimilation of West Cameroon instead of unifying with her were started by Ahidjo (of blessed memory) and continued by Dr. Biya who is still hanging unto the reigns of the dictatorial power handed over to him.

A return to the 1961 Foumban accord would not only be a return to justice and legality but a return to a distinct cultural, educational and administrative legacy that is in many respects far superior to the Francophone legacy but that is in danger of completely dying out. Anyone who has properly experienced both systems can testify that the West Cameroon educational system, administrative system, judicial system, audit and accountability system, policing, work ethics and what have you, are by far superior

141

to their Francophone equivalents. This legacy, like the English language itself, is part of an emerging global legacy and world culture. Thus, if East Cameroonians, owing to their historical background, are still reluctant to adopt these, it stands to reason that if they are preserved in West Cameroon, East Cameroonians might, in the fullness of their own time, be very grateful to benefit from them. In this sense, the liberation of West Cameroon would signal the liberation of all Cameroonians.

Federalism is compatible with decentralisation in general but the two must not be confused. Decentralisation should concern all Cameroonians. It clearly appears to be a more rational and more satisfactory way of running a plural and highly complex country like ours. We can all join in the debate for decentralisation, but we should not confuse it with Federalism. The Federalism issue strictly concerns only West Cameroonians who, as a self-determining people with a common historical experience, opted freely to join East Cameroon, under certain specified conditions. In other works, a return to Federalism will not hinder decentralisation in any way. If the return were effected today, we would have two federated states as before, the State of West Cameroon and the State of East Cameroon, the former composed of two provinces and the latter of eight provinces. Of course, more provinces could be created in either or both of the two federated states. Each province would enjoy a certain amount of administrative autonomy and self-determination as well as preserving a homogeneous linguistic and cultural heritage. Definite areas would be centralised. But apart from these, the movement towards a totally homogeneous national culture would be left to evolve with time.

In such a set-up, there is no question of some West Cameroonians having to abandon properties in East Cameroon or vice versa. We will all remain Cameroonians, with the theoretical right to settle and own property anywhere within the national territory, as has always been the case. No one will lose his job. Rather more job opportunities will be created everywhere. North Westerners will not oppress South Westerners nor vice versa any more than they are doing now. So, what is the reason for this cacophony of voices over this Federalism issue?

50

CAMBANK Is Still Owing Me
(Published Pay 27, 1992)

How was Cambank ruined? The answer to this question may not be blowing in the wind, but one day we shall surely know. In fact, I do have fairly definite guesses. Don't we all now know how SCB was ruined? The virus may be traced to a single common origin because he who pays Paul to rob Peter would equally rob Peter to pay Paul. Howbeit, I am particularly concerned about the ruination of Cambank, not only because it was a credible bank under a fairly credible management, but because its ruination has affected me very directly. And I'm sure that here, I am speaking for thousands of other customers like me.

At the time the ill-advised liquidation of CAMBANK was announced, I had 100.000 francs in my Saving Account. I hadn't touched this money since 1985 and I intended to "tie-heart" and leave it there until 1990 as a type of security, since it should yield appreciable interest. At a normal interest rate of 05 %, my capital should have been yielding me an average interest of 60.000 frs. *per annum*. That means that by 1990 my savings should already have earned me 360.000 francs as interest. In other words, if I had decided to close my Savings Account in 1990 as planned, I should have collected 460.000 francs. Saving is a form of investment. It requires time and perseverance, but, all over the world, (Cameroon excepted?) it is supposed to be the safest and most secure form of investment. With an initial capital of 100.000 francs in 1985, any astute businessman or investor would surely be counting millions today. But I didn't feel like an astute entrepreneur; hence, my decision to invest hard-earned money more "safely." It may not be irrelevant to mention here that I earned the money in question through sweat and tears, literally carrying concrete. I have never won State lottery in my life.

So, imagine my fury when, on 17th May 1991, I received the following insult to add to my injury, from the so-called liquidator of

Cambank. He sent me the following letter: "We acknowledge receipt of your declaration dated 02.06.90 for 10.000 FCFA. Along with the following documents: *Livret d'épargne*. We reject your declaration entirely. Reason: *Debiteur de 200.000 FCFA*." My wowo French did not at first permit me to understand the last sentence, which was written only in French without the usual English translation is small characters below. But I soon confirmed beyond all reasonable doubt that "*Monsieur le Liquidateur*" of Cambank was telling me in black and white that I was owing the defunct *Cameroon Bank* 200.000 francs. "*L'impossible n'est pas Camerounais'!* I shouted.

Well, after due reflection, I came to the conclusion that politeness is an altruistic moral virtue. So, suppressing my justified furry, I sent back the following reply: "Dear Sir, Thanks for your letter of 17th May, 1991, regarding my Savings Account with Cameroon Bank which stood at 100.000 FCFA as at the time the bank was closed down. You are certainly mistaken to state that I am indebted to the Bank to the tune of 200.000 FCFA. I have never, repeat never, in my life taken a loan or asked for credit facilities from Cameroon Bank nor from any other bank for that matter. Please rectify your error and kindly pay me, without any further delay, my legitimate dues, non-payment of which has already caused me untold hardship. Yours Sincerely, Rotcod Gobata."

It has taken exactly twelve months since I submitted the above polite protest before "*Monsieur le liquidateur*" finally answered me last week. During that that period, I've been there to follow up my "*dossier*" no less than 48 times! My experiences during those visits must be reserved for another occasion. The present letter (now written completely in English) reads: "Sir, we have received your letter by which you transmitted to us the justifying documents of your claim on Cambank. After verification we wish to inform you that we have taken the following final decision as regards your claim: Full acceptance for: 100.000 FCFA. Thank you."

So, after 7 years in a blocked Savings Account, Cambank is proposing to pay back my 100.000 francs with a "Thank you"? Walahi! The interest on my money should now be standing at 420.000 francs since 1985. Thus, Cambank owes me 520.000 francs. They are now proposing to pay me 100.000 francs. Where is the rest of the 420.000 francs? Gone just like that to construct someone's dream palace, not so? While I don't have even a thatched roof over a wall anywhere in my name and can scarcely feed my wife and kids.

I have been planning to go to the Human Rights Commission but some students of Uniyao have just informed me that, if I go there, the big man of the Commission will dash me 1000 francs and beg me to please keep quiet. Cameroon is a country where blatant injustice and oppression walk around in broad daylight, because the crime busters are themselves the criminals. I intend to fight for my legitimate rights and I am inviting all those in a similar situation to let's join hands together. If I don't get all my dues from Cambank, then one of these days, when I run out of patience, and go down there and ask to be shown the creature called "*Monsieur le Liquidateur*," then he will learn that the other side of the impotence of power is the power of impotence. Haba! Enough is enough!

51

Albert Mukong, Federalism and the SDF
(Published June 1-8, 1992)

The pace and tempo of evens in this country, at present, are simply too fast for all of us. The return of Albert Mukong, after two years of voluntary self-exile on our behalf, should have attracted a critical notice from a columnist of my timber and calibre. Mukong is a patriot whose sincerity and commitment have gone through the acid test and baptism of fire. He is a patriot whose patriotism is beyond all reasonable doubt.

His sincerity notwithstanding, however, he has sometimes made errors in practical matters. Sincerity is not criterion of rightness. The late Bernard Fonlon is reported to have once described Mukong as a "prisoner without Discretion" clearly re-echoing the latter's *Prisoner Without A Crime*. Some of Mukong's numerous arrests and detentions could have been avoided had he learned to use more supple and subtle methods. A person fighting with monsters must learn not only

145

the art of standing upright and running but also the arts of gliding, docking, crouching, crawling and even lying down flat on the ground. The adoption of these various strategies at appropriate times can in no way be considered as abandoning the fight, even though it would finally be won standing bolt upright. I have followed the differences between Mukong and the other Founding Fathers of the SDF from the very beginning and it seems to me that this is where the "Prisoner Without A Crime" goes wrong even within his rightness.

I have already treated "Federalism" in this column (see *CAMEROON POST* May 6-13, 1992). I will not go back to what I said in that piece but I recommend it for your re-reading. It is really amazing to realize the type of conceptual confusions that are accompanying the very simple and straight-forward case for a return to Federalism. Invariably, the call is being mistaken by both supporters and opponents as a call to secession. Mr Mukong's interview published in *Cameroon Today* of May 19, 1992, shows that he himself lacks conceptual clarity on this issue or, at any rate, that he identifies it with secession. That is why he says that he disagrees with Gorji Dinka's idea of "Ambazonia" only because of the "procedure." According to him, "we will need to create and train an army and go into the *'maquis'* in order to assert our independence." He further declares: "I am today against the ten-state Federation option, for these provinces or states cannot be autonomous – and I mean real autonomy with every state controlling its finances and internal security."

I can confidently assert that what the majority of Cameroonians want at this point in time is not secession but a return to the pre-1972 Federal system implying relative or partial rather than absolute autonomy. What would be the point calling ourselves a single nation if each of the states composing the nation is absolutely autonomous? There must be a central authority with certain matters under its jurisdiction among which, for example, would be allocation of revenue to the states, worked out and agreed upon by all using such parameters as land mass, population, resources, contribution to common revenue, etc. Each state can then run its own allocated budget autonomously to its good or ill.

The most muddle-headed contribution on this Federalism issue that I've read in print is an article in *Cameroon Life* of April – May, 1992, entitled "The Argument Against a Federation" by George Atabong. The author's main argument against Federalism is that "In a Federation, if you happen to be a Southwesterner, notwithstanding your background, you will have guaranteed economic life. This is because the Southwest would come out as the richest of the newly created Federated States. Other provinces which are without natural resources would be relegated to the status of banana republics." Apart from the unclear nature of what this author understands by Federalism, it is hard to see why he thinks that the economic life of any Southwesterner would be automatically guaranteed, irrespective of his background (whatever that means) if the Southwest became a state, even an absolutely autonomous state. This would be a dangerously delusive dream in any situation. Funnily enough, the author under consideration styles his piece "an epistemological argument." Its epistemological limitations are indeed glaring although it need not "annoy" or "hurt" any reader, which fear the author repeatedly expresses.

Federalism is not incompatible with integration (not assimilation, however) as Mukong thinks. A return to Federalism now doesn't mean that we cannot gradually and more honestly evolve from there towards a more integrated system. The issue of a return to Federalism, correctly understood, is one on which all Anglophones, whatever their party affiliations, can be unanimous. The Cameroon Anglophone Movement (CAM) does well to champion and spearhead the demand, because it is a non-partisan organization. People like yours truly, who in principle would not identify with any party, can be openly committed members of CAM. In fact, I see ALBERT Mukong as belonging more to CAM than to any political party. He shouldn't insist that he is a member of the SDF, if he disagrees with the party's principles and manifesto. The fact that his central idea was rejected, albeit *in absentia*, shows that he is a founding member of the party only on a generous understanding of the term.

The SDF doesn't reject the idea of Federalism but, as I understand their problem with Mukong, they have always wanted to keep it as a back burner so that they could improve their chances of gaining power at the centre, which seems more important as a starting point. And this might be a very sound strategy. We need Federalism. But we can never achieve it as long as the Biya regime continues in power. First logical thing therefore is to help boot them out power, no matter who replaces them. And if it happens that the next regime had been even secretly sympathetic to the cause, what a fortune would that be for us. There is absolutely no need to counter-pose CAM and the SDF. We must learn to use different strategies and methods to achieve our aims. If Fru Ndi had followed Mukong into exile, would we already have advanced so far from our "advanced dictatorial democracy"?

52

Solomon Nfor Gwei's Tribulations
(Published June 10-17, 1992)

When I wrote on Honourable Nfor Gwei and his Human Rights Commission (see *CAMEROON POST*, April 2-9, 1992) I was almost certain that I would come back to the subject sooner than later. In fact, Human Rights can be considered as the barometer by which to gauge a just, democratic and civilized society.

In my former treatise, oh Solomon, I expressed sceptical doubts about the Commission of which you are Chairman and tried to point out certain gaps in your programme, as elaborated by you then. A regime which is hanging on to power and ruling by sheer physical force cannot be expected to create a Human Rights Commission. It doesn't make sense; it is not logical. That is why, to make sense out of it, one was forced by logic to conclude that creation of the commission was simply a smoke screen to conceal Human Rights abuses. And this tactic has a precedent in the case of democracy, where Cameroonian airspace has been filled with shouts of *"Democratie avancée! Democratie avancée!,"* while the instruments of dictatorship and repression were being perfected and tightened.

Within this framework, the regime not doubt, expected that you would play ball with them perfectly because of the unquestioning loyalty with which you have served the dictatorship in the past thirty years, always ready to "tear 880" at the slightest snap of the fingers to do its bidding. They might also have calculated that you would badly want a Chieftaincy title, now that you are past the age of retirement. So that if you co-operated very well with them, the next thing we would hear is a Presidential decree appointing you the Paramount Chief of Nkambe or something like that. In all this, however, they were not considering (pagans that they are!) that spectacular religious experience that could change a Saul into a Paul. That is why, in spite of my own analyses, I still gave you personally the full benefit of my justified doubts.

Listening to you recently (03/06/92) over *"News Focus"* as you told the pathetic story of what befell you and members of your Commission at the Gendarmerie Legion in Yaounde, I felt justified in my earlier analysis of the situation as well as in my having given you the benefit of doubt in that situation. Naivety is not a reproachable character trait. You went to the Gendarmerie armed with the Presidential decree which created your Commission and conferred it with certain powers, only to discover that the decree was not worth the paper on which it was typed. Not only were you prevented from doing your presidentially – commissioned duties, but you and members of your Commission were rough-handled and detained against your will. Do you know why they did not shave your hair with a broken bottle and ask you to roll in mud and eat soil like the unfortunate students you were seeking to see? Well, if you don't know, I can tell you. It was simply for fear of public opinion and possible reaction.

As a Churchman, you surely remember the Biblical lines: "Physician, heal thyself." If, as the presidentially-decreed Chief of the Human Right Commission, you have no way of preventing abuse of your own rights, how are we, ordinary mortals, supposed to believe that you would help us protect ours? If you are unable to help yourself, how are you going to help us? Don't get me wrong. These rhetorical questions are not calculated to bewilder you but simply to highlight the gravity of our common situation. In this country, those trained and armed at public expense, ostensibly to protect the citizenry, can wantonly break into any domicile, drag out the occupant and, without telling what s/he has done wrong, force him/her to roll in mud and eat grass before the inevitable broken-bottle hair-shave and incarceration. Even supposing that the person in question were a suspected criminal, what is the relation between this and rolling in mud or eating grass and dust? But, of course, people who can throw hand grenades in the midst of peacefully marching children would consider such things as harmless fun. You have loudly complained as you should. But if anybody even gets punished for that sacrilegious act, then either this is no longer *La République du Cameroun* or I am not Gobata's son!

The impression one sometimes gets is that a powerful group of terrorists has taken control of this country and holding even the Presidency of the Republic to ransom. For, suppose, just suppose that Dr. Biya decides not to return again from his present "private short visit" abroad. Would that really change anything for us? What we need is a change that begins from the roots and affects all the branches via the trunk. Such is properly called a "radical" change. To be able ever to arrive there, the foundation must be laid with freedom of expression and respect of Human Rights. And then a free and dynamic press is an absolute desideratum. That is why the recent clamp down on the Private Press which, for a while, had been breathing fairly freely, is likely to send us back several nautical miles from shore. Let the press inform, educate, entertain and conscientize. Let the press report facts and nothing but facts. I, however, disagree with Pa Aletum, who said on "CC" last Sunday morning that the press should report only facts for which they have proofs. That would rob us of information to which we are entitled. Journalists are not detectives. If it is alleged, for example, that the Emperor's goat or the Emperor himself stole cocoyams from the central barn, this allegation is a fact in itself and should be accordingly reported by the journalist together with the sources of such allegation. It cannot be considered part of his duty to prove the allegation true or false, because he is not equipped to carry out such a task. But the person accused has the right and sometimes even the duty to react to the allegation through the same medium. That is freedom within the context of a just, democratic and egalitarian society.

53

Wanyetoh Resurfaces*
(Published June 17-24, 1992)

Hope you did read the story of Wanyetoh, which I strongly recommended for your reading as far back as October, 1991. (See *CAMEROON POST*, October 4-11, 1991). Wanyetoh was first and foremost a clever trickster. When badly cornered red-handedly, he could successfully feign humility, friendliness, responsibility, illness and even death. His general attitude and comportment were always those of a magician. "Now you see me, now you don't see me. The more you look, the less you see." His most permanent attribute was arrogance. After a disquieting absence during which his enemies and rivals might have jumped to the wishful conclusion that he had vanished out of existence, Wanyetoh would quietly resurface, just as if he had just gone over to the neighbour's compound to beg for salt.

From where has our modern-day Wanyetoh so suddenly, smoothly and quietly reappeared, after causing us sleepless nights for almost 30 days? And this is not the first time nor shall it be the last, from all indications. Recall that after the *honoris causa* doctoral ceremony at Eastern Shores last year, the man disappeared without trace, in transit between USA and Africa.

How can the Head of a modern State be missing twice in less than 24 months? This is really a serious matter and the levity with which most Cameroonians are treating it worries me. The whole issue must be looked at within the context of power, responsibility and accountability. The fact that the pilot of our ship of State can abandon the steering wheel for more than a month, while the ship is drifting directionlessly, without any explanation, let alone justification, completely belies the induced illusion that we are moving, no matter how slowly, in a democratic direction. Democracy is a system in which, among other things, power is subject to accountability and ultimate control by the rabble. A ruler who can quit his Kingdom for an unknown or vague destination, for an indefinite period of time, for purposes that are only a subject of wide and varied speculations among the subjects, rules like an autocratic tyrant.

Within a democratic set up, absences of that type not only have to be explained but justified. We don't vote people into power so that in addition to all the privileges we accord them, they can go on indefinite and unjustified safari holidays at our expense.

Our Prime Minister, Achidi Achu, has set himself the task of restoring the authority of the State. We can deduce from this that the State has lost its authority over the citizens. How and why did this happen? I don't think that the P.M. has addressed himself seriously to this double-barrelled question. Would citizens rebel against a Government they support? If the citizens don't support a Government, then in whose name and under what mandate is it governing? The payment of taxes is a very important civic responsibility without which no modern State can function. Within a democracy, one of the tacit implications of the contract between the rulers and the ruled is that every citizen would fulfil his/her civic responsibilities, foremost among which is the payment of taxes. Any supposedly democratic Government which is unable to collect taxes without using excessively coercive and repressive methods should do one thing: resign with immediate effect and automatic alacrity! But this suggestion would, no doubt, be considered by the regime as preposterous. And this proves that it is an Auto or Pluto-cratic dictatorship and not a democracy as is being pretended.

There are two very significant indicators in the present task of restoring the authority of the State. Some of the recalcitrant communities which have been refusing to pay their taxes have reportedly declared that they are waiting for one of the opposition leaders to "open the way." This shows that they fully recognize their civic responsibilities. Their point is clearly that the Government collecting taxes has no legitimacy in their eyes. I predict that once there will be a real, meaningful and popular change in the Government set-up, no campaign will be needed before people pay their taxes. Some people have also pointed out, quite significantly that the State terrorists forcing "taxes" out of people at gun point are collecting the money not for State coffers but for their pockets. Ask any motorist. The second significant indicator is that the P.M. erroneously tags his campaign "the rule of law." This is a disastrous mistake. THE RULE OF LAW means that absolutely no citizen, including the Head of State, is above the law. In other words, under the rule of law, I should as a citizen have been able to file a suit in court against Paul Biya, for his one month of unexplained and unjustified absence which injured me as a loyal citizen, and he would have to answer before the courts. How can you open fire in a village market in the name of collecting taxes and call it an attempt to restore the rule of law?

*The title and sections of this piece were censored in the published Newspaper, thereby rendering it incoherent and incomprehensible in parts. It is here published as was written.

54

Mbella Was Right and Wrong
(Published July 2-9, 1992)

The contradiction in my title for today is only apparent, not real. In one of his immortal Reggae pieces, Jimmy Cliff sings that "you can't be right and yet wrong, no matter how hard you may try." That is simple Aristotelian logic. In relation to one and the same thing, you cannot be right and wrong at the same time in the same respect. But of course, you could be right in one respect and wrong in another, right from one perspective and wrong from another, right from one point of view and wrong from another, without any contradiction, because the part that is right is not the same part that is wrong. It is in this way that my title is to be understood.

In his "BEWARE" (*Cameroon Life,* Special Edition, May 1992) Mbella Sonne Dipoko has made a contribution that should not be passed over in silence. He is an excellent poet and novelist. He is a frontline Cameroonian writer and one of the few to have gained world-wide recognition. Have you ever read *Because of Women, A Few Nights And Days, Black And White In Love, etc.?* These are all highly delicious artistic creations, compulsive reading of the type which immediately transports you into a very real unreal world, making it difficult to put down the work once you've started. Mbella is a writer in the strict literary sense. Now, a writer in this sense always writes prescriptively; he writes *sub specie eternitati,* that is to say, s/he is committed to recommending a reality, a world, a state of affairs which s/he perceives as either better, truer or more beautiful. A writer in this sense is not just one who is expressing personal idiosyncratic opinions, feelings, and preferences of the type covered by the expression *"de gustibus non disputandum."* By choosing for himself, the writer is at the same time choosing for everybody else. That is why her/his pronouncements cannot be treated with levity.

In "Beware" Mbella makes a very important point, namely, that all human beings are sinners. We are all fallible beings. We are also limited with regard to our knowledge and capabilities. These

154

limitations are ineradicable. We can therefore only learn through experiences. In fact, we can only learn through our mistakes. No human being is a saint and those who pretend to be are likely to turn out to be devils. No human being is in a position to promise others heaven on earth, because such a promise is not fulfillable. We must therefore always take the promises of politicians, whether those in or those out of Government, with a healthy pinch of salt. In other words, we need always to be thoroughly critical in our attitude, not gullible or naïve.

But to say that all human beings are sinners is not to say that they are all equal in their sinfulness; it is not to say that some are not better than others. In the political realm, we can only know a Government from its performance. Among the several alternatives, we cannot know beforehand which will perform well although that is not to say that there are no indicators which can guide us. But we are sure of those which have failed. If there is such a thing as a Government which performs well, then among the several alternative possibilities, there are some that can perform well, although we may not be able to know for certain which that one is, although again we can make a guess on the basis of the evidence available to us.

All this shows that the most fundamental right of a people should be the RIGHT TO CHANGE A BAD GOVERNMENT. No one can claim the right to install an infallible Government. No one can claim the right to do an impossibility. Mbella started off very well and I thought and I thought he would continue in this wise to warn us to already start being on our guard against the next regime, ready to criticize its failings and to change it if it doesn't redress them progressively. Instead, Mbella ended up sounding like a subtle apologist of the Biya regime, trying to rationalize his incomprehensible continued membership of the ruling party.

If Mbella sincerely believed that he could change the Biya regime "from within" one can only exclaim: "How could someone like Mbella be so mistaken!" He must have been operating from within the illusory world of his own artistic creations. Is it this regime which disperses peaceful demonstrators with hand grenades that Mbella is going to change from within? And where is his "within"? Is it the completely abandoned town of Tiko where he informs us he wanted

155

to be a CPDM parliamentarian? Is that his "within"? Did Mbella not follow the efforts of Ekindi, Melone, Sengat Kuo, Simon Munzu, etc., to change the CPDM from a "within" that was really within?

Mbella seems to have an unavowed serious axe to grind with some individuals within the opposition ranks and, because of that, he blankets them all as "the opposition" or "the opposition chaps." The opposition is a generic term. All critics are in the opposition, even though some of them, like yours truly, don't belong to any political party. And all political parties are not equal. Some are equaller than others.

Anybody who is convinced that the Biya regime has failed and should quit so that another regime can have a try is in the opposition. The opposition has not been peltering "the palaces of power with sterile stones" as Mbella would have us believe. I consider it a demonstrable fact that, but for the launching of the SDF in May 1990, and increasing critical awareness among the masses, our "palace of power" would continue to be monolithic , autocratic and thoroughly dictatorial beyond the year 2000.

The fact that Leninist Bolshevism also failed after replacing Tsarist capitalism does not mean that Tsarist capitalism, should not have been overthrown. That Castro also developed into a dictator after having overthrown the fascist dictator, Batista, does not mean that the latter should have continued in power. That the opposition may also fail after replacing the Biya regime is no good argument for allowing the regime to continue in power. A possible evil is a lesser evil than an actual one.

I hope that Mbella will continue to remain in the CPDM when, as is more than likely, according to his own admission, it becomes the opposition. I hope he would not maintain his preference "to preach the need for change not from outside the ranks of Government, but from within…" If he maintains such a preference, he would always have to change to the winning side. Now, that is properly called "calculative Machiavellian expediency."

55

Cherchez Le Mot (For My Censors)
(Published July 9-16, 1992)

Consonne D, voyelle E, consonne R, voyelle U, consonne S, consonne N, voyelle E, consonne C. Yes, Jingo, what did you get? CENSURED. Good. Now quiz time: Who can perform the impossible feat of writing an empty page? Absolutely right! Bate Besong!! Full marks.

Gentlemen, (since I can't imagine any decent lady amongst you fellows), this thing is getting out of hand. Do have a sense of proportion. Do you want to make us the laughing stock of the world? And just when we thought we had successfully forded the river and were safely on the other bank. Just when we had come so close to convincing the civilized free world that we too are a free and democratic liberal society.

Please, for your information, *NO TRIFLING MATTER* is a cool, level-headed contribution towards the cause of a more liberal, democratic, united and prosperous Cameroon. It is presented every week, completely free of charge, to all the 12 million Cameroonians. Is it fair to rob them of this free gift? Of course, you might be sincerely convinced that you too are working on behalf of the same 12 million Cameroonians in the cause of unity, peace etc. You are certainly entitled to your own convictions. But since we cannot agree between us, why not let those on whose behalf we both claim to be working to be the judge? You may be trying to annoy me. Suppose you succeed and I stop writing altogether, what then will you be censuring? Has it occurred to you that you might get out of job through redundancy and have to join millions of jobless Cameroonians? So, I say, let's treat each other nicely. I can say without fear or favour, pride or humility, that the son of each other nicely. I can say without fear or favour, pride or humility, that the son of Gobata is a completely de-tribalized, de-provincialized patriot, who can neither be bribed nor bullied, nor cajoled, nor blackmailed, nor lapiroed.

The analyses in this column are highly technical and thoroughly researched treatments of people, issues, places, events and ideas, whose importance is sometimes underestimated in the manner of every vital thing that comes completely freely. If I "vex" and stop it, everyone and the nation as a whole will be the poorer for it. I hope you people were not the ones who prevented the very strategic advice I offered Dr. Biya free of charge in November 1990 from reaching him (see *CAMEROON POST*, Monday, November 19-26, 1990). Do you think that if Dr. Biya had followed my advice then he would have got to where he is today?

The philosophy of this column is clearly spelled out in "GOBATA ON GOBATA (*CAMEROON POST*, July 16-23, 1991). What can you have against such a sensible project and philosophy of action? And suppose you succeed in stopping me, what are you going to do about the ideas themselves? Has any method yet been discovered by which what has been thought can be un-thought?

Ladies and gentlemen (I am now addressing my readers), don't mind them! "*De pickin whe he say him mama no go sleep...*" Do they realize that by fighting your cause I am equally fighting theirs? Time will tell. We shall see the past tense of this shit. But, not to worry, everything is being preserved for you. All the contributions of Bi Gobata are being put together for your delight in the not-too-distant future. If you doubt me, ask Chief Bisong Etahoben, the Editor of *CAMEROON POST*. Faithful readers are hereby called upon to suggest a title for the anticipated collection and to book for their copies well in advance.

In the meantime, let us continue with the game of scrabbles. It could be very exciting. You see, if Bate Besong writes a story, well, that is just one definite story, finite, and circumscribed forever in space and time. But, if Bate Besong writes a completely blank page, then there is an infinite possibility of different stories. In other worlds, the story you decide to read into Bate Besong's blank page is completely up to your own imagination. So, here, only your imagination can place limits on the story you decide to read in the blank page. We could thus possibly end up with 12 million stories. Wouldn't that be a more interesting and exciting world than the real world?

The censors of *NO TRIFLING MATTER* of June 25-July 2, 1992, left enough clues for those who are adept at playing *"cherchez le mot."* Could you fill the blanks? If you could not, then you are certainly not good at the game. But, like with all other games, practice will surely make perfect. Hope our censors will not spoil things by discontinuing censorship and thus stopping the game abruptly. If they do, we will be missing so much fun.

For the time being, try your hands at this little quiz: supply the title and missing paragraphs of *NO TRIFLING MATTER* of June 25-July 2, 1992. Members of the censorship board and their families are not eligible. Answers, appropriately sealed, should be sent to: *CAMEROON POST*, B.P. 1981, Yaounde. Winners will be announced during the launching ceremony of Gobata's collected articles. Good luck!

STOP PRESS: This column would like to recognise the passing away of (Honourable) Fonka Shang Lawrence. He is said to have died of a broken rib of which he was not aware! For someone who, apparently quite honestly, did not seem to see anything wrong with the Biya regime, it is not surprising that Fonka Shang could also be carrying around a fractured rib without realizing it. He was basically a naïve villager among sophisticated crooks. We propose the following epitaph for his grave: "HERE LIES FONKA SHANG LAWRENCE. HE WAS NOT A CROOK." Would that much be said of any other member of this catastrophically kleptocratic regime? The answer is blowing in the wind.

56

From Extreme to Extreme
(Published July 17-24, 1992)

One thing that is wrong with our ruling dynasty is what I have before described as "lack of a sense of proportion." Would you go for a sledge hammer to kill a mosquito? If you do, you would be showing lack of a sense of proportion and, in fact, of rationality. If members of the armed forces use hand grenades to disperse civilian demonstrators or open automatic gun fire in a village market, in the name of collecting taxes or restoring the authority of the State, this betrays a grotesque lack of a sense of proportion.

The Biya regime is not first and foremost a dictatorship as some people erroneously think. Anyone who lived under the Ahidjo regime should know this. No matter how restrictively we choose to define "dictatorship" the Ahidjo regime would pass the definition. That was a dictatorship! although that is not to say that it lacked democratic elements. But such elements were either used in the service of dictatorship or were merely its effects, corollaries, consequences etc. That the Biya regime would go down in the annals of Cameroon history as basically a kleptocracy should already be clear to all contemporary historians, chroniclers and critical commentators. Future generations of Cameroonians are going to marvel how it came about that, for over a decade, such a pack of... (a seven-letter word which I have censured myself) could rule over 12 million supposedly rational Cameroonians. But the regime has not been devoid of dictatorial and democratic elements. But these, by obversion to the Ahidjo regime, have been either used in the service of kleptocracy or have been its effects, corollaries, consequences, etc. And the problem has not been with stealing as such but rather with lack of a sense of proportion in the act.

In Cameroon, as elsewhere in the world, people would readily ignore moderate stealing by people in power, let alone undue privileges and advantages. There are people who even honestly believe that it is humanly impossible to wield real power over public property and resources without pinching from them. So the problem has not been with stealing *per se* but with complete lack of a sense of proportion in stealing. In fact, instead of stealing from public coffers, these people have attempted completely to empty public coffers. To borrow a metaphor from China Achebe, they stole so much that the owner noticed.

One of the consequences of this situation is the emptiness of State coffers, resulting in the inability to carry out development projects or even maintenance of existing structures anywhere in the country. But, with approaching elections, which the regime badly needs to win so that it can continue to give protection to its kleptocrats, members the regime are all over the place, visiting long-abandoned projects and communities and making the most fantastic of promises. The abandoned Tiko airport and wharf, the Victoria natural deep seaport, the horrible Kumba-Mamfe-Ekok road, the abandoned Besong-Abang airport, have all been visited with noisy fanfare by Ministers. This is all calculated to create the impression that something will soon be done about them. In fact, one Minister went as far as boldly declaring that the Tiko airport is fully functional and operational! Sure? So who has been using it? You feel like shouting: "Who do these fellows think they are deceiving?" The possible answer is: "Cameroonians." Cameroonians seem to be such slow learners, such easy forgetters, that any demagogue can trifle with them at will and raise them to the very heights of ecstatic excitement with the most unbelievable of illusory promises.

We also hear rumours that eight universities will soon be announced: two in Yaounde, two in Douala, one in Buea, one in Ngaoundere and one in Bamenda. If we have not yet discovered the correct way of running one university, would creating seven more help us in this regard? What does Yaounde need another university for, in addition to the existing two (remember the Catholic University)? These frantic election gimmicks could do a lot of harm to this country. We also hear that university students would be made to pay registration fees at the following rate: 100000 francs for ordinary university students, 350000 for students doing professional courses (ENS, Polytechnic) and 450000 francs for medical students. At these rates, there is no doubt that only the sons and daughters of

161

public thieves would be able to attend university. This matter needs very careful handling. I warmly refer the authorities concerned to my two papers: "Blueprint for University Studies"(*CAMEROON POST* Feb. 7-4, 1992) and "Blueprint for University Studies (2)," *CAMEROON POST* Feb. 19-26, 1992).

57

A Tale of Three Parliamentarians
(Published July 24-31, 1992)

Today, permit me not just to refer you to what I wrote before, but to actually quote myself at some length. In doing so, I am conscious of the danger of boring some very faithful readers of this column. But I am convinced that the possibility of such a danger is more than compensated for by the importance of the issue and the benefit to those who, for one reason or another, might never have read the piece from which I am about to quote. The piece under reference was entitled "SHALL THEY MAKE OR MAR?" (*CAMEROON POST,* March 13-20, 1992).

I prefaced the above-mentioned piece with the following statements: "As the euphoria over the hasty legislative elections subsides, it is urgent to remind all Cameroonians that the main task facing our generation at this point in our history is that of placing our country on a firm and unshakable socio-political and economic foundation. The task is no mean task; for what is at stake is our collective survival. As I have remarked several times before, our country is, from all indications, a potential paradise, if only we can perform this task well – that is, thoroughly, objectively, disinterestedly and unselfishly, rationally. Before this task, SHALL WE MAKE OR MAR?

"The 180 parliamentarians who should be sitting in the Ngoa-Ekele glass house by the time you are reading this, have a special responsibility before history in the execution of this task. Shall they make or mar? The son

of Gobata hereby solemnly calls on these assemblymen, irrespective of the party banner under which they have been elected, to take this task seriously. Let them eschew garri politics, short-sighted egoism, political horse-trading, unprincipled compromises and all forms of corruptibility and bribability."

At the time I wrote the above lines, I didn't, of course, know that the regime's policy of Government though bribery and corruption would combine with the MDR factor to make the new parliament little different from its monolithic predecessors. Did any of our parliamentarians read my piece which was specially addressed to them? The answer is blowing in the wind. But what can be said without fear of error is that none of the pitfalls and dangers I laboured to warn them against has been avoided. What we have witnessed in the past four months include "garri-politics, short-sighted egoism, political horse trading, unprincipled compromises and all forms of corruptibility and bribability," and even more. By the time I wrote "SHALL THEY MAKE OR MAR?" I had no idea that the CPDM would manage to secure a simple majority in Parliament and that the leader of Parliament would be someone with two *"yeye's"* in his names. In fact this parliament can aptly be described as a *yeye* parliament. It is a mixed bag, an odd collection of some of the most ununiform and heterogeneous Cameroonians. If not, what is someone like John Tatah doing, sitting opposite a personality like Sona Elonge or Thomas Melone?

This brings me to our three parliamentarians in question. They are by names: Sona Elonge, Akum Fomum and John Tatah, in descending order of excellence. I have never met any of these "Honourables" and know next to nothing about any of them. My comments here are based solely on their voices as I heard them though *"Cameroon Calling"* (CC). Intellectual honesty thus behoves me to state that my comments are only preliminary and provisional. Further investigations and further evidence would either confirm or disconfirm them.

Sona Elonge gave me the impression of someone with a good conceptual grasp of our political situation and problems and of his own role as a representative of his own people. In "SHALL THEY MAKE OR MAR" I had told the newly elected parliamentarians the following: "You are representatives and the interest of those you are representing must always be foremost in your consideration. The day you exchange this sacred duty for blind support and propaganda for any regime, you have missed your calling and have no more justification to consider yourself a parliamentarian." If, in addition to what came through of Honourable Sona Elonge, he is also a morally upright man, then my verdict would be that he is the calibre of persons we need as parliamentarians.

Honourable Akum Fomum sounded very expansive and eloquent indeed. He had a forthright and ready answer to every question he was asked, but left the impression of a clever crook trying to sell his own personality. I would put him in the category of those who can live quite comfortably with their own contractions. His vision of politics seems to have no anchor in morality. Politics for him seems to be no more than mere cleverness. He would justify any morally reprehensible action by declaring: "That is politics, that is the game of politics." For him politics is a mere game.

Honourable John Tatah must be one of the greatest curiosities of the present parliament. A parliamentarian who can sit down before a radio microphone and calmly declare that he is in parliament to represent and protect Government interest as opposed to that of his own people, a parliamentarian who calls his own constituents "vandals" and "hooligans" exhibits a level of political illiteracy that is unparalleled anywhere in parliamentary history. In my *njangi* house, the other day, someone was marvelling how a highly scholarized area like Bui Division could send someone like John Tata, who can hardly communicate in English ("when you sick…you take coy shot…") to represent it in parliament.

Dear Honourables, if you feel provoked by this column today, please, don't run to your godfather to report. Answer back in writing in your own recognizance. That is how the democratic "game" is played in all liberal societies all over the world. *NO TRIFLING MATTER* is at your disposal. In fact, someone like Honourable John Tatah might kill two birds with one stone by answering in writing. By answering in writing he might prove sceptics wrong by demonstrating that he can communicate in written English. So, over to you, my Honourables.

58

Of the General Born on Banana Leaves 55 Years Ago
(Published July 31, 1992)

This might have been a book review but it is not. I will not tell you the title of the book that I might have reviewed but I will give you a good clue in the manner of our *"cherchez le mot."* There is a newspaper called *"Le Messager"* which members of the ruling class love to hate because bitter truths are bitter. Once, they banned the newspaper; but the publisher is a smart guy so he immediately created another called *"La Messagere."* But they also banned it. Why were they so much against it? Answer: Because *"Le Messager"* always has a "message" and they had their own opposite message in their heads which they hoped to write down as a book someday. Get the point?

The author of this book, whom we hope is also its writer, is an Army General who was born "on a banana leaf," according to his autobiography, 55 years ago, precisely, on 21st June 1937, under the astral sign Gemini, in the famous *Arrondisement* of Djoum, in the Dja and Lobo Division. This hyphenated-General, that is to say, Author-General, has constructed a magnificent villa on the very spot where he was born on the banana leaf. You can even see a picture of the dream-villa in his 80-page book which, ironically enough, has been banned! I will not call his name so as not to give the censors a lot of work in wiping it out throughout my text. But if you don't know whom I am talking about, and if you are a Cameroonian, then call yourself a yamhead.

Now the question is: why has this little book been banned? The answer is blowing in the wind. The book is full of measured praise of Paul Biya whom the author describes as "the most insulted President in the world" and of protestations of the author's own loyalty, fidelity, honour and nationalism. It is equally full of lightly veiled xenophobic opposition and invectives against *maquisards,* agitators for Federalism, collaborators with the private press, mediocrity and laxism within the army. But since the book has been banned, how come it is still available at exorbitant prices? Might the

165

banning not be a trick to better disseminate the General's message as well as make him a multi-millionnaire?

In the book the General presents himself as an ideal Cameroonian: highly intelligent, disciplined, strong, virile and patriotic. He testifies to the beauty of Cameroonian women of all types and claims that his in-laws stretch from Mbouda through Bafang to Kumba. He says "and even Kumba" but unfortunately does not elaborate at that point at which I was really excited because that is the closest he came to also being my *moyo*! The General is the father of many children who like himself are ideal Cameroonians. His first son, who is perfectly bilingual, got his Bac at Montpellier, France, his first degree from Oxford and Cardiff and his Master's degree in Business Administration (MBA) from the United States of America: "A well-trained public servant, useful to his society." Does the General know how many Cameroonians with a better profile are hanging around jobless?

There is nothing in this book to justify its banning. Except, perhaps, that the General's Generals (for every commandant, a commandant until the uncommanded commandant!) might have taken strong exception to the statement that he is disciplined and available but that he can easily become a rebel if badly handled. That sounds like a threat and when a General rebels, the consequences cannot be predicted.

What you will not find in the book is any concern for moral issues or sympathy with the plight of suffering Cameroonians. Is the General aware that many Cameroonians, also born on banana leaves like himself about the same time as himself, cannot boast of even a hut over the spot where they were born? Is he aware that while he can afford junketing to Europe, USA, Japan, Thailand etc. to observe marvels and the enormous progress made by the people of those lands, that many Cameroonians, working here in Yaounde, cannot afford to visit their villages because they have not been paid their wages for nearly one year?

Sometime ago, the Cameroon Bishops asked the following disquieting questions: "Why are the banks empty? Who have emptied them? Where are those who emptied them?" The Bishops have since got loud and clear answers to their questions. But we have not heard from them again. Have their Lordships gone to sleep or have the answers to their questions so shocked them that they have all fainted or something?

Is this General with a message not the same one mentioned in the Messi Messi papers? Why are some people excited at his redeployment? Would he not be replaced at his old post by another Atangana? What is the difference between glucose and glucode? Or, if you don't get that, is there any difference between Zebedee and the father of the sons of Zebedee?

59

Meditation on Death
(Published August 7-14, 1992)

This year would seem to be a bad year for Cameroonians or, more precisely, for prominent Cameroonians, the well-known big-(wo)men in the public eye. The *massa damnata*, the Fanonian wretched of the earth, have never had it any better; they have never stopped dying. When it has not been from gun-shots, hand-grenades or beatings, it has been from epidemics, endemic diseases or famine. The death of the big ones has one initial lesson for all of us, namely, that, in spite of cosmetic differences, all human beings are exactly equal and that no one can run faster than God. Death levels all human beings. It no longer matters how much power you wielded, how many sky-scrapers you built at home and/or abroad, how much stolen or honest money you have in your Swiss account.

In nearly all cultures, posthumous flattery has been raised to the status of a fine art. Let some well-known scoundrel die and you would be surprised at the exaggerated eulogies heaped on him/her at the grave-side and the number of healthy people who will display grief to the extent of threatening to follow the dead into the grave. Elaborate funeral ceremonies are part and parcel of this scenario of post-mortem flattery.

In my view, the Moslem practice of burial comes closest to being the most rational. When someone dies s/he should be buried as quickly and as simply as possible with dignity devoid of sundry cumbersome contrivances. For this purpose, it is enough that the corpse be wrapped up in a mat or blanket and put in the earth within the context of some brief religious ceremony. But most people would do everything to have an expensive casket (to boost their own vanity) and to have the burial ceremony performed, if possible, by a whole college of bishops, if not cardinals. It would seem reasonable to give a religious burial to any deceased person on the simple request of the closest relatives, no matter how the person in question lived or died. Once dead, every individual is out of the reach of all mortals and face to face only with God. To deny any such person a religious burial for whatever putative reason is also to try to run faster than God. Christian churches in particular usually insist that, to receive a Christian burial, someone must have been a practicing Christian in addition to dying a good death. This insistence, I believe, is wrong. In practice, of course, rich people, even if they lived as notorious polygamists or criminals and died by their own hands, somehow always manage to get an elaborate Christian burial. My suggestion is that the ceremony should be severely simplified and also extended to the poor including pagans and apostates. This, I believe, would be Christian.

As I am writing this, Madam Biya is being buried in their palace in Mvomeka, within the context of a Christian religious ceremony involving six bishops and countless priests. Since her sudden death three days ago, (nine days ago at the time of publication. – Editor) there has been an undeclared competition among groups and individuals to send the most flattering messages of condolence. All very reminiscent of those orchestrated "spontaneous" motions of support. It is very significant that these messages are not sent to Mvomeka but to the radio houses and read on the television screen. This clearly indicates that those sending the messages are basically performing a public relations exercise for themselves. Hence, the senseless exaggerations and misuse of language.

To say that the death has turned all of us into orphans or that everyone wept at the news is a silly exaggeration. The death was, of course, shocking in its suddenness but that is not to say that it shocked everybody. It cannot also be properly described as 'brutal' without any evidence. It, of course, concerned everybody, being the death of the First Lady. But people were concerned in different ways for various reasons. There are those who opened a beer to celebrate a "good riddance" and there are those whose main concern is that the key witness in the Messi Messi mess is no longer available. If you want to condole with a man for losing his wife, just condole with him for losing his wife." For how, as a third party, can you know that she was either beloved or loving? Someone even went as far as describing the late lady as a model of moral integrity and rectitude! If care is not taken, she might be beatified and canonized before the end of this year!

From the point of view of our contemporary history, the strange circumstances of Mrs Biya's death will surely be recorded. (Maybe when all the dust settles, history will provide a reasonable explanation). First of all, its suddenness is remarkable. She was well enough to have posed for a "family picture" with black American musician, Stevie Wonder, a few days before and to have been scheduled to open a mushroom farm the very day she died. What she died of has not been disclosed. The younger sister died two months before. What did she die of? Is there witchcraft within the family? Mr Biya, who normally doesn't attend even OAU summit meetings, was absent, having left the day before to attend the ECOWAS summit in Dakar even though Cameroon is not a member of ECOWAS. News of the death was officially announced with a celerity and promptitude that is very un-Cameroonian and the burial performed with uncharacteristic speed.

Many people have testified to Mrs Biya's simpleness and generosity. But, since she had no visible means of income herself, her generosity may have been based on "robbing Peter to pay Paul." But we believe the simpleness part of her nature and would accordingly like to propose the following epitaph for the spot where she is being buried: "UNDER THIS EARTH LIES A SIMPLE WOMAN WHO DID MANY UN-SIMPLE THINGS IN HER DAYS."

60

Keeping Yaounde Clean
(Published August 14-21, 1992)

One of the depthless aphorisms of the mundane political wisdom of Biya Bi Mvondo, for which he will long be remembered states that "When Yaounde breathes, Cameroon is alive." Well, what Yaounde has been breathing is highly polluted air. Yaounde is a city literally drowning in dirt, filth, garbage. Acrid smoke from burning garbage is oozing out from every street corner in Yaounde. Unable to clear the garbage, the authorities concerned are trying a clumsy method of recycling it on the very spots where it is dumped by setting it on fire. This might even have been understandable, if most of the garbage were combustible, but it is not.

Some six months ago, when the city was nearly submerged under mountains and mountains of garbage, the authorities in charge took one of their usually panicky measures. They ran to their Master, the French, and arranged a contract of several hundred millions for a French company to collect refuse for six months. Of course, for such a contract, they must have got their normal kickback, be it in hard cash, bags of rice and flour or crates of wine. At the time, I asked the following question: "Are these people crazy? Do we need to go and bring French people to help us clear our own refuse? And at what price? And what will happen when the contract terminates?"

This contract was evidently a political gimmick at the time, similar to the action by which ministers are presently going round with trumpets and alarm bells, paying farmers money they have been owed since 1989. But the contract has now come to an end and Frenchmen are no philanthropists. The authorities concerned don't seem to know what to do next since the little money in public coffers has other more urgent needs. They seem to have exhausted their originality and ingenuity with the erection of their gigantic posters on which they could not even inscribe an intelligible message: TO MAKE DIRTY IS GOOD, TO GATHER DIRTINESS IS

GOODER. I recently passed by what has been christened "Carrefour Emah Basile." The garbage pyramid is half-way up the skies again!

Every city in the world has its own personality, its peculiarity, its most striking feature which every visitor remarks and retains as a souvenir on the walls of his/her memory. That of Yaounde is garbage or more abstractly, dirtiness.

In their "Proposals Relating to Reform of the Constitution" Drs. Simon Munzu, Carlson Anyangwe and Mr Sam Ekontang Elad propose the creation of a "National Capital Territory" in the following articles:

Article 25: There is created in the area of Yaounde, a National Capital Territory the boundaries of which shall be defined by an Act of Parliament.

Article 26: The National Capital Territory shall be the capital of Cameroon and the seat of the Government of Cameroon. All lands comprised within the National Capital Territory shall belong to the state which alone shall determine the use or uses to which they may be put.

Article 27: The provisions of this constitution shall apply to the National Capital Territory as if it were one of the provinces. However, the National Capital Territory shall come under the direct rule of the authorities of the Republic and shall accordingly, be independent of the Regions.

The creation of such a National Capital Territory is indeed very necessary. But Yaounde should not be designated such a territory for several reasons among which pride of place should be given to its insanitary condition. We should learn a good lesson from Nigerians and create our National Capital Territory on suitable virgin land, which meets certain specifiable criteria and which can be developed over a period of time, according to a specific blueprint. That way, we will end up with a capital city we can all identify with and of which we can all be proud. I don't know of any inhabitant of this stinking hell called Yaounde who would not be happy to get out of here for a breath of fresh air anywhere else.

The sanitary situation of Yaounde reflects very accurately the moral condition of the country's leadership resident in the city. People who are completely unmoved by moral dirt cannot be

171

expected to notice its physical counterpart, let alone doing something about it. Let these people GET THE HELL OUT OF HERE, so that more sensible and sensitive Cameroonians can try to put things right again. But, from all indications, they intend to stay where they are at all cost, by all means. Have we not already been listening to those teleguided and carefully orchestrated messages of support calling on Dr. Paul to call early Presidential elections and to stand as candidate? Let him not think that he can do it by remote control as usual this time around. It is not only pot-bellied ministers, well-fed businessmen or rosy-cheeked CRTV journalists who will be voting. The Cameroonian masses will be the ones deciding. Dr. Biya will be testing his popularity and acceptability to these masses against individuals like Ni John Fru Ndi, Bouba Bello Maigari, and I don't know who else. From Victoria through Kumba, Mamfe, Batibo, Bali, Bambili, Babessi to Ndu and Nwa, Cameroonians are anxiously waiting for Biya to come and campaign. They will push his Presidential limousine through the impassable parts of the roads, for a moderate fee. The other presidential candidates are not campaigning from a distance. To stand any chance at all, Bi Mvondo must do likewise.

61

Matters Arising From the CELLUCAM Affair
(Published August 21-28, 1992)

The CELLUCAM scandal dates back to the first week of July 1992, when the French language weekly "*La Nouvelle Expression*" (No .056 of 30th June-6th July), hit the newsstands to shock our collective consciousness with screaming headlines and a most carefully documented story. I have written the word "scandal" above without any quotation marks because, whichever way you look at it and whichever way it turns out, it is a veritable scandal. In other words, if it really turns out that a newspaper of the calibre of "*La nouvelle Expression*" could fabricate such a carefully documented story, simply

172

to tarnish the image of an innocent Minister who has been doing his best to "help Cameroonians," then this is in itself a press scandal comparable to the purported politico-financial scandal that the paper was presumed to have uncovered. Such a press scandal would be severely sanctionable by the "Press Council" if it existed.

If any newspaper could just on a whim, pick on any innocent and hardworking Cameroonian and string together such a scandalous story with coordinated evidence gathered in Douala, Yaounde, Paris, London, Anvers, Bruxelles and Singapore, about him/her, then we should really talk of "press terrorism."

Since the CELLUCAM scandal broke out, I had refrained from commenting on it in this column for two principal reasons. First of all, the documentary evidence produced by "La Nouvelle Expression" to buttress its story, looked so good, so thorough and so complete that I kept wondering how a common journalist could manage to lay hands on such sensitive and accurate documents. I have all along been having the sneaky suspicion that it might turn out that these documents were careful forgeries with which someone might have deceived the newspaper. But the "Honourable" minister at the centre of the scandal has himself now confirmed the authenticity of all the corroborating documents, all the material elements of the case. In other words, the difference between the Minister and the newspaper at this point in time is not about the facts of the case but about how these facts are to be interpreted.

The second reason that I have so far refrained from commenting on the scandal is that Mr Rene Owona, the Minister at the centre of the scandal, is someone I used to admire very much and to consider as a sort of lily among brambles, within the ranks of his ministerial colleagues. I liked his wretched, lean and hungry look. Please, don't laugh. I'm quite serious. He really looks like one of us. Those of them with pot-bellies and rosy cheeks always tax my credulity when they pose in their three-piece Parisian suits to talk about helping us, out of the economic crisis, whereas their very appearance betrays them as the most likely cause of the crisis. You start imagining their fat bellies as the "banks" into which all our money is disappearing.

After one and a half months of an embarrassed and embarrassing silence, following the story of *"La Nouvelle Expression,"* the

'Honourable' minister has now reportedly come out with a 74-page document telling his own story. I hope that this document would be made widely available. I for one I'm dying to read it. Now we have a clear cut case: "*La Nouvelle Expression*" versus Rene Owona, 'Honourable' Minister of State for Trade and Industries. It is time now to hand over the case, with all the respective supporting documents to an independent commission of inquiry which, after careful study, would publicly cross-examine both parties before deducing its own conclusions and findings. An impartial senior judge with no vested interest in the case, with no extra-judicial ambitions such as becoming a paramount chief, and with a demonstrable record of incorruptibility, should be charged with leadership of such a commission, whose other members should also be persons of like timber and calibre. The National Assembly had already called for an inquiry into this affair and might be able to put in place such a commission.

In the meantime, the 'Honourable' Minister's presentation of his own version of the story and his press conference raise some very pertinent and important preliminary issues. First of all, the minister's side of the story has been given wide propagandistic coverage in all the organs of the public media-radio, television, press. The story of "*La Nouvelle Expression*" although containing very grave allegations against a public figure, was never mentioned in any of those organs. In fact, the newspaper itself was seized from the newsstands and some of us had to read the story from the photocopies of those who had managed to somehow secure copies. Objectively, this is unfair. It reinforces the notion that truth can only come from above and never from below. Suppose the Minister's story is simply a sophisticated cover-up carefully constructed over six weeks, how would we know?

During his press conference, the Minister was playing the role of innocent accused as well as that of judge, even issuing threats. This should not have been the case. It is only when we get down to the truth of the matter that sanctions can be prescribed. The idea that there are foreigners who come here to "help us" out of the economic crisis is completely false. Colonialism and slavery have made us always to take as gospel truth whatever a white man says. All these foreigners always seek their own interests and most of them are also crooks. Few of them are philanthropists of the Mother Teresa of Calcutta type. We need always to be on our guard when bargaining with them.

The Minister admits that he did import rice but that he did so on the orders of the President to help Cameroonians. This is, so far, the most difficult part of the Minister's story to digest. How come Ghudam Gharam was coincidentally involved in the transportation of this rice? And how has it helped Cameroonians? How does duty-free rice imported by *Camtraco* help Cameroonians? Is *Camtraco* a philanthropic company? Should a Minister of State also double as a rice importer? Does the President of the Republic really concern himself with such minutiae as who should import rice and flour? Those who are really sympathetic to the story of *"La Nouvelle Expression"* would not fail at this juncture to conclude that the mention of the Head of State only indicates that he has his fingers in every messy pie.

Let's avoid both press and state terrorism and get down to the truth of this matter. It is so important for the future of this nation.

62

Governement by Trial and Error, Bribery, Corruption and Manipulation
(Published August 28-September 4, 1992)

The tax-defaulting and tax-evading « business » men who were selected to intone the Government-composed and Government-sponsored chorus that BIYA should call anticipated Presidential elections and stand as candidate actually anticipated me. I had been having it in mind to call on Biya to call early Presidential elections, so that Cameroonians could rid this Nation of the greatest plague, the greatest catastrophe that has ever afflicted it, seeing that, in spite of the anticipated legislative elections of last March, we are today firmly back into an autocratic dictatorship. No need to have added that he should stand « as CPDM candidate. .'' How could it be otherwise?

The CPDM constitution is even quite clear on the point: its Chairman is, by its constitution, its presidential candidate. Except perhaps that that constitution, just like the constitution of the country at large, means nothing to Paul Biya. But, in any case, the clause under consideration is not one that he could possibly want to violate.

It is really an amazing historical irony that Dr. Paul Biya would most like to be remembered as the person who brought democracy, among other good things, to Cameroon. As I pointed out long ago in this column, (see *CAMEROON POST*, July 30-august 6, 1992), his concept of « *la democratie* » even when further qualified as « *avancée* » is antithetical and nearly polar-opposite to democracy in its ordinary meaning and acceptation.

Just look at the CPDM itself. As a party, it has never ventured to try democracy the way the SDF, for example, did recently during its Convention in Bamenda. The CPDM has never risked any democratic procedure such as spontaneous open debate or balloting. Nearly all those within the party who have been anxious to see the instauration of democratic practices within the party have been frustrated out. When recently there were vacancies in the central committee of the party, an election was not held to fill them. The people were appointed and their names, as usual, read over the radio. Someone well-known to me was appointed in this way and people were rushing to him to congratulate him for having achieved what? When the Meme section executive of the party had some problems, a brand new executive was appointed right from Yaounde and imposed on the people of Kumba. *Est-ce que cela c'est la democratie ?* It is astounding that these are the people Cameroonians are banking on to conduct free and fair democratic elections.

This country is now like a boat drifting aimlessly and directionlessly on a turbulent sea. Government has become a matter of trial and error. The Government is hanging on precariously and hoping to continue and consolidate its grip on power though bribery, corruption and careful manipulation. These days, if the Government owes you any money it will only pay it as a bribe in exchange for sycophantic support, and this now includes normal salaries and wages for all categories of workers. Why should farmers whose money the

Government has been keeping since 1988, nearly five years ago, be paid now with propagandistic fanfare as if they were being done a very special favour? If these farmers were wise and aware of their rights, should they not demand for the interest that should have accrued on their dues over all these years? Is there anybody who is not aware of how much a big amount of money would yield in terms of interest in an average bank, let alone a *njangi* house, over a period of one year? In fact, abroad, where these monies have usually been kept, interest is calculated on a daily basis. This means that what the farmers are actually being paid now may be only the interest on their original dues. Ditto for every other person that is being owed money that was already earned long ago.

The Government is indebted to GCE markers since 1984! And recently, in order to break the deadlock over the GCE imbroglio, we were told with shameless bravado that the Government has managed to get some money to pay « part » of the entitlements of the markers. Haba! Does it mean that over all these years the Ministry of National Education has been preparing its budget without taking into consideration the fact that conducting and marking examinations is part of its main duties? The part payment now being offered to the markers is, no doubt, calculated as a bribe to lure them away from their more important demand of the immediate creation of a credible examination board for the GCE and allied examinations. Will they fall for the bait?

Today, the Government is owing just about everybody. Monies which have already featured in past budgets. University students, for instance, who are entitled to bursary, have received only about 10% of what they were due for the last academic year. Now it is being whispered around among the students that they would soon be paid « something » through the private generosity and magnanimity of the President of the Republic. Yet another bribe. But where is the money coming from? Is it part of the 490 billion that Omram Adham has allegedly paid into Dr. Biya's private account as a kick-back from ten years of mortgaged Cameroonian petroleum? The answer is blowing in the wind!

Some extremely rich businessman called Victor Fotso has recently been reported to have donated a school to the Government.

Is it a business deal or is the man known to be a philanthropist? How much would his « good gesture » earn him in terms of tax relief and monopolistic import licences? The Government has immediately announced the conversion of the said gift into a University of Technology. Was the Government planning to establish a University of Technology at Bandjoun but only lacking the physical structures or did it suddenly get the bright idea when it received Fotso's gift? If that is how it works, then I would also like to donate a very flat piece of land, which my father left me, for the construction of an international airport behind our compound. Abi? Why is the donor supposed to run his school again for two years, after donating it, before handing it over? We hope that the whole thing is not a gimmick. We should know after two years. But one thing is clear, now. Together with the other eight universities that we have already talked about, it is abundantly clear that this regime does not have the slightest idea about what a university is.

To faithful readers of this column, it should be no secret that the son of Gobata considers this incumbent regime as basically a kleptocratic kakistocracy, or, if you prefer, a kakistocratic kleptocracy. I am dying to see the instauration of democracy in this country. You can jolly well guess where I will be casting my vote, come the anticipated Presidential elections. Let the whistle be blown. What are they waiting for again?

63

Critical Moment of Decision
(Published September 4-11, 1992)

August 25th 1992. Time: 8.00 p.m. From what is possible, nay likely, to be Dr. Biya's last televised address to the Nation, I have retained two short phrases which have continued ringing in my ears : ... *J'AI DECIDÉ*...and ...*JE SERAI CANDIDAT*... As the echo of these words fade in the ears, it should mark for us the end of a veritable nightmare, the end of egocentric, egoistical autocracy and dictatorship, the end of misgovernment and mismanagement, the end of power without responsibility and accountability. This hopefully last televised address to the Nation, from the point of view of form alone, had certain positive elements. It was brief and to the point and the man managed to keep his usually dancing eyes and frantic hands under control. In short, he looked composed and confident.

Was this purely accidental or did some good advice miraculously penetrate to him? Your guess is as good as mine. But one thing is clear: the man has daring and audacity! After what he has done to the economy in the past ten years, after the Messi Messi and other scandals, after all other things that we cannot yet speak about and must therefore pass over in silence, after very recent windowerhood, after all these and more, to appear on national television, dry-eyed and unblushing, and calmly declare that he wants another 5- year term of dictatorship, clearly exhibits a level of audacity, temerity and sheer effrontery that must be admired even by his bitterest opponents.

Very few people understand Dr. Biya. He seems to be eternally elusive. Even those we imagine to be very close to him often shock us by confessing how inaccessible and unreachable he has been to them. He remains like a jigsaw or Chinese puzzle whose linking elements lie hidden in the bosom of time, a quadratic equation with several unknowns. For anyone who knows the disaffection and unpopularity he « enjoys » among the Cameroonian masses, it is hard to imagine what could possibility be the source of his confidence vis-

179

à-vis the upcoming precipitated presidential elections. Does he have confidence in those « spontaneous » motions of support manipulatively initiated and paid for by himself? Is he banking on some super-human source of power and efficacy? Has he mapped out a fool proof strategy for rigging? The answer to all these questions is blowing in the wind.

But I can predict one thing with confidence: Dr. Biya will not dare step out on the campaign trail as should be normal and expected. The reason is that, by now, he must have run out of false promises. Imagine him, for yourself, standing on a dais, say, at Buea or Bamenda. What would he say? Would he re-promise the Victoria sea port, Buea University (on the famous Anglo-Saxon model) and the Bamenda Ring Road? Would he re-swear: "*JE M'ENGAGE PERSONNELLEMENT*"? Very unlikely; so unlikely as to be a practically excluded possibility. A more likely course of action is to bribe and manipulate chiefs, lamidos, businessmen, ministers, elites and other such adventures to do his campaign for him. We should take careful note of these adventures because we shall hear of them again come the new dispensation. If my prediction turns out to be false and Dr. Biya comes out of the comfort of this Mvomeka'a palace to campaign, I shall voluntary accompany his campaign trail, free of charge, right from Victoria to Nwa.

I consider the oncoming Presidential elections as rare spilt chance offered Cameroonian to rescue this potentially great country from its descent into hell. To do otherwise is to opt for national suicide. No one can afford to be indifferent. We must all rise up like one man and seize our destiny from the hands of political lunatics and then make sure that destiny remains firmly in our own hands by the instauration of democracy.

This columnist must applaud Garga Haman Adji, who last Thursday, 27th August, 1992, did what Sadou Hayatou hadn't the guts to do, by quitting the sinking ship of the Biya regime. Garga Haman, together with the former Minister of Posts and Telecommunications, Sanda Oumarou, were generally regarded by the Cameroonian masses as having sufficient personal credibility in spite of being members of an evil regime. Garga Haman's press interview over his resignation as Minister of Public Service shows how absolutely impossible it has been to reform the regime from within. It also shows that there are many skeletons locked up in cupboards which will shock us whenever they come to light. As Garga Haman himself recognizes, he stands in the same tradition as Bernard Fonlon, the very first Cameroonian ever to have resigned a ministerial appointment on principle. If there still are other Cameroonians the calibre of Fonlon and Garga, then this is the crucial moment of decision for them. Let them stand up to be recognized and counted. After this, it would be too late. Those who dare are welcome into the ranks of the opposition, the ranks of those who would count no cost in the task to salvage this country and set it on the firm and unshakable path of democracy, unity and prosperity.

For readers with a Hemmingwayan-type detective mind, here is a puzzle: What is the connection between the ritual murder of the former Archbishop of Garoua, the sudden and mysterious death of Cameroon's First Lady, the ritual rape and murder of two aged Reverend Sisters in Sangmelima, and the fixing of precipitated Presidential elections on a Sunday? Sealed answer should be sent to the *CAMEROON POST*. We will get back to you when history uncovers the correct answer.

64

How the Opposition Can Proceed
(Published September 11-18, 1992)

The opposition parties should sink their differences, overcome their prejudices and premonitions, and form a united front against the Biya regime in the forthcoming Presidential elections. The reason for this is not that it is impossible to beat Biya in the elections if they don't unite. Given a fair electoral code and a credibly neutral electoral commission, any of the main opposition parties is capable single-handedly of beating Biya and his CPDM. Biya does not need to be beaten. He needs to be disgraced. What the opposition needs is not just victory. It needs an earthquake victory!

In spite of what some people are made to declare before television cameras and radio microphones, I don't believe up to a thousand Cameroonians can be counted who would sincerely before God and their own conscience take their own hand and vote for Dr. Biya to continue in power. In fact, in my optimistic moments, I sometimes think that, given the chance, Dr. Biya would vote against himself. Is it not possible that he is giving the precipitated Presidential elections mock seriousness as a neat and honourable way out of a very embarrassing fix, where advancing has become as difficult as retreating? Consider the matter yourself. Dr. Biya has himself stated that the precipitated Presidential elections are necessitated by complete loss of faith by both foreigners and citizens in the Government. There is an air of eternal uncertainty and tentativeness, which needs to be remedied to restore credibility and confidence. So, how would confirming the same person and same regime responsible for the loss of confidence in power change the situation? If in ten years Biya has been unable to redress the economy, by what magic would he be able to do it in a further five years? So, the slim chance is there that the man is trying to use the Congo formula of Denis Sassou Ngouesso. This latter made sure he lost the Presidential elections woefully. That way, in spite of having been a notorious crook, like the rest of his African counterparts, everyone would forget and leave him alone to enjoy his loot in peace and quiet.

But the Cameroon opposition should not take any chances. I suggest the following procedure as a *modus operandi* for their consideration. They should agree on a simple and minimal programme and field a single candidate for October 11th. The programme should be a firm agreement that whoever is fielded as Presidential candidate would set up and head a transitional government whose main task would be to put in place firm and unshakable democratic structures within two years. Democratic elections can then be organized. But the transitional President and all the members of his government must not, under any circumstances, contest in these elections. This must be made abundantly clear to all those who are now hustling for presidential nominations. They must understand from the onset that they would be required to commit political suicide, as it were, after two years.

Some people have been seriously canvassing that His Eminence, Christian Cardinal Tumi, should be approached to accept standing as the opposition candidate. I don't think that the Cardinal would accept to stand election for any party or group of parties. But once a transitional Government comes into power, I could see him accepting to chair a national conference or constitutional assembly. For his well-known firmness and fairness without any vested interest, he would be an ideal person for such an important and delicate job.

Now, how should the opposition proceed in selecting, its unique candidate? This again should be very simple. Given the provisos already specified, each of the participating opposition parties should send, say, five delegates including its own proposed presidential candidate to an all-opposition-party congress. The unique candidate should then be selected from the list of hopefuls by all the delegates, through a simple and transparent democratic process.

Given such a procedure, those who nurse serious political ambitions and whose unavowed calculations have been making it difficult for the opposition to reach consensus, would better be advised to lie low for now until the transitional period is over. If the opposition parties could come to an agreement like this, I'm sure that the independent press would take it up upon itself to be the custodian of the agreement on behalf of the silent masses, so that its terms are never flouted. That way too, there would be more time, within a freer atmosphere, for the public to know each of the presidential aspirants and their true positions and views on all the burning issues of the day.

65

Very Fraudulent Procedures
(Published September 19-26, 1992)

Whichever way you look at it, the middle name of the Biya regime must be FRAUD. In that domain, the regime has really distinguished itself and created an all-time unbeatable record. And yet the evidence on the basis of which we are led to make this judgement must be only a tip of the iceberg, given that the regime is in total control of everything. It is only the very extremely flagrant frauds that have filtered through to attract the notice of the public.

Just take this presidential election thing. After secretly preparing for it very carefully in every way, Dr. Biya suddenly announced Presidential elections out of schedule, thereby taking potential rivals completely by surprise and giving them scarcely more than one month to prepare and face him at the polls. Such tactic of "surprise, attack and vanquish" is very fraudulent indeed. It is like going to wake your wrestling opponent from sleep early in the morning after secretly training all night and insisting that the wrestling contest scheduled for the evening should take place there and then in the courtyard, already ringed round exclusively by your own supporters. Very unfair!

Notice again that this surprise and unconstitutional decision is first announced in a nation-wide broadcast, specifying date and all before being submitted to parliament for approval. A very strange procedure! The fact that parliament rubber-stamped such a crazy decision clearly shows that the present so-called pluralistic parliament is as powerless and irrelevant as its monolithic predecessors.

One of the intended aims of the surprise announcement and short notice was, no doubt, that the really powerful opposition parties, which have always insisted on clear and fair rules of procedure, would refuse to participate so that the incumbent could be fairly unanimously hand-clapped into a third consecutive five-year term of dictatorship. But that failed as all opposition parties seemed ready and willing to rise up to the challenging situation. This unexpected reaction of the opposition parties became embarrassing to Dr. Biya. Campaign would be necessary. But given all the false promises he had made in all parts of the country before, how cold he dare step out to campaign? What would he tell the people who now know him to be a shameless liar, *inter alia*? It was thus necessary to craft more frauds. Chiefs, businessmen and elites are always the easiest groups to corrupt and manipulate. Hence, ask them to invite you to come and visit them in their province. Let them plead with you on their knees, with tear in their eyes, as if their very survival and continued existence depended on your visit. Give them enough money to cover the cost of your visit, give them some more money to donate towards your visit as if it were from their own pockets and, of course, something for their own pockets. A perfect formula that could never fail. And thus, the chiefs, elites and business people of the West province were chosen to set the ball rolling and they nearly deafened all of us with their cries for a Presidential state visit for the second time within one year. The relay baton will surely be handed to the white-turbaned Lamidos and businessmen of the North and so on and so forth wherever possible.

The question I ask is: why can Dr. Biya not go out boldly and honestly to campaign for his re-election? Is he really such a coward? Why does he need to hide behind the idea of a "state visit" which he is "persuaded" to perform in order to do his electoral campaigning? But, of course, it is all part of the fraud. By pretending that it is a state visit and not electioneering campaigning, state coffers can be emptied with apparent justification to finance it, and all state institutions mobilized to support it. Civil servants can even be blackmailed into attending. Dr. Biya and his CPDM have taken complete control of the public mass media, financed by all tax payers, for his exclusive use. Programmes and journalists who strive for objectivity and fairness such as "Cameroon Calling" have simply been immobilized. Independent newspapers which usually tell things as they are have been banned. This way, the stage has been set for subverting the collective will of the vast majority of Cameroonians.

Another question I ask is: where are the Americans, Britons and French, who told us they would leave nothing undone for the instauration of democracy and liberalism in Cameroon? Our armed

185

forces continue playing zombie. Where are our own Sanni Abachas and Babangidas? Not even a young Valentine Strasser, who could be counted on to salvage the situation, if it becomes necessary?

I hope the Minister with Anglophone ears is also reading this with his Anglophone eyes. I am sure he would be carrying his Anglophone ears around with Dr. Biya in his invited "state visits." Say, Mr Minister, have your Anglophone eyes ever seen the like of this? Have you ever seen the like in London or America? To your Anglophone eyes, does it not all look rather strange, Sir?

We also watched another Anglophone Minister narrating the marvels Paul Biya has done for us in the past ten years and assuring us that he is the only one who can lead us into an earthly paradise. But when we looked at the fellow we understood. Even as he was preaching to us, he was opening his mouth with considerable difficulty, on account of the sheer weight of his jaws. His neck is heavier than that of a fattened cow, and his ebony black skin is glowing from the effects of prolonged cocoa butter treatment. Why would a man like that not kill and even be ready to die so that the "New Deal" regime may continue in power? Is that how he was before Biya invited him to the banquet table? The answer is blowing in the wind.

66

Ben Muna's Aborttive Bid
(Published September 24-October 1, 1992)

Ben Muna's bid for the SDF Presidential ticket took many political observers by surprise and caused a near-panic among many grass-root supporters of the party. Ben Muna is, of course, well known to SDF militants. The diligence, courage, efficiency and apparent selflessness with which he has served that party since its epoch-marking launching at Ntarikon park on May 26, 1990, are all very remarkable. He has been one of the Chairman's closest right-men and his perfect bilingualism has, no doubt, been a valuable asset to the party's hierarchy. Personally I had made a mental bet long ago that leadership of the SDF would one day fall on Ben Muna. But I must have been thinking about this the way Mr Bouba Bello Maigari seems to be thinking regarding the possibility of an Anglophone President in Cameroon. When questioned in Bamenda on the issue, Mr Maigari answered that he could very well see an Anglophone becoming the President of this country "in future." I caught my heart. Honestly, I had expected him to answer: "The next President of this country could be Anglophone!"

Back to Ben Muna. When I quietly bet that he would one day assume leadership of the SDF, I realized at the same time that there would be formidable odds against him, but noted with satisfaction that there would be formidable odds against him, but noted with satisfaction that the good work he was doing, if sustained, would dispel all the prejudice people hold against him for being his father's son. I am an ardent advocate of personal merit. Nevertheless, Ben's bold bid also jolted me momentarily. The mind naturally flashed back to Shakespeare's Julius Caesar: Lowliness is young ambition's ladder; to which the upward climber turns his face. But once he has attained the desired height, unto the ladder he turns his back; now looking scornfully on the low steps by which he ascended. That is Shakespeare, in my own words. These thoughts could not help flashing through the mind, at least momentarily, but there was no justification for screaming: "Another Muna? God forbid!!" as some people did. Children should not be held responsible for the actions of their parents. People should be judged on the basis of their own qualities and actions. Our obsession with blood, clan, tribal and provincial relationships are completely misplaced and, in fact, irrational.

I recall that when the SDF had its first democratic congress in Bamenda some people were seriously objecting to Dr. Siga Asanga's re-election to the post of Secretary General on the grounds that he is a blood relation of Ni john Fru Ndi. *"Is it a family business?"* some people were asking. A very silly and unfair way of thinking. When Asanga and Fru Ndi risked their lives to give us democracy, did anybody ask if it was a family business or complain that two blood relations were risking their lives? I have noted before how it has become fashionable for people to claim to have been one of the

Founders of the SDF. To me the matter is very simple. Any person who dared to be present at Ntarikon Park on May 26th 1990, during the launching of the SDF, is a Founding Father/Mother of the SDF and consequently of democracy in Cameroon. To avoid "the advantages of theft over honest toil," anybody who was not there present on that occasion can only be a "founder" in a metaphoric or associate sense.

Back again to Ben Muna. Ben Muna's attempted challenge of Fru Ndi, for the presidential candidacy of the SDF, was quite in order and shows the SDF to be a genuinely democratic party beyond all others. But the bid was pre-mature for at least two reasons. Ben Muna probably underestimated what it takes to dispel deep-seated prejudice. A plausible picture can be painted of Solomon Tandeng Muna as a political opportunist. Some Anglophones unfairly blame him for all their present woes. As a political leader, he cannot of course, escape all blame from mistakes. All human beings are fallible. Human fallibility is such that even now we are liable to making mistakes which we shall only realize retrospectively much later. But whatever the case, and whatever our own appraisal of the facts, the truth remains that Ben Muna is not Solomon Tandeng Muna and should accordingly be judged entirely on his own merits. But this is logic, and prejudice and logic never go together. Had Ben realized this, he should have taken more time to prepare his attempted assault of the summit. Secondly, in spite of being an insider, Ben Muna probably doesn't know all that makes the SDF tick. The SDF' popularity is very much related to the charismatic leadership of Ni john Fru Ndi, the bookseller of Bamenda. The thing about charisma is that it is usually fortuitous and undeserved. Fru Ndi seems to be quite aware of this. Last year he declared in Wum that he is a sinner not an angel. Charisma is strictly personal and un-transferable. On our present political firmament, Ni John Fru Ndi has no peer. He is a lone star shinning in a dark firmament. Those we were placing at par with him have recently surprised us with their selfish manoeuvres. While Ni John had long declared that he would fully support any Presidential candidate uniquely chosen by the opposition to help oust the Biya regime, the other opposition leaders, after dilly-dallying and shilly-shallying, are now going, each into his own curriculum vitae, to specify acceptable criteria for a unique Presidential candidate. Imagine someone specifying *"experience in treating dossiers"* as a necessary criterion for a good Presidential candidate! I nearly crushed my ribs laughing at that one. If one of these people were in Biya's place, he might have proposed in the electoral code that, to stand for Presidential elections, you must have been a President before!

If Cameroonians want positive change, NI JOHN FRU NDI IS THEIR MAN FOR PRESIDENT. Quote me!

67

The Comedians on Our Political Stage
(Published October 1 – 8, 1992)

Since the struggle for democracy was launched in Cameroon a little more than two year ago, we have lived through alternating moments of irremediable despair, euphoric hope and lackadaisical lethargy. These varied situations have been regularly punctuated by comic relief, whose value for the psyche cannot be underestimated. I have always followed with the corners of my eyes the comedians and jokers who have provided us with these moments of comic relief. They are the clowns and court jesters on our national landscape. Do you still remember Lapiro de Mbanga? Were it not that people like yours truly were quick to add to the English language the new verb "to lapiro," you would surely be forgiven if you have completely forgotten Lapiro de Mbanga. For quite a while he appeared like a folk hero with a massive following among the *massa damnata*, our populous, "wretched of the earth," who stand to lose nothing from change except their chains and tribulations. But a few millions of the regime's blood money transformed him overnight and ended a very promising artistic career.

Remember Mandenge? Temporary paucity of contracts within the CPDM regime made him to decamp with a bang from that party to the SDF. But discovering that the SDF was a mass movement with no contracts in sight, and reflecting soberly over the hunger in

189

his belly, he re-de-camped with the same fracas back to the CPDM! Prodigal back home. Have you forgotten Dicka Akwa? What is that his other name which sounds so musical? Yes, Bonambele. Where on earth is the Douala prince? I loved his hat! You cannot have already forgotten the likes of Honourable Tamfu and Tatah. Their mere presence in the National Assembly is comedy itself. For one of them, the remote cause of his present situation is said to go back to the fact that he used to be Dr. Foncha's houseboy. He was so good in the art of "passing chop" that one day Foncha simply promoted him from a houseboy to a Minister! Not really so astonishing. "Minister" means "to serve," you know. But in this case, should we also list Foncha among the comedians? Decide for yourself.

The list is long. But, if we leave aside the amateurs and concentrate only on the professionals, I would award the gold medal to someone whose name I'm not very sure of but who is unmistakably well-known to both you and me. He could make millions of dollars at Hollywood, just being himself. The name sounds something like WRONGLY MASSACRE. Is this a show name? Your guess is as good as mine. He has one unmistakable identification mark: an extremely funny hat which marked him out from the very beginning as a master comedian. It is rumoured that he goes to bed with his famous hat on and even takes his bath without taking it off. One day it would be interesting to know what is concealed under the hat. He registered a party. His party is one of several others which I once described as "paper parties" most of which were sponsored by and formed as secret satellites of the CPDM, to cause confusion and havoc within the opposition ranks. Mr Wrongly (if that is his name) is very fond of press conferences. Whenever he announces a press conference, many people, especially youngsters, would always go there to admire his funny hat and he would mistake them for political supporters. Recently, he appeared on national television to announce that his party had decided to support the candidature of Paul Biya in the Presidential elections. Was this news to anybody? But the question is: where are his militants?

The silver medal for these awards goes to Mr Frederick Augustin Kodock, the Secretary General of one faction of the UPC, who was beaten to the gold medal by mere split points. It must be mentioned here in passing that, if these awards were being made on a party basis, the UPC would probably have bagged both gold, silver and bronze, leaving rival parties only with consolation prizes. Mr Kodock started off as a fire-spitting spokesman of the UPC, the oldest revolutionary mass party in Cameroon, and the only one until the birth of the SDF.

From the beginning, those who knew Kodock's messy record as General Manager of Cameroon Airlines, started warning us that the man was a fake. But many of us mistook his red eyes and sharp rhetoric for signs of a revolutionary. Until he astonishingly subverted the eligibility of the UPC's own very presidential candidate, professor Hogbe Nlend, at the National Assembly. After that, there was no longer any shadow of doubt that he would soon announce an alliance with the ruling CPDM. Sacrilege of sacrileges! Would the martyrs of the UPC over the years not all spin in their graves to learn that the UPC has formed an alliance with the twin-brother of the CNU? To whatever impression that must be formed of Kodock on the basis of what he did as a former high-ranking member of the incumbent regime, must be added the clearly dictatorial tendencies that he has exhibited as Secretary General of the UPC. He insists on being the only genuine mouthpiece and ex-cathedra oracle of the party. Never once have I heard the Chairman or leader of that party make any declarations. According to Kodock, Prof. Hogbe Nlend, the ineligible presidential candidate of the UPC, has no right to go into alliance with the UNDP. *Kodock locuta, omnia finita!*

The bronze medal goes to the Lamidos of the North and the Fons of the Northwest, who in their clownish sycophancy have dealt the heaviest blow to traditional kingship as we know it. When Lamidos were still Lamidos, who were you to see the Lamido at short notice, let alone getting the Lamido scurrying to come and see you at the snap of the finger. Shake hands with the Fon? A real Fon of the Northwest? Who would you have to be? Yet, we watched in disbelief as the Fons of the Northwest, in their traditional regalia turned into comic costumes, bowed their heads to the ground in reverent abnegation, as they gratefully shook the hand of a Lilliputian non-royalty.

Though falling short of medals on account of the fierce competitivity, both Louis Tobi Mbida and Gustav Essaka must come for honourable mention in these awards. The former, who is the spineless offspring of a noble name, cannot but keep close to actual power. The latter's ambition for tenancy of the Etoudi palace was frustrated by lack of the caution fee of 1.5 million francs. Something that should not have surpassed any candidate who could boast of up to 150 supporters, contributing only ten thousand francs each.

We can see clearly now. The grain has been separated from the chaff, the men from the boys. Let the so-called leaders trade horses and cross carpets. We, the commoners, know where our interest lies, and it is not in two places. We anxiously await October 11th.

68

As the Countdown to Zero Hour Begins
(Published October 8-15, 1992)

A flash of lightening. A clap of thunder. A ferocious lion (monarch of the forest and open savannah alike!). And the affirmation: PAUL BIYA, MY PRESIDENT. That is the genius, the *l'idee original*, of some Frenchman, on behalf of Dr. Biya's re-election campaign. The fellow has done great harm and an incalculable disservice to Biya. The idea is simply weird and revolting. I thought it was the English who were supposed to have such a diabolic sense of humour. Representing Dr. Biya as a terrifying ferocious lion, a predator even on predators, which itself lives a life of absolute idleness, but feeds on all other animals, trampling with careless arrogant abandon on their fundamental animal rights, is simply too damaging. I don't think that any Cameroonian, even the greatest Biya-hater, could have conceived such a thing. May be it serves Dr. Biya right for having refused to follow his own advice: *consommez Camerounais.*

The sad thing is that this imagery, which paints Biya as a marauding ferocious king of the jungle, at the second moment of perception and reflection, is quite apt and appropriate. What the

Frenchman has done in effect is to translate into powerful symbols one half of the Machiavellian political philosophy that MIGHT IS RICHT. But this diabolic descendant of the Gauls forgot that even Machiavelli himself said that the political leader should combine these qualities of the lion with those a fox. Because even though the lion is all powerful, it is not intelligent enough to recognize traps, whereas the fox, which is weak and powerless, is a master at recognizing and dodging traps. If Dr. Biya had any of the qualities of a fox, he wouldn't be seeking re-election; he would long have been enjoying his retirement in peace, tranquillity and affluence. Naked power has its limits. Bribery, corruption, blackmail and intimidation have their limits. Trickery and lies have their limits. Even fraud has its limits.

As zero hour approaches, minute by minute, when our near-future ex-President will cross the narrow divide between potentiality and actuality, when his "is" will change to "was," the son of Gobata cannot help casting a retrospective glance at his own efforts towards that long expected mutation. Since the inception of NO TRIFLING MATTER, Bi Mvondo has come in for a fair share of my caustic, destructively constructive criticism. The approaching zero hour has been awaited in the manner of the messiah, and with its advent, I can chant my *nunc dimistis* with one side of the mouth, because the struggle will surely continue, though on a different gear. Personally, I have nothing against Dr. Paul Biya. If inscrutable fate had not catapulted him to the summit of dictatorial power, with disastrous consequences for all of us, he might, in fact, be among the more likeable type of Cameroonians. But as a leader/dictator, he has been an unmitigated disaster. My critical comments are objectively aimed at the Cameroonian society at large. I will continue in the same spirit when Ni John Fru Ndi or whoever else replaces Biya at unity palace. I hope that he would, unlike Biya, listen to advice and benefit from honest criticism.

It was as far back as 1986 that I saw in one prophetic-like flash of intuitive insight that the Biya regime was driving Cameroon down a slope into hell. By then most Cameroonians were still naively living in a fool's paradise. The situation is very different today, happily. I remember an evening towards the end of 1986 when some young

193

ladies in whose company I found myself in a 'chicken parlour' nearly beat me up for daring to make some severely critical remarks about their idol, Paul Biya. They all affirmed how handsome he was (is). In fact, one of them frankly and shamelessly declared that she could have an orgasm simply by looking at his picture. I failed woefully in my attempts to convince them that, even though handsomeness is a desirable quality generally, it cannot be listed among the particular qualities desired in a head of state.

Yesterday again, as I was waiting for a taxi opposite one of Biya's giant election posters, a young lady remarked in French that Biya actually resembled the lion placed beside him. She then affirmed: "Truly he is handsome, but he must go!" I was so happy with this remark. For me, it showed a very positive mutation in the consciousness of the Cameroonian woman. Anyone who does not limit himself to the radio and television propaganda of the regime but who is in contact with ordinary Cameroonians at the grassroots' all over the national territory, knows that Dr. Biya will lose the Presidential elections with a landslide. That should give him a chance to try the world of international modelling; a different world, where he really seems to belong. With his impeccable French suits and remarkable ties (never once have I seen him in an African dress) and his handsomeness, he would surely be a hit success in that domain.

It is, however, not impossible that the impossible should happen and we find the Dr. still occupying the Etoudi palace after October 11th 1992. Members of the National Democratic Institute for International Affairs (NDI) are here to witness the elections. I hope that they will not be witnessing them only from Hilton Hotel. I hope that they are taking note of the rigging that has already taken place before the vote. Nearly half of the eligible electorate is unregistered and those anxious to register so that they can exercise their fundamental right of franchise, have been bluntly refused registration, because the regime rightly suspects for whom they would be casting their votes. In this case, it is very interesting to see the apologists of the regime hiding behind the very law which they have violated and continue to violate at will to achieve their aims. Do the gentlemen and ladies (?) of the NDI know of anywhere in the world where the person in charge of the overall conduct of democratic elections, the referee in the game, is also an open partisan of and campaigner for one of the parties? ; Where the chief of NATIONAL SECURITY is not only a campaign manager for one of the parties, but openly engages in acts of violence and intimidation against rival parties? Does the NDI know of any precedent in the history of democracy where one of the Presidential candidates has been systematically and forcibly prevented from simply telling the electorate why he deserves their votes? Does the NDI know of anywhere else in world where the entire state machinery, including the armed forces and public treasury are mobilized to serve the cause of one out of many competing parties?

The naked truth is that we have here a very peculiar form of fascism. Fascism masquerading under democratic rhetoric and double-speak. We only hope that the NDI would take all this into consideration before giving their report to the international community on the nature of the 11th October elections in Cameroon.

69

God Has Not Yet Cast His Own Vote
(Published October 16-23, 1992)

We are in such a nervous state of suspense that, for once, the son of Gobata has found it extremely difficult to pick up his biro and continue with his self-imposed duties on behalf of the Cameroonian people. The rapid alternation of hope and despair seems to be driving many people to the very brink of madness. I would like to appeal that we should all keep our cool and maintain our psychological balance. God has not yet cast his own vote. Recall that I did ask before why these precipitated elections were fixed on a Sunday in flagrant violation of the constitution. The answer to that question is still blowing in the wind. But remember that Sunday is a day of rest for God. So he could not have voted yet. Maybe one reason for fixing the elections on Sunday was to steal victory while God was resting and run away with it. I don't know. But, as I once remarked, no human being can run faster than God. That is why God takes his time, and God's time is not our time, but God's time is the best.

Maybe you have not yet read the prophecy of Ezekiel in Ezekiel 29: 1-6. If you have not, you better do. It is someone called R. Ewane who drew attention to it in the weekly newspaper "*L'ami du Peuple*" No. 12, of 9th October 1992. The prophecy stands remarkably fulfilled in our context both from the sacred and from the purely profane-scientific points of view. We don't need any Old Testament prophet to prophesy the fall of Dr. Biya Bi Mvondo for us. His fall is a scientific certainty, no matter the number of pyrrhic victories he may seem to be winning now. Remember that those whom the gods want to destroy, they first make mad with power. No individual can win a war against the collective will and conscience of the overwhelming majority of his own people.

Some things about these elections have really shocked me, in spite of the fact that I have very good shock-absorbers, by virtue of usually being able to correctly anticipate developments. One of these is the fact that Mr Andze Tsoungui, the Minister charged with the overall conduct of the elections, Mr Jean Fochive, the overall boss of National Security and Mr Douala Moutome, the Minister of Justice, all went out to campaign for candidate Paul Biya and did so with a fanaticism quite close madness. I expect any neutral observer to be shocked and scandalized by this fact. Has any of the NDI people noted this?

As if that was not enough, these very fanatical partisans are sitting in judgment over the results of the vote. How on earth can they be expected to be clean and fair? It is simply not humanly possible. Going by what we heard from their own mouths on the campaign trail, it is evidently quite impossible that Biya could lose while they are still alive. That is why they have turned the announcement of results, over which they claim exclusive right (contrary to the electoral law), into a continuation of the campaign. How does Mr Tsoungui know that the people of Sanaga Maritime voted overwhelmingly for Bouba Bello because of Hogbe Nlend? Is Mr Tsoungui the Holy Spirit? How can he be making calculations on the basis of so-called provinces where Biya is traditionally strong when the results which should determine who is strong where are not yet in? Were we not repeatedly assured that Biya would draw 100% everywhere in the West province? What did the reality turn out to be?

When during "Luncheon Date" of Monday 12/10/92, the reporter from Douala was cruelly censured in mid-air, I knew that something quite serious was going on and that we were in for some nasty surprises. Is this the total freedom of expression which "Zero Mort" promised us as from October 12th?

The unholy trinity of Tsoungui, Fochive and Kontchou, with the legal logistical support of Moutome, seem to be specially charged with the task of seeing that Biya "wins" at all cost. For them it seems to be a task that must be done even if the whole country perishes. The electioneering campaigns and the elections themselves must have clearly indicated to Biya where exactly he stands with the Cameroonian people. I'm sure that he cannot have any illusions about this. So the question I ask is: Suppose Biya takes the courage of the lion without the common sense of the fox and imposes himself on the Cameroonian people (like a jigger stuck in the toe) how does he hope to be able to govern for five years? By ruthless repression? Whatever the case, we are watching. And I hope that people will now understand retrospectively why some of us tried to insist at the beginning on an independent electoral commission, a fair electoral code, and clear rules of procedure. The insistence was worth all the agony of the "*Villes Mortes.*" In trying to run away from present inconveniences, we store for ourselves greater future agonies. Unfortunately, most human beings cannot, without the benefit of experience, use reason alone to discern what is right and good for them.

70

Under the Magnetic Spell of the Bookseller
(Published October 23-30, 1992)

The followership behind the "illiterate" bookseller of Bamenda, as at the present moment, is simply mind-boggling, even for people like yours truly who were converts from inception. Recall the parable of the mustard seed. From little acorns mighty oaks do indeed grow. I remember one of the Chairman's mammoth campaign rallies. A commotion ensued, after the uncovering of a hired assassin, who was surreptitiously taking an appropriate position for carrying out his diabolic mission. A stampede was about to begin when the Chairman raised his hands and called for calm. Everything stood still including the wind. He motioned the crowds to sit down. And we all sat down there in the dust. Around me I could see University lecturers and professors, medical doctors, business tycoons, writers, journalists, technocrats and high-society ladies, civil servants, hawkers, taxi drivers, jobless people, men, women, the young, the old, the not-so-young and the not-so-old. In all honesty, I have never before been part of a crowd of that magnitude. I left there knowing, yes I say knowing, fully well that Ni John Fru Ndi had won the presidential elections, no matter what the regime might subsequently declare.

Faced with this reality, it is quite understandable that the regime should panic quite visibly. In their secret high-powered meeting they would exclaim: *Qu'est-ce que ce phénomène de Fru Ndi?* To which question none of them seems to know the answer which is clearly blowing in the wind. So using the mass media under their exclusive monopoly, they decided to inundate everybody with the "revelations" that Fru Ndi is an ordinary bookseller, an illiterate with no experience in high matters of state, which should be left to doctors, an Anglophone secessionist, an incarnation of Adolf Hitler, etc. But why the crowds should desert the doctors and professors with their bagfuls of stolen money and follow this mendicant is what they could never understand. Just like in the days of the Messiah, the Christ. The learned Scribes and Pharisees, the Priests and Sadducees, the Doctors of Law, could not understand how an apprentice carpenter and son of a carpenter could be the messiah.

Well, let us tell it again as it is. Leadership has got nothing to do with academic qualification (or any other type of qualification for that matter) nor has it got anything to do with experience. The only requirement for good leadership is moral integrity (which breaks down into such simple virtues as honesty, courage, fairness, sympathy, charity, truthfulness, reliability, humility etc.) backed by good old common sense. I would prefer a stark illiterate farmer as Prime Minister or Minister of Information and Culture to a professor who boldly tells incredible lies publicly to the nation without blinking. Just recall Dr. Biya's address to the nation, before the October 11th Presidential elections, and contrast that with John Fru Ndi's own address shortly before, under the programme *"Expression Directe."* In a gist, what Dr. Biya was telling us was that he was the most suitable candidate because he was clever and experienced. He said some of his competitors know nothing about matters of state while others had been in the administration before but had shown their "limits." The way he sounded, one had to be grateful that he was willing to lead us to paradise, where only he could lead us. By contrast, John Fru Ndi said: "I am an ordinary Cameroonian like all of you. Some people say I am an ordinary bookseller. So be it. But I have a magnificent dream for this country, which we can realize together, if you cast your lot with me." You could immediately see a statesman. He won many hearts that night.

As we face a most precarious and uncertain future, I keep wondering why Dr. Biya ever thought it wise to engage in democratic rhetoric. As far back as June last year, (see *CAMEROON POST*, June 20-27, 1991), I had stated: "If Dr. Biya had continued with the dictatorship that he inherited from Mr Ahidjo, we should be living in peace, even if such peace is closer to that of the grave yard. But by dishonestly toying with the idea of democracy and at the same time tightening his grip on the instruments of dictatorship, he has brought our security and collective existence seriously into jeopardy."

No one may be able to say now what further price Cameroonians are still to pay for democracy. But what is clear is that the process is now absolutely irreversible. Trying to stop or reverse it now is like trying to stop the waters of a broken dam with bare hands or trying to put out a raging dry-season bush fire by farting towards it. If you don't believe me, go out and take a census of Cameroonians who are quite willing and ready to die for Chairman Ni John Fru Ndi.

71

Let's All Avoid Mass Hysteria and Do It Again
(Published October 30-November 4, 1992)

We must all try to avoid mass hysteria in the present crisis because, when sustained, mass hysteria inevitably leads to war, the greatest of evils, characterized by killing or being killed for no other reason than that if you don't kill "them" they will kill you. By the time any war breaks out, especially civil war, no one again remembers the original reasons for the conflict. It is very important to remember that what we are having is a POLITICAL CRISIS and not a regional, provincial or tribal conflict. There are Bamilekes who are fanatical supporters of Dr. Paul Biya and there are Betis who are fanatical supporters of Ni John Ndi. Anglophones, who continue to be regarded by some people as if they were a single tribe, belong variously to all political parties and all shades of political opinion. In Biya's own village, there are several people who would have voted for Fru Ndi and in Fru Ndi's own village there are several people who would have voted for Biya. So, the problem presently on our hands is neither a problem of *Beti* versus *Anglos* and *Bamis* nor a problem of certain provinces or regions versus others or the rest of Cameroon. Once the problem begins to be presented under this light, you know immediately that someone is desperately gambling with the collective existence of people for private political ends.

I have read the tract jointly signed by *"Action Directe," "Croix de Sang," "Front de Libération du Peuple Beti"* and *"Delta Force,"* calling on Bamilekes and Anglophones to pack and go or else their blood would be used to purify Yaounde. Do the people giving this ultimatum realize that they are asking, among others, people like Augustin

200

Kontchou Kouomegni and Achidi Achu to pack and go? Do they realize that these two and many other Bamilekes and Anglophones like them, have done more for their idol, Biya, than most Beti? The mass hysteria likely to be aroused by the attitude behind such tracts is very dangerous indeed. In the South Province, where this attitude first began, immediately after the results of the 11th October presidential elections started coming out, the purported reason was that the Bamilekes had deceived and disgraced Biya. Forgetting that there, nevertheless, are several Bamilekes - the Fotsos, Kamga's, Fonnings, Kontchous etc., who are quite willing and ready to die for Paul Biya.

The natural opposite reaction and backlash to this hysterical attitude would be against Beti (indiscriminately) in some other regions, forgetting that there are Beti who are fanatically opposed to Paul Biya and all he stands for. This attitude is extremely dangerous in that it may not only lead to a situation where people attack others who have done them no harm or done no harm at all, but also to a situation where people harm their own supporters. I know a Nigerian ex-soldier who, during the Nigerian civil war, mistakenly wiped out his own entire family, including wife and seven children, with his own machine gun. The family had escaped under bombardment from his own village across the river Niger to take refuge in another village within the rebel territory. Our man's military contingent later got there with orders to wipe out every living thing.

In the present crisis, it is very regrettable that the CRTV has done a lot to worsen the attitude of mass hysteria by not reporting accurately on events and, especially, by not reporting at all. The CRTV remains the best proof, for any objective observer, that we are very far from democracy, because it has remained a propaganda organ for the regime in power. By refusing to report on the events in the South Province, for instance, the news that reached people through those escaping from there and through the rumour mill was that all strangers in the South Province had either been killed or chased out to Gabon and their properties destroyed or looted; and exaggeration of the truth.

A provincial Governor resigns in the heat of the presidential elections. How can the mass media possibly ignore an event like that?

The CRTV ought to have been the first to give Mr Achu Mofor an interview in Bamenda to let him tell Cameroonians the reasons for his resignation. If his reasons are selfishly political, it will always come out when you push him to explain himself.

What the Biya regime does not perhaps know is that if many people today, including many neutral observers, believe Biya's proclaimed victory to be fraudulent, it is thanks largely to Kontchou Kouomegni's press briefings, from which it became very clear that the regime was up to a sinister manipulative game. Had Kontchou not given any press briefings, I'm sure that very few people would believe Fru Ndi's claim that he is the winner. How do you explain the fact that, since the proclamation of Biya's victory, the CRTV has shown us everybody who is either happy with it or willing to let it go "in the interest of peace" but has never shown us Fru Ndi to let him explain to the nation his claim that he is the winner? In fact, we most needed to listen to him and Biya.

I have a simple suggestion to make to resolve the present crisis. First, let us stop pretending that there is no crisis. We are in danger of having two Presidents: one with legitimacy minus legality and the other with legality minus legitimacy. Neither of these will be able to lead us to the expected Promised Land. It is quite shocking that the Supreme Court listed a catalogue of irregularities connected with the elections and then said that the law did not allow them to do anything about it but only to declare as winner the person who scored the highest number of votes, as submitted to them. In other words, we don't yet have a Supreme Court. It is inconsistent to admit irregularities and yet accept the results.

My suggestion is this: since this election is seriously contentious, both because of the rules and their application, let us simply cancel everything and redo it more carefully. Our collective survival and well-being depends on it. So we should invite others who are more used to this thing called democracy to assist us (the U.N., the OAU, etc.). In the meantime, we will all submit ourselves to President Paul Biya who, luckily, has not yet completed his last mandate. He still has until March next year, so those with over-sensitive legalistic consciences can sleep soundly.

Over and above passion, this is the solution that stands most to reason, if we love Cameroon. But should the actors on our political arena fail to see this reason, I believe that a patriotic army which, as an institution should always be above partisan politics, would be right and, in fact, morally obliged to step in and impose it. This point of view is inescapable for anybody genuinely interested in democracy in this country and in the collective well-being of all Cameroonians.

As I was completing this piece, the Association of Pregnant Cats and Dogs of my *"quartier"* here in Djongolo wanted to send a message of congratulations, through this column, to His Excellency the new-old, (or is it old-new?) Supreme Court proclaimed President. But I reminded them that this column only deals with *NO TRIFLING MATTERS* and referred them to the CRTV.

72

Remember Nelson
(Published November 4-11, 1992)

Well, you can also REMEMBER RUEBEN, if you like. But it is Nelson Mandela particularly that I want you to remember today. To remember Nelson Mandela is to remember his heroic struggle against apartheid and racism which engendered, sustains and nourishes it. It is to remember the struggle for democracy, liberty and human dignity in South Africa. The story of Mandela is the story of an iron will and unbendable determination, in pursuit of justice and fairness, in the face of blatant injustice, daylight robbery and iron-fisted repression. It is the story of a man who refused to be bribed or bullied out of the straight, narrow and often lonely path of rightness, not to say righteousness, with its overly religious flavour.

Any struggle against the forces of evil must be ready for many a set-back and for patience in the face of postponement of the day of victory. When victory seems to recede, like the horizon with every step forward, the freedom fighter needs patience, determination and stick-to-itiveness; in short, he must keep his eyes on the sparrow. In the history of human affairs, the darkest and longest night has always ended in day break.

Nelson Mandela was jailed by the forces of evil against which he was struggling in 1962 and only released two years ago in February 1990. He thus spent 27 long years, spanning the most youthful, virile and creative period of his life, behind bars! But that was not enough to break him or make him give up his cause. And, when finally released, he could not sigh and say "*mission terminée.*" No, it was to continue the struggle. And he has done so without calculating the sacrifices that have been and will continue to be his, until final victory. Mandela's very charming wife, Winnie, of whom he once said that it was because of her that he could bear the terrible privations of prison life, had time to discover (who can really blame her?) the wondrous marvels that every virile young man can offer any love-starved middle-aged woman. So, no sooner had Nelson got out of prison, all grey and senile, than Winnie deserted him. But, ever with his charming smile and determination, he continues with his struggle, and who doubts his assured victory?

The story of Nelson Mandela should be a lesson and act as great encouragement to all of us. By the time you are reading this, Dr. Paul Biya Bi Mvondo would already have been sworn in for a third consecutive term of office as President and Head of State, (*ceteris paribus*). I am writing this before the event, but I am quite sure that the occasion will be one of the saddest days for the overwhelming majority of Cameroonians. But then, I remember the story of a man on whose door robbers knocked in the dead of night. He was not a weakling. So, grabbing his matchet, he shouted: "*Who be that? If you are still there by the time I open this door, we will know who owns this house!*" But before he could open the door, it had been kicked open and he discovered that he was not dealing with a single thief but with a whole company of heavily armed robbers. Given their number and the sophistication of their weapons, our man could only offer a token resistance, before watching helplessly as they carted his stuff and property away and left him with bruises to help him remember the occasion. Did that make the robbers the true owners of his property? No. Our man's head was only bloodied, not bowed.

To accept our inability or limitations in the face of certain hard facts, to accept our inability to change an unacceptable situation is not to accept that situation itself. And so, for us, the struggle must continue by all means possible. Those who would now give up and start chanting psalms and canticles to our LEVIATHAN, in exchange for a share in the form of juicy crumbs falling from the banquet table, belong to the second group of Cameroonians which I delineated as far back as March 1991 (see *NO TRIFLING MATTER* of March 20-27, 1991). I delineated two camps of Cameroonians: those who would prefer death to slavery and those who would accept slavery to avoid inconvenience. For those in the first group, whose numbers are increasing in leaps and bounds daily, the struggle must continue until *"La Democratie Avancée?,"* which proceeds via marshal law, catches up with simple plain democracy, as I intimated in *NO TRIFLING MATTER* of July 30-August 6, 1991.

Our *L'homme Courage-Lion-Président* could not help coming out finally, resplendent in all his true colours. The sharpening of our contradictions foreshadows their resolution in an acceptable synthesis. With the benefit of retrospective hindsight, some of us might become more credible in what we say. When before, I described our system as a very peculiar form of fascism, who believed me? Now who would doubt me? Unless you have never read George Orwell's *"1984."* Just consider the bold lies and the conversion of realities into their opposites. It is we who are shot at and hand-grenaded who are the vandals. It is John Fru Ndi who is the fascist. He is being incarcerated for his own good and in his own very interest. As for our democracy, it is one of the best in the world. We have nothing to learn from anybody. When we invited the NDI people here, it was to teach them democracy. At this rate, before the present five-year term goes half way, we will all be worshipping Satan and calling God a devil. Mark my words!

73

There Can Never Be Peace without Justice
(Published November 14-18, 1992)

You can quote me on that. If you want peace, forget about peace and seek justice and you will find both justice and peace. There can never be peace without justice. Justice is the indispensable condition for peace. Peace, in fact, is simply what results when there is justice and fair-play all around. And justice and fair-play have their home base in TRUTH.

Two years ago, I missed His Lordship, Archbishop Jean Zoa's famous pontifical high mass against democracy and multiparties, during which Alhajis (allegedly) entered the cathedral with their caps on the head and (allegedly again) filed up for holy communion at the appropriate time. Being a sceptic by natural bent and experiential instruction, I dismissed these stories, as the flagrant exaggerations of his Lordship's detractors, who were envious of his ever privileged situation *vis-à-vis* the top brass of the ruling regime. So, when another pontifical high mass by his Lordship was recently announced over the CRTV, I vowed not to miss it this time around. The purpose of the (Holy?) Mass was to pray for peace.

So, Sunday morning, 1st November 1992, there was I among the distinguished congregation of Our Lady of Victory Cathedral in Central City, Yaounde. For sheer ceremony and solemnity, you can never beat the Catholic Church. I was having the optimistic premonition that His Lordship, the Chief celebrant, would combine the considerable immunity offered by the Cassock with the prophetic courage common throughout Church history to call on *"L'homme Courage"* to be really courageous and, in the name of justice, fair-play and peace, return, the stolen Presidency to its rightful owner, the simple bookseller of Bamenda. I was encouraged in my optimism by the décor of the whole ceremony, part of which was this display of a group of kids, two from each of the ten provinces of the Republic. I recalled one of Biya's catchy phrases: "What type of Cameroon do we want to bequeath to our children?"

206

But his Lordship's speech (I dare not call it a sermon) when it finally came, was so disappointing that I left the Church immediately after, without waiting for holy communion. It sounded exactly like a government propaganda tract: respect the law, legality and authority. Not a word about truth and justice and fair-play. True to its divine mission, I believe that the Church should always be in a state of eschatological tension with profane authority. Once churchmen become too chummy with or agree to serve as apologists for civil authorities, you know that that divine mission has been violated. On all crucial occasions, his Lordship, Jean Zoa, has proved to be no more than the Episcopal accomplice, apologist and defender of the regime.

Now, looking back, and considering that this mass was repeatedly advertised on CRTV, the Government propaganda organ, it is no longer surprising. Today, one sure way of detecting propaganda or lies is if you hear it over the CRTV .When, for instance, I heard the memorandum of the infamous quintuplets: Agbor Tabi, Egbe Tabi, Ebong Ngole, Ephraim Inoni and Ayuk Takem "on *behalf of all South Westerners*" being read during prime-time news, as part of the main newscast over CRTV, I knew it was a monstrosity even before angry disclaimers started coming in from more credible South-Westerners. Why have none of the disclaimers been read over CRTV? The answer is blowing in the wind!

I once said that there are West Cameroonians who can sell their mothers into slavery in exchange for political posts. Many people said my language was too harsh. Today, does anyone still disbelieve me or think that my language is harsh? If anything, was my statement not an understatement, seeing that there are West Cameroonians who are quite ready to stir up fratricidal civil war in their own community in order to retain their political posts? Notice that the bond binding the Tabis, Egbes, Ngolles, Inonis, Takems, Achus, Ngus, Nkwains, Ayafors, Yuongas, Kontchous, Mbappes, Moutomes, Owonas, Tchoungis , etc., is by far stronger than any blood, family, tribal or provincial bond.

For quite some time now, they have deafened us with peace talks, while at the same time preparing for and engaging in war. When they ransack a place, carrying half its able-bodied population into concentration camps and driving the other half into hiding or exile, they proudly call that "peace." The other day, Fai Henry Fonye showed us deserted and desolate streets in Bamenda, through his T.V. camera, and called it "dynamic peace." A piece of insane propaganda, which really makes one wonder how it ever come about that this journalist who had made his mark and established an enviable record of professionalism could, towards the end of a meritorious career, completely sell his soul to the devil. About two weeks ago, Fai Fonye pleaded with the irascible populations of the North West to allow them, as journalists, to do their work of informing Cameroonians objectively about the happenings in the North West province. But, as things turned out, he was only pleading to be allowed to film the horrendous scenes which the regime has since been using as part of its propaganda to justify the state of emergency imposed on the North West province. As an objective investigative journalist, why did Fai Fonye not investigate the story, rife in Bamenda, that Alhaji Tita Fomukong's death is traceable to a vindictive gang of thugs and brigands who were on his pay roll? And what about the hundreds of innocent citizens, arrested, brutalized, tortured and incarcerated? What about the beatings and rapings and lootings? Does investigative journalism stop short of all these?

There can never be peace which is not built on truth and justice. Everywhere now, the magic word seems to be "dialogue." There certainly must be a way forward from the present impasse (though Kontchou says there is no impasse) which might be discovered through dialogue. But dialogue must also proceed from truth and not from carefully constructed falsehoods. Let me state very starkly a few of the basic truths on which real reconciliation dialogue can be based. 1. The last Presidential elections were marred by several irregularities. 2. Biya did not win the elections. 3. Even though Biya did not win the elections, he was officially proclaimed the winner. 4. The elections were followed by violence in several provinces, occasioning deaths, destructions, tribal conflicts and general insecurity. With such stubborn facts as a base, useful dialogue can surely be engaged by all concerned.

I am writing this on November 6th, the day when, ten years ago exactly, Alhaji dealt this country a mortal blow, by handing over absolute power (which corrupts absolutely), on a platter of gold, to Biya Bi Mvondo. Ten years ago, Cameroonians all had the illusion of being in paradise. Today, they all know they are in hell. Between illusion and reality, a viable future can only be constructed on reality, no matter how unpleasant.

74

What of Our So-Called Human Rights Commision?
(Published November 19-25, 1992)

Where now is Dr. Solomon Nfor Gwei and his so-called Human Rights Commission? The blood-curdling atrocities being inflicted on the populations of Bamenda and the North West Province in general have been going on now for about three weeks, without as much a murmur from Dr. Nfor Gwei's (Human Rights?) Commission. The last we saw of Nfor Gwei was on Television, a few weeks ago, receiving free furniture for his Commission from the Britons and, in Oliver Twist fashion, expressing the fervent hope that the good gesture of the Britons would be the beginning of a regular series of more free gifts! What does the Commission need tables and chairs to sit on and be doing when their work should be in the field where Cameroon is firmly back into a Hobbesian "state of nature," characterized by the nastiness, brutishness and shortness of human life?

From the very beginning we had serious misgiving about this Government-created Human Rights Commission, especially at a time that independent Human Rights Associations were being proscribed. It didn't appear logical that a highly repressive regime would voluntarily create a genuine Human Rights Commission to check its own abuses. That did not just seem possible. We were therefore led to the inexorable conclusion that the so-called Human Rights Commission was a clever device for covering up human rights abuses. Nevertheless, we were quite prepared to give the said Commission the benefit of the very slight margin of error on our

209

part, as an act of faith in the personal integrity of Solomon, a Christian and a preacher. For with God through Christ, nothing should be deemed impossible. But the present total silence of the Commission in the face of unprecedented human rights atrocities all over the country, clearly shows that we were right in our original scepticism.

Nothing justifies the state of emergency imposed on the North West Province, when we consider that comparable violence and destruction were equally registered and, in fact, continue to be registered in other places: Ebolowa, Mbalmayo, Sangmelima, Douala, Kumba, Muyuka, Mutengene, Limbe, Yaounde, Bertoua, Bafoussam etc. The state of emergency in the North West was thus evidently calculated to punish that Province for pioneering and spear-heading the challenge to monolithic dictatorial power and the demand for pluralistic democracy. The way things are going in the North West Province gives room for reasonable fears that a Lake Nyos-type of disaster, on a larger scale, is what is envisaged for the Province. The Goebbels of the regime had already publicly announced with characteristic glee that the state of the emergency was not yet the worst possible. According to him, there is a further stage *"pervue"* by the law of the land, called the "state of exception" in which people would be lined-up and shot, simply on the orders of His Excellency, without the need to bring them to justice.

Recently, Mr Jean Fochive, the Delegate for National Security, appeared on television and, with a faint sadistic grin playing on his lips, declared that only (!) 50 persons are in detention in the North West Province and that the only person that has been arrested and detained outside of the North West is Dr. Hameni Bieleu, who was allegedly inciting people to revolt. Nearly everyone in Yaounde has a fair idea of the number of people that have been arrested and detained. Kondengui and the various Commissariats are overflowing with detainees. Is it credible to suggest that no one has been arrested and detained in Douala and the other cities? That apart, it is very significant that Fochive himself could publicly admit that up to 50 people are in detention. Within the context of the *"Zero Mort"* mentality, it would be reasonable to assume that over 5000 innocent citizens are languishing in concentration rooms, behind bars. Besides, that is the news that is reaching us through mouth-to-ear rumour, the most assured source of information in Cameroon today.

So do you believe Fochive's assurances that those being detained are not tortured or maltreated in any way? If you do, you must be a wonderful yam-head. If you are not a yam-head and you still believe him, then consider the following: we have been repeatedly assured that the troops in the North West are there to ensure the security and to protect the lives and property of all, without discrimination. Is this consistent with the attempt to starve Ni John Fru Ndi and the other 200 people imprisoned with him in his house to death? Or, if you can, take a walk down Foncha Street in Bamenda and have a good look at the residence of the Sendzes, a lawyer couple who are both among the detained. See for yourself what the forces of protection and security have done to their magnificent mansion and the property therein.

Recently, firm instructions have been circulated to all diplomats in Yaounde not to travel out of Yaounde, without the prior permission of the regime, which must be sought in writing at least two weeks prior to the intended date of travel. You can call that "City Arrest" by analogy with Fru Ndi's house arrest. It is unprecedented in diplomatic history. But the intention is quite in rhyme with the logic of the situation. By all means, the international community must be kept in the dark of what is happening in Cameroon today, because it is extremely shocking. I don't even know what possible help the international community could offer Cameroonians today even if they knew the truth about what is happening. It all seems too late. The international community should have listened and done something two years ago, when many of us were shouting from here that we did not believe people who were dispersing peaceful demonstrators with hand grenades intended to introduce democracy. Did the son of Gobata not cry out from this column?

75

The Pre-Conditions of Reconciliatory Dialogue
(Published November 25-December 2, 1992)

The South African Archbishop, Nobel Peace laureate and President of the African Congress of Protestant Churches, Desmond Tutu, has paid us a "pastoral" visit and gone back. Even before the famous Prelate took off from our shores, some people were already claiming that his visit had achieved a break-through of the political impasse, which the whole world knows about but which Government spokes-people continued denying existed. I think that it is too early to assess the impact of Bishop Tutu's visit. There is as yet no sign, two days after his departure, as I am writing this, that he achieved a break-through. The feeling that he did may turn out to be based on wishful thinking on our part. Let's keep our fingers crossed as we await the first signs of the positive fruits of Desmond Tutu's peace mission.

But one thing we can say for Desmond Tutu: he must be a diplomat of rare calibre. On landing, he insisted on the "pastoral nature" of his visit. The press statements he made gave some of us cause for concern that his visit might be part of the Government's propaganda strategy. But as it turned out, the Archbishop kept his press statements fairly vague and ambivalent, but reserved his most powerful prophetic punches for the pulpit. I realized this when later, I listened to a recording of his sermon at the Messa Church here in Yaounde. I had missed the service. Listening to the sermon, one really wonders how all those Government ministers and functionaries could sit there in church and listen to all that without either storming out or undergoing radical conversion. Desmond Tutu's finest stroke was being able to wangle a *laissez-passer* to go to Bamenda and meet Ni John FRU NDI. When you consider that the Government had gone as far as restricting all diplomatic personnel within the city of Yaounde, so as to conceal from the external world what is happening in the North West Province, you have to doff your hat to Tutu. Given the rare chance to ask Desmond Tutu a question in Bamenda, some senile CRTV journalist could only think of the following idiotic

212

question: "Your Grace, you have seen some houses which were destroyed. So what do you think about them?" To which His Grace responded devastatingly: "I'm used to all that."

Desmond Tutu has emphasized dialogue and reconciliation as a way out of our present impasse. He has begged us, with tears in his voice, to turn back from the slippery slope of violence because, once started on that path, it is very difficult to regain firm ground again. The South African freedom fighter and human rights crusader knows what he is talking about.

For there to be reconciliatory dialogue, the Government, which has a monopoly of all the most potent facilities for violence, which alone can decree state of emergency and house arrests, must make the first unambiguous move. What dialogue can a prisoner, (with or without a crime), have with his gaoler? Suppose a gang of armed robbers breaks into your house at night, what type of dialogue could you possibly have with them, a gun pointed at your brains? The least minimum preconditions for dialogue in our situation, then, would have to be the lifting of the state of emergency in the North West Province, the freeing of Chairman Ni John FRU NDI, and the releasing of all political prisoners and detainees.

Unfortunately, even as I am writing this, news is reaching us from Bamenda of yet another detainee who has died from the effects of torture and brutality. May his blood remain indelible on the hands of his torturers and murderers! The United Nations "Convention against Torture and other Cruel, Inhuman or Degrading Treatment or Punishment" adopted by the General Assembly on 10th December 1984, lays down in articles 2 and 4 as follows: "No exceptional circumstances whatsoever, whether a state of war or a threat of war, internal political instability or any other public emergency, may be invoked as a justification of torture. An order from a superior officer or a public authority may not be invoked as a justification of torture.... Each state shall ensure that all acts of torture are offences under its criminal law. The same shall apply to an attempt to commit torture and to an act by any person which constitutes complicity or participation in torture; each state shall make these offences punishable by appropriate penalties which take into account their grave nature."

Cameroon is a signatory of all United Nations Conventions. But evidently, it signs these things as a mere formality. Worse still, it uses these things, at the rhetorical level, to cover up sordid flagrant violations of them. There is a glaring difference between Anglophones (West Cameroonians) and Francophones (East Cameroonians) in their respective attitudes to this matter of State Terrorism. As a legacy of continuing French colonialism, East Cameroonians seem to take state terrorism simply for granted. It seems to be part and parcel of Francophone culture. But it is the most scandalous and intolerable thing for an Anglophone with an Anglo-Saxon cultural background, where even a suspect must be presumed innocent until proven guilty. In my village, everybody remembers our first introduction to gendarmes, sometime around December 1961, shortly after Reunification. I was a kid then. The gendarmes were on mission to arrest some criminal in a neighbouring village. But right from my village, through which they were simply passing, they started beating everybody they met. If you were an adult male, they insisted that you were the criminal in question. If a woman or child, they insisted that you must know the criminal and should go and show them. Reaching a small local market, where old women and children were selling groundnuts, bananas and other edibles, they not only seized the things to eat on their way, but destroyed the vessels and containers for the merchandise. We had never imagined such wanton wickedness possible with uniformed "law enforcers." After that experience, we all knew we had made a serious error by massively opting for "reunification" in the recent plebiscite. If today some West Cameroonians are advocating secession as the best option, it is not so much because of economic exploitation as this matter of state terrorism and wanton violation of fundamental human rights. We will surely return to this theme in future.

214

76

Punishing the Innocent, Rewarding Criminals

Last time I was telling the story of our very first encounter with gendarmes in my village. "Introduction to Gendarmes" you might call it. I told the story rather skimpily and incompletely. But it is really very significantly indicative of the difference between Anglophones (West Cameroonians) and Francophones (East Cameroonians) on the issues of state terrorism and abuse of fundamental human rights.

So, (to continue with the story from where I stopped it last time), while the gendarmes were wasting time, beating and brutalizing everyone on their way, someone ran ahead to Jokwei's village. ("Jokwei" was the name of the suspect criminal they were after). The 'good Samaritan' met Jokwei sitting in the sun in the courtyard, doing nothing of great importance. He informed Jokwei that death was on its way to him and that it might even take others along the way before reaching him. Jokwei barely had enough time to pack and hide his scanty personal effects, and then climbed up to hide in one of the big kola-nut trees in the compound, before the gendarmes arrived, with one of the people they had beaten and kicked until he agreed to go and show them Jokwei's compound.

Through the leafy branches of the kola-nut tree, Jokwei watched, with barely restrainable amazement, as they rough-handled and brutalized his aged mother, who all the time was swearing that she had not set eyes on her son, Jokwei, since he disappeared from the compound several years before. They brought out her cooking pots and smashed them on the courtyard. They then warned her that they would be coming back the next day and that, if she didn't produce Jokwei, they would burn down her house. But, in fact, they never came back.

Jokwei remained on the tree until nightfall, then came down, took his bag and set off for Nigeria. He had been a trader of sorts and used to carry kola-nuts on his head from Cameroon to Yola or Maiduguri in Nigeria. It was on his return from one of such trips to Nigeria, as we now learned, that he was intercepted by gendarmes, who discovered some guns and ammunitions in his luggage. They suspected he was supplying them to the *maquisards* in East Cameroon. They tortured him and locked him up in prison. But one fine day, he disappeared from prison. That is why they came after him to his village.

Now, notice that although the gendarmes harassed and brutalized many innocent people and wantonly destroyed many things, they never achieved their primary objective of arresting Jokwei, a suspect prison escapee. Had they gone about their job more gently, without oppressing and brutalizing innocent people, they would have got Jokwei sitting lazily in the sun in front of his mother's house. It is precisely their *modus operandi* which enabled him to escape. Just recall, by contrast, how quietly and smoothly the West Cameroon police, especially those belonging to what they used to call the "Criminal Investigation Department (CID)," used to operate. They were always gentle and polite, even with criminals or suspects they intended to arrest. But in East Cameroon, guilt by mere association has always been the practice. If a suspect comes from some village, everyone in that village is held equally guilty. In this country, we know of cases where whole villages have been wiped out because it was suspected that a few political dissidents were hiding there. And woe betide you if you happen to bear the same name as some wanted person. When I read Boh Herbert's incomparable report from Bamenda, I was struck by the prevalence of FRUS and NDIS among the detained. In typical East Cameroon mentality, you cannot be called Fru or Ndi without being a relation of the Chairman.

If it were in the former West Cameroon, those who actually killed Alhaji Tita Fomukong and those who actually burnt or destroyed houses following the announcement of the fraudulent Presidential elections would already have been openly tried. But we know this will never be the case in today's Cameroon. Most of those now being tortured in concentration camps have nothing to do with these events. In fact, one of those already killed in detention was nowhere near the scene of arson and destruction. They were arrested simply for being supporters of Ni John FRU NDI. But, once you have been arrested, you would be tortured until you "confess" whatever they want you to confess. Did you read the letter of the Bali-Kumbat

216

detainees, smuggled out of their detention cell in Bamenda? Well, they were offered their freedom and even a little financial incentive, if they would agree to act before CRTV cameras, as trained gorillas of the SDF. Typically Cameroonian!

It needs repeating and emphasizing that this matter of Government terrorism, official fraud and wanton abuse of fundamental human rights, is what separates West Cameroonians most widely from their East Cameroonian brothers and sisters. This should change, un-negotiably, with immediate effect and automatic alacrity. Or else, let us all accept that the experiment in reunification has been a complete failure, if not an unmitigated disaster, and quietly, peacefully, go our separate ways and return to the *status quo ante*. Marriage is never by force.

Apart from sheer arbitrariness, the other identification attribute of the Biya-dynasty is punishment of the good and the innocent and reward of crooks and criminals. The just announced "Government of National Unity" clearly proves this. All those thrown out of Government, with the possible exception of Niat Njifendji, are people who, because of their natural shyness and introversion, were not sufficiently convincing in their fanaticism for the regime. Such certainly is the case with John Niba Ngu, René Owona and Jacques Roger Booh Booh. Not that anyone would possibly be missing any of these. Who would miss Niba Ngu, with his *wowo* French or René Owona, with his wretched ascetic looks and stiff Cassian smile? Besides, they won't be left in the cold for long, if the regime is able to maintain its iron grip on power. In fact, it is reasonable to suppose that they have been released from their ministerial functions to enable them handle other equally important functions. Owona would now probably take full charge of Korean rice and wheat flower, while Niba Ngu should help to complete the surreptitious sell-out of Cameroon companies and parastatals to Frenchmen, fronting for members of the regime.

All those rewarded with ministerial portfolios are people who displayed insane fanaticism, Machiavellian cleverness in fraud, ran unbelievable personal risks or denounced their own mothers on behalf of the regime. Those picked from outside the regime are all people who have displayed consuming personal ambitions, double-

217

dealing tendencies and a clear lack of principles of any sort. Let them reign for a hundred years, if they like. They will all end up in the rubbish heap of Cameroon history. My confident prediction.

www.ingramcontent.com/pod-product-compliance
Lightning Source LLC
Chambersburg PA
CBHW032131020426
42334CB00016B/1114